W9-DIV-657

". . . changing and elevating behaviors
is not an intellectual exercise.
It's the business of the heart."

Praise for *Do Big Things*

"I love this book. I love it because it's refreshingly original and unique. I love it because it's delightfully well-written. I love it because it's full of captivating tales that bring to life the struggles and triumphs of high-performing teams. I love it because the practices and principles are based on years of up-close-and-personal experiences and empirical evidence. And I love *Do Big Things* most of all because Craig Ross, Angie Paccione, and Victoria Roberts remind us that successful teams are not about star players or outsized talents, but about relationships where people exhibit caring, humanity, and heart. They show us how it's the human imperative that builds and sustains excellence. If you want your team to do big things, it's imperative that you read and apply *Do Big Things*."

> —Jim Kouzes, coauthor of *The Leadership Challenge* and the Dean's Executive Fellow of Leadership, Leavey School of Business, Santa Clara University

"People don't mind being challenged to do better if they know the request is coming from a caring heart. *Do Big Things* has a clear message: People in high performing teams need to care for one another. We can do big things together when we understand that relationships are just as important as results."

> —Ken Blanchard, coauthor of *The New One Minute Manager*® and *Collaboration Begins with You*

"We all know that teamwork is important work . . . but it's also hard work! Craig, Angie, and Victoria have somehow cracked the code with the Do Big Things framework. Not only do they challenge us to rethink our beliefs about what makes a successful team, but they have also given us a powerful set of easy to use practices that any organization can use, if they are courageous enough."

> —Andrew Collier, Head of Leadership Development, Nestlé

"*Do Big Things* is a clarion call to think big and accomplish feats that matter. This book can serve as your guide to changing your attitudes and actions to bring your farther down the road to success."

> —Daniel Pink, author of *Drive* and *To Sell is Human*

"This book captures the magic of extraordinary teams and gives you a roadmap to navigate and accomplish your toughest challenges. I've seen the tools equip good teams to become great teams—by shifting how teams move from an individual focus to a collective force to achieve amazing results."

> —Lisa Bacus, EVP Global Chief Marketing Officer, Cigna

"*Do Big Things* offers a simple and heart-based approach to elevate teams beyond high performing. If you want to open hearts and minds in your business, arm your team with this book . . . and maybe you'll all live a little more deliciously."
    —Chip Conley, NY Times bestselling author of *Emotional Equations*,
    Airbnb Strategic Advisor for Hospitality & Leadership

"This book serves as validation and a how-to for successful teams that are beyond high performance. The teams that master this approach are unstoppable."
    —Marshall Goldsmith recognized as a Top 10 Most Influential
    Business Thinker in the World, best-selling author of
    What Got You Here Won't Get You There* and *Lifestorming:
    Creating Meaning and Achievement in Your Career and Life

"The Do Big Things approach and steps are very powerful and transformative. Leaders and teams who choose to apply them can make a huge difference to their business and organization. It is a must-read for any leader wanting to play big with high impact."
    —Anne Watson, Global Human Resources Leader,
    Fortune 500 Company

"Ross, Paccione, and Roberts cut through the typical to the atypical, with an approach that embodies effectiveness and engagement, wrapped in—of all things—heart! A must-read for those who want and need their teams to do big things."
    —Lynn M. Gangone, Ed.D., Vice President, ACE Leadership

"*Do Big Things* is different. Because of our commitment to following the steps in this book, I am seeing how collectively, as one team, we will re-invent the way we innovate. These steps are simple, immediate, and authentic. The tools shared in this book have become a common language that allows us to lead with clarity and optimism like never before."
    —Franck Leveiller, VP, Head, R&D Surgical Franchise, Alcon

"Craig Ross taught us the power of comradery. In this new book, the authors teach us about the power of chemistry. It's powerful."
    —Jack Stack, Founder and CEO of SRC Holdings, author of
    The Great Game of Business

"Unlike other teaming books I've read, this book immediately improved the way I interact with colleagues. Ross, Paccione, and Roberts have inspired me to focus on the process and even more on the people—to lead less from my brain and more from my heart."
    —Mariah Burton Nelson, MPH, CAE, is in charge of innovation for
    ASAE: The Center for Association Leadership

"The practical Do Big Things Framework gives teams a map to be their best—and accomplish innovation by working across the business on a shared goal. I've seen this book come to life and it's powerful and a game-changer when you experience more potential being activated in your leaders and teams."
—**Kevin McEvoy, Former CEO, Oceaneering International, Inc.**

"*Do Big Things* contains simple yet powerful tools that are timeless and work for any team. I've seen and personally experienced teams achieve incredible innovation and organizational transformations by applying the principles outlined by Ross, Paccione, and Roberts."
—**Terence Calloway, Vice President R&D, Chief Technology Officer, Energizer**

"*Do Big Things* is a guide for any team. Grounded in research focused on the human element, *Do Big Things* combines a trusted process with proven tools to serve as a catalyst that inspires teams to reach amazing heights."
—**Mike Bloomfield, Former NASA Astronaut, Shuttle Commander**

"*Do Big Things* includes an approach that supported our team in navigating market conditions, being agile, and shifting our strategy—and doing so in a way that improved the lives of our team and community. It's equipped us to live, lead, and care while successfully having the greatest impact on our culture, community and business."
—**Patrick Criteser, President & CEO, Tillamook**

"The Do Big Things approach equipped our team to leverage our solid foundation in culture to achieve even greater business results (sales and margin growth)—with leaders showing up wanting to be their best ever, transforming our organization, and moving us forward faster. If you're not using these tools, you're already behind."
—**Matt Reid, CEO & President, SupHerb Farms**

"Few books offer quick insights that impact teams immediately. *Do Big Things*, and the approach in its pages, shifts teams in dramatic ways. I've experienced first-hand the power of these tools in support leaders and teams to be adaptable."
—**Eric Stockl, VP, Ecolab**

"I am a big believer in giving the 'how' to managers and individuals alike. There are too many articles and books that address the 'what' and many individuals are floundering because they agree with that, but don't know the steps necessary to make the change. Thank you Craig, Angie, and Victoria, for making this a great 'how' book and providing enough examples that resonate with any leader or any individual in any team in any organization. Wow!"

—**Beverly Kaye, Founder: Career Systems International; Co-Author:** *Love 'Em or Lose 'Em: Getting Good People to Stay* **and** *Help Them Grow or Watch Them Go: Career Conversations Employees Want*

"The introduction of this terrific book lays down the gauntlet: 'We . . . are not here to be inconsequential or do small work.' You already up for that challenge, I know. But you can't do it alone. You need good people with you. You need a team. And sadly, good teams are hard to find. 70 percent of employees report being part of a dysfunctional team. If you'd like to change that up, this may be the book for you. Do Great Work, Do it with a great team."

—**Michael Bungay Stanier, author of** *The Coaching Habit* **and** *Do More Great Work*

"You will find not only practical ideas that can be implemented immediately, but evidence-based strategies that provide a compelling framework for action. Look elsewhere for the usual management bromides in which talk is a substitute for action. This is a book about decisions—deciding to be great, deciding to take responsibility, and deciding to make a difference."

—**Douglas Reeves, Ph.D., Founder, Creative Leadership Solutions, author of the best-selling** *The Learning Leader*

"Using real-life examples from their multiple decades of consulting, Craig, Angie, and Victoria deliver a pragmatic way to inspire and earn high performance from every organization's most precious asset, the human beings who work there. I recommend this book to anyone looking to find the precious balance between high performance and humanity."

—**Henry J. Evans; Co-Author of Amazon Top 10 Business Book** *Step Up-Lead in Six Moments That Matter,* **and author of the best-selling** *Winning With Accountability-The Secret Language of High Performing Organizations*

"In life and business every new undertaking is a venture into the unknown. Craig, Angie, and Victoria have written a book that serves as a valuable roadmap for any leader who's looking to do more and be more. This book shows a way to achieve greater results with deeper satisfaction."

—**Bryan Miller, author of the forthcoming book,** *Power, Productivity & Peace*

DO BIG THINGS

THE SIMPLE STEPS TEAMS CAN TAKE TO MOBILIZE HEARTS AND MINDS, AND MAKE AN EPIC IMPACT

CRAIG W. ROSS / ANGELA V. PACCIONE / VICTORIA L. ROBERTS

WILEY

Cover image: Amy Shenton
Cover design: Wiley

Verus Global® is a registered trademark of Verus Global, Inc. WE EQUIP TEAMS TO DO BIG THINGS™ is a trademark in process.

Published by John Wiley & Sons, Inc., Hoboken, New Jersey.
Published simultaneously in Canada.

For general information about our other products and services, please contact our Customer Care Department within the United States at (800) 762-2974, outside the United States at (317) 572-3993 or fax (317) 572-4002.

Wiley publishes in a variety of print and electronic formats and by print-on-demand. Some material included with standard print versions of this book may not be included in e-books or in print-on-demand. If this book refers to media such as a CD or DVD that is not included in the version you purchased, you may download this material at http://booksupport.wiley.com. For more information about Wiley products, visit www.wiley.com.

Library of Congress Cataloging-in-Publication Data:
Names: Ross, Craig W., author. | Paccione, Angela V., author. | Roberts, Victoria L., author.
Title: Do big things : the simple steps teams can take to mobilize hearts and minds, and make an epic impact / Craig Ross, Angela V. Paccione, Victoria L. Roberts.
Description: Hoboken, New Jersey : John Wiley & Sons, Inc., [2017] | Includes bibliographical references and index. |
Identifiers: LCCN 2017019102 (print) | LCCN 2017029984 (ebook) | ISBN 9781119361169 (pdf) | ISBN 9781119361176 (epub) | ISBN 9781119361152 (cloth)
Subjects: LCSH: Teams in the workplace. | Organizational behavior. | Organizational effectiveness.
Classification: LCC HD66 (ebook) | LCC HD66 .R6685 2017 (print) | DDC 658.4/022–dc23
LC record available at https://lccn.loc.gov/2017019102

Printed in the United States of America
10 9 8 7 6 5 4 3 2

DEDICATED TO OUR FAMILIES.
YOU INSPIRE US TO DO BIG THINGS.

Greg   Angie   Victoria

CONTENTS

READ ME FIRST

We are now ready to start on our way down the Great Unknown. We have an unknown distance yet to run; an unknown river yet to explore. What falls there are, we know not; what rocks beset the channel, we know not; what walls rise over the river, we know not.

—Major John Wesley Powell, in 1869, as the crew of
explorers at his command descended into the unexplored
Grand Canyon of the western United States[1]

Your team is expected to deliver—big. Like Powell's crew nearly 150 years ago, perhaps you're even embarking on an ambitious plan to do something that's never been done before. Your Grand Canyon in front of you is deep and fraught with risks. And if you're like most, you begin your journey amid swirling changes and scarce resources.

Even though you may believe you personally have what it takes to deliver on your responsibilities, you wonder: Is every person on the team truly committed and capable of bringing their best? Will the members of the team productively work together and become larger than the sum of individuals? And will the team be able to work its magic in a company culture that at times lacks alignment and is careless about valuing the people doing the work?

Does your team have a chance to succeed?

"I have no question that a team can generate magic. But don't count on it," observed renowned team dynamics expert and professor of psychology at Harvard, Richard Hackman.[2] Volumes of research on the topic support his claim. As a sampling, consider that 70 percent of the workforce say they are a part of a dysfunctional team,[3] while **the experts who assess team effectiveness say 75 percent of cross-functional teams function below their potential**[4]—in some cases, by significant margins.

Is your team telling itself the truth? The fact is, in most cases the odds are stacked against you and your team. But it's not like you're going to throw your hands up and quit. Within you is the belief that big things can be achieved when the right things are done. This powers you internally. So you choose to step forward. (Doing so makes you feel alive.)

Your team doesn't have to meet an inglorious fate. History, including as recently as yesterday, includes teams that have overcome the odds and achieved extraordinary feats. We know this, because we've spent over two decades obsessed with teams that do big things. Specifically, we've pursued answering one question: How do they do it? Specifically, how do members of a successful team function together—in the midst of churn and constant change—to succeed when it seems they don't have a prayer of delivering your business imperative?

We found the answer. As a part of an expanding team of professional development specialists, consultants, and coaches, we've invested over 65,000 hours observing and studying what teams do (and don't do) to deliver on their business imperative. Our work includes supporting leaders and teams at global companies including P&G, Nestlé, Novartis, Cigna, Ford, Harley-Davidson, and others, as well as start-ups and those in academia, government, and nonprofits. In addition, we've studied teams in the world of sports, exploration, entertainment, and more. In each case, we found a common and undeniable pattern of steps, a code, successful teams use on their way to making a meaningful impact.

Just like Powell's team left us all with a map we can now use to safely navigate the Grand Canyon, so there is a replicable framework with clear steps that your team—any team—can take to succeed and do big things. We want you to have and experience that process. That's what this book delivers.

Teams that are ignorant about the severe odds they face, or choose to deny the facts, risk more than business results by rushing to their boats shouting, "We *have* to succeed!" Because such teams are ill-prepared for the perilous whitewater rapids that are most certainly ahead, the careers and happiness of teammates are at stake.

Your solution is more than people-centered; our work with leaders and teams around the world makes clear that big success occurs when the best of each teammate is brought forth in relation to the people around them. To that end, your team can and should be one of the greatest levers to improving the leadership of every team member.

Whether you're curing cancer, building buildings, developing software, selling widgets, organizing a charity, mobilizing first responders, coaching Little League, or huddling with financial experts, your team is influencing your organization's health in significant ways. The imperative is that this is done productively, where your team impacts other teams in ways that enable them to also do big things.

This book, and its valuable map for team success, is designed and written for you. Whether you're a team leader (or aspire to be), or you play a different role and are committed to doing your best to help your team succeed, we've delivered the content so theory can more easily be put into practice.

We as human beings are not here to be inconsequential or do small work. We are here because we matter. And we want to matter more. It is in our control to do the extraordinary, and it is our fortune to do so as a team.

While history creates its heroes out of individuals (insert your favorite here), even their work would be forgotten if it hadn't been for a team coming together around or behind them to do something more significant than any one of them alone. Indeed, people working together—a team—is usually the only reason big things are achieved.

Your team can make an epic impact—and in the process have an epic impact on you. Your Grand Canyon awaits.

Disclaimer!

Because the proven methodology in this book works, as your team quickly begins to do bigger things, your team is going to stand out. And here's why.

This book doesn't conform to the established thinking and doctrines of most other business books. For starters, being a high-performing team is not the ultimate objective. There's more. (Heresy? Perhaps, but you're about to prove that today's teams must go beyond mere basics to succeed.) Nor do we pontificate about the importance of trust, communication, alignment, accountability, and every other well-studied dynamic of successful teams.

That's because we have proven that teams that do big things don't do what's normal. They do what is exceptional. Specifically, developing your team to be trustworthy, communicate more effectively, and so forth isn't what your business is asking you to do. (More heresy!) Your business is demanding results.

Transformation occurs when you enable your team members to better deliver what has to get done by equipping them to be their best, bring out the best in others, and partner across the business to deliver shared objectives. **When people are enabled to be their best, the business does its best. Now, because of your boldness, you will see an increase in the greatest practices of humanity, including trust and all the other values your team and organization cherish.**

This is about the heart of the matter—being who we all know we can be—together. That's how big things are done.

1 Teams That Do Big Things

Those who know history increase their ability to make it. Here's a brief look at a team that made an epic impact. These seemingly unexceptional people demonstrated that together most any team can do big things. And they left a map for you to do the same.

At 1:00 P.M. on May 24, 1869, a team of 10 explorers pushed their boats into the water and floated away from Green River Station, Wyoming. They were determined to do something that had never been done: travel and chart the Green and Colorado Rivers of the western United States. At this point in history, the details of the nearly 100-year-old country's map were largely complete—except for one conspicuously large space. In an area the size of France, cartographers had simply written "unexplored." The region was unknown. And for good reason.

Downriver, danger lurked. To begin with, the desert terrain was nearly all rock and sand. Native Americans roamed the untamed and unknown territory. And the river—it was already legendary. Tales were told of waterfalls that made Niagara look small. Others claimed the river disappeared completely like an enormous snake vanishing down a hole.[1]

The last portion of the journey would take the explorers through what is now known as the Grand Canyon, a gouge in the earth 277 miles long, 18 miles wide, and a mile deep. Today, tens of thousands of people apply for the chance to raft the river for sport; occasionally, some lose their lives as they do so. But to the team pushing their boats into the water that day

1

some 150 years ago, the wild Grand Canyon wasn't there for fun. It was a job, something they were hired to do. It was something they had to do.

The leader of the band was a short, one-armed Civil War veteran named Major John Wesley Powell. As a would-be scientist, he had little experience in the Wild West. Still, he beamed with optimism. He'd assembled nine other men, all with varying degrees of experience as explorers and hunters, to complete the party. Some joined the team just days before their launch, motivated by the need for adventure and a paycheck. Altogether, these men weren't the best of their time, but they were all Powell could afford.

Prepared with supplies and food to last 10 months, the team reflected their captain's confidence. What they didn't know—couldn't know—is that they had prepared for the wrong trip. Their approach and planning were suited for entirely different circumstances. How they thought about their environment and each other was based upon the only resource they had: past experiences.

But there was nothing like the land they found themselves in. No river could compare to the one they were floating down. To achieve their objective, they'd have to do what they'd never done before.

The purpose of the expedition was to map unknown territory. For Major Powell, there was an additional objective: fame. The big thing he wanted to accomplish was earning a reputation as a legitimate scientist. While celebrity and fortune appealed to the members of Powell's crew, their primary objective was altogether different, yet equally clear: survival. While they'd never been on this particular river before, they knew enough from legend that they would be tested and pushed like they'd never been before. Success was not certain.

We'll return to Powell's journey into the great unknown shortly. First, though, consider the team you're on or the team you lead. What's your Grand Canyon? What's the significant objective the team must accomplish to positively and meaningfully impact the business? What's the transformation or big change or launch or innovation the organization is demanding you deliver?

And now, the question this book will equip you to answer in the affirmative: Is your team equipped to deliver big things?

A word of caution: Many who have gone before you into uncharted territory have mistakenly thought that the key to their team's success (survival!) was a matter of equipping themselves with a new structure, software, process, (quick, make another Gantt chart), or rearranging where people sit or dine. Most of those teams have not been heard from again. Their work was at best marginal, and therefore, forgotten.

That's because it is not merely how your team is structured or the equipment and resources in your hands that you'll need for success today. It's something more—much more.

Why Many Teams Can't Do Big Things Today

Well-intentioned organizations everywhere are sending their teams into the great unknown future riding inflatable floaties—the same type you give to children in the backyard pool. Companies spend an inordinate amount of time determining what they must accomplish, then slap acronyms on those goals, like S.M.A.R.T. (specific, measurable, achievable, relevant, timely) and WIGs (wildly important goals).[2] Knowing your team must conquer its Grand Canyon, without being equipped with how to do so, however, is reckless (if not madness). Teams are increasingly desperate for knowing *how* as humans they'll achieve the *what*. We're functioning in what the U.S. military coined a VUCA (volatile, uncertain, complex, and ambiguous)[3] world. The disconnect is obvious: Employers are pulling employees together, calling them a team, giving them a directive, and expecting them to deliver results quickly.

But such teams can't. This isn't an inflatable backyard pool your team must get across. Your objective today is its own Grand Canyon. The way teams came together before won't work in today's intense, fast-changing world. When organizations fail to grasp the wisdom that the method for teaming successfully has changed, their approach can look like the antiquated change model depicted below:

- Step 1: Announce the new initiative the company needs to meet lightning-quick changes in the market.
- Step 2: Form teams and assign people to roles.
- Step 3: Tell people what to do and give them half the resources needed to do it.
- Step 4: Remind everyone of the company values (optional).
- Step 5: Apply external motivations in the form of rewards or penalties.

- Step 6: Try to overcome the resistance or confusion created in Steps 1 through 5.

- Step 7: Identify who is to blame for missed deliverables, milestones, and budgets.

- Step 8: Disband the teams or change personnel and repeat Steps 1 through 7.

This common approach never gives teams a chance to do something significant. In moments of fatigue, as people are shuffled from project to project while enduring new demands, it's easy to think the bosses have gone mad, while the bosses get mad. They can see what needs to get done, yet can't find a way to get the team to operationalize the new vision.

Is it any wonder why so many people avoid eye contact and hurry back to the isolation of their workspace feeling despondent?

Is Your Team's Whole Heart in It?

Who are we kidding? Nearly all of us lose a bit of ourselves each time we're forced through the eight dysfunctional steps of the antiquated change model. It's an unsustainable formula: We diminish ourselves while the magnitude of our work increases in volume, complexity, and speed. We used to finish the work we started; we used to celebrate jobs well done; we used to have meaningful relationships with those with whom we worked. But now? What used to make us feel alive is too often absent for too many. We are sapped of a certain sort of energy necessary to do big things.

It's clear that there's a new requirement to succeed as a team today. The solution is refined and raw, sophisticated and practical, genius and basic, elegant and simple: It's heart. The ability for teammates to be at their human best and become bigger than anything they face. This is what many teams are starved for.

Is your team's whole heart in it? It's not enough for one or two individuals to have heart on a team of 10 people, as an example. In fact, that's tormenting as emotions usually erupt or apathy sets in. Teams rise above this and significantly increase their odds of achieving big things when their whole heart is in it. Defined, this is the point at which the members of the team fully commit to bringing their full self to the team and its efforts to ensure successful outcomes—unconditionally. Now, with the personal integrity of each team member in action, the purpose of the team transcends personal position, ambition, and recognition.

Whether your team has been together for years, you're a newly formed team, or every team member only knows each other virtually, can you quickly develop this whole heart, where the best of each person on the team is amplified? Teams we've observed functioning at this level describe it this way:

- Whole heart occurs the moment we act on the wisdom that we are stronger together.
- It's the valor and collective grit that shows up even when times are tough.
- It's the juice we experience when we're up against severe odds, yet somehow summon the strength to win.

This whole heart is what collapses the idealistic into the realistic. Teams that possess it passionately own their plan to deliver on the big thing in front of them. They get off the fence and refuse to allow the circumstances to determine their thinking and actions. They say no to whatever tempts them away from their goal. These are the teams where people speak straight, and remain optimistic when the data say they shouldn't—because they know what they are capable of and what's possible.

This ability for any group of people to quickly unite and operate with a shared, energized focus that brings out the best in all of us is the defining need of our time. If we all tell ourselves the truth, this need transcends business. In too many arenas and communities, people are experiencing self-inflicted wounds through persistent attacks on each other. The tolerance for divisive actions in humanity is reaching a breaking point.

As all of us drop deeper toward our own Grand Canyon, we recognize and agonize over the wisdom inside of us: We are better than this. Our leadership, talent, culture—in other words, who we are as people—all merge at a space called *team*. It is here that we discover our darkness and our brilliance. It is only here that we get serious work done.

WTF (Want the Facts)

In case you have a teammate who's been out of town for a while and missed what's going on, and they want the facts to better understand the reality of the situation faced by all, share this data with them:

- 84 percent of employees are "matrixed" to some extent, meaning they serve on multiple teams.[4]

- 21 percent of executives are confident in their ability to develop cross-functional teams.[5]

- 92 percent of companies are going through reorganization.[6]

- 70 percent of transformation efforts fail.[7]

- When team members were asked to describe their team, fewer than 10 percent agreed about who was on it.[8]

How Legendary Teams Succeed in Doing Big Things

Take this quiz. Consider these now-classic tales of glory and identify what they all have in common. What exactly enabled these teams to succeed?

- The Apollo 13 space mission team, including those at mission control in Houston, Texas. After an explosion on board, the astronauts had to scrap their plans for exploring the surface of the moon and divert all their resources to getting a hunk of malfunctioning metal—and the lives it carried—safely home. In what some consider a miracle, they prevailed.[9]

- The 2016 Chicago Cubs. They faced a history book full of 108 years of failure that said they were losers. But in this magical season they made it to the championship of baseball, the World Series. After four games in the best-of-seven series, they found themselves down three games to one. With perseverance, they overcame long odds and fought their way back, forcing a final and deciding game. In what became an instant classic, the game required extra innings to determine the winner. The Chicago Cubs dug deep and found the strength to win.

Legions of fans around the world could finally say: Our team is the best.[10]

- The team called the "brain trust" at Pixar, the computer animation film studio known for producing smash hits like *Toy Story*, *Finding Nemo*, *Monsters Inc.*, and many others. Pixar founder Ed Catmull says, "Early on, all of our movies suck."[11] Yet, the brain trust and other teams within the company have the remarkable ability to produce and deliver feature films to the market that regularly win Academy Awards and almost always make the list of top 50 world-wide highest grossing animated movies.

For more than two decades, we've been obsessed with answering one question: How do you equip a team to deliver big things? We've studied teams like those just mentioned and observed and worked with thousands more—with a singular lens: What is the *how*? Specifically, the *human* how? In other words, how did they create the behavioral dynamics that make the team seemingly superhuman?

When teams are enthralled with an idea, they are relentless in their learning, experimentation, and practice. We certainly are, which is why we've insisted on going far beyond team basics in our work. For example, nearly everyone knows that for a team to succeed they need a purpose, agreed-upon goals and objectives, a strategy, customer, charter, resources, role clarity, clear responsibilities, processes, and all the other fundamentals.

Here is the key question, though: If each of us knows these basics, and many teams fulfill those requirements, why do so many teams still fail to do anything significant at all? The truth is that a lot of organizations are in peril for one striking reason: Dynamics exist that stop employees from being who they really want to be: great people, particularly in relationship to the other members of their team.

Good teams can repeat back a strategy they've read on paper. They can watch the slides and listen to leaders at the town hall gatherings. But if the team's plan isn't reflected in their hearts, they're likely doomed to be overwhelmed by an avalanche of priorities and mixed messages about how they should do their work. In addition, the seemingly ever-changing direction of the company creates a dizzying swirl of confusion. A pressure to reinvent oneself while still delivering what the team was told to do yesterday overwhelms capacity and crushes confidence.

Under such circumstances, even though executives can see the strategy clearly on the whiteboard, without the ability to be better together, employees with glazed eyes ask with increasing frequency: Where are we going? Who are we becoming?

Going Deeper Than Behavior Basics

It's painfully clear that it's far more than revising the team charter or redesigning the reporting structure that's going to get any of us through this. As well, the solution requires going further than platitudes about needing to model organizational values.

The answer to what's necessary for teams to do big things today lies in going deeper than the behavior basics. A first step is examining how the members of extraordinary teams behave together. For example, let's go back to the quiz of legendary teams. What did you see as the common thread in the success stories cited earlier? Most people come up with a list that includes these behaviors:

- Trust
- Collaboration
- Respect
- Vision
- Strategy
- Accountability
- Empowerment
- Communication

These characteristics or behaviors indeed are demonstrated in nearly every story of team success. (Come on, though, admit it: Did you have a sense of déjà vu when you read the list? We did because it's a list distributed nearly word for word in countless books and within organizations around the world.) There's no surprise here: These qualities are necessary for a team to succeed.

But there's more. (And once you see and apply it, everything changes.) These values and behaviors are inherently intangible. **What's necessary**

are reliable methods to create tangible behaviors. In nearly every success story, there's a pattern—a way the team approaches their objectives and team members interact with each other—that serves as a mechanism by which the behaviors on the list above become a reality. Those who can see this pattern and these dynamics and replicate them dramatically improve the arc of the team's destiny.

The key to seeing the pattern requires understanding that the values and behaviors we've all been conditioned to believe are the Holy Grail (in other words, if you have them, the world is yours) aren't the end-all resolution. The values and behaviors successful teams demonstrate, while important, are in reality just one of two steps toward the solution. To illustrate, consider pi.

$$\pi = 3.14159265$$

- The values and behaviors we listed for successful teams are not wrong; they're merely incomplete. For example, if you ask someone, "What's pi?" and she answers, "3.14," you wouldn't jump up and down and claim she lied or was incorrect. Likely, you'd explain that there's more to the numerical value: It's 3.14159 . . . and so on from there.

- Recall that we asked what exactly enabled these exemplary teams to succeed? At that moment, most of our brains did the same thing. It defaulted to describing *what* the teams did to succeed (3.14 = trust, courage, collaboration, and so on). To complete the answer, however, we must dig into *how* the teams functioned to create the *what*, the trust, courage, collaboration, and more (3.14159 = the how).

What's important is rarely achieved until a team knows how to do it.

A System for Creating the Thinking, Actions, and Outcomes Necessary for Success

None of us have been told a lie. The talented people in HR and organizational development know what they're doing. Values and behaviors and characteristics and capabilities—identifying them is critical to success in any endeavor. And if you are as passionate about developing and being a part of teams that do big things as we are, you've likely reflected on the list of values and behaviors and asked yourself these critical questions:

- Why does it seem everyone keeps talking about the same behaviors but little changes in people's actions?

- Why is it that many professionals could look at their bookshelves and see pages upon pages promising the characteristics identified on this list, yet these same people are challenged to demonstrate these qualities when under pressure?

- Why is it that nearly every person in today's workforce can define and describe the virtuous behaviors they believe their team needs to demonstrate to win—yet are unable to consistently model the behaviors?

We know why. (And so must every team with big aspirations.) And here's why we know why. Together with our team of specialists, we reverse engineered what successful teams, including those highlighted earlier, were doing as they achieved big things. Specifically, we looked at the outcomes–actions–thinking (in that order) demonstrated by the members of those teams. **Thus, we cracked a code: how to shape *thinking* that creates the *actions* necessary for any *outcomes* you desire.**

The knowledge of incredible thinkers has powered our work. This list includes Aristotle (thinker who needs no introduction), Viktor Frankl (Holocaust survivor and psychiatrist who helped humans find meaning in even the cruelest form of existence), Daniel Goleman (the psychologist who looked beyond IQ and explained the skill set called EQ or emotional intelligence), Daniel Kahneman (another psychologist whose life's work has focused on judgment and decision-making), and David Cooperrider (professor and innovator of appreciative inquiry into leadership).

By pulling the research and wisdom together of those who study how we behave—and holding it up as a lens to view how teams quickly and effectively change their behaviors so they can do big things—a clear pattern of thinking and actions became obvious.

For 25 years, we've tested this pattern through various applications and constructs. We've analyzed results, adapted our models, and then applied them again. Our empirical data are collected from partnering with teams from 37 countries in 25 different industries, those on the Fortune 500 list, multinational companies, and small businesses alike.

As we saw the pattern reveal itself, we wondered: Does the methodology work more effectively with a certain type of thinker than another? And across all functions of a business? Using a phenomenological approach to answer those questions, we've tracked applications and outcomes within teams made up of multiple age groups, representing those in commercial, production, research, finance, legal, and in multiple industries. Additionally, we've broadened the scope of work to include nonprofits and those in government and academia. By so doing, we captured the experience and developed a thorough, contextualized description of the process teams were using to do big things.

No matter what culture, country, industry, function, or team, the results have always been abundantly clear: We've tapped into something profound. Regardless of the circumstances within or around the team, there are specific steps successful teams take to create the thinking–actions–outcomes necessary to do big things.

These forces of success, now obvious upon post-assessment, can be purposefully used as a system of success for teams today. Why wait until after your team has done something significant and then share stories of glory? It's far more useful to tell those stories in advance; you reduce risk (and its sibling, stress) when you know how a story ends. By naming and simplifying this method, the outcomes can be replicated and scaled within your organization and team. Now, your aspiration of doing big things is actionable.

The Do Big Things Framework

Here it is. We won't make you read to page 127 to get what you're looking for. Let's get busy being who we know we can be. Right now.

It's called the Do Big Things (DBT) Framework. It's the method teams practice (whether they know it or not) to transform how they think and act together so they can deliver transformative outcomes. The DBT Framework provides the language teams use to transform and quickly elevate their power and effectiveness. It's how everyone on the team aligns to a powerful and singular focus necessary to achieve the big objective in front of them—and deliver the greatest impact to the business while seizing the opportunity to be better human beings along the way.

Importantly, the Do Big Things (DBT) Framework is how team members realize the best of themselves and the team's collective significance. Now, the whole person is showing up in big ways.

The steps within the DBT Framework equip any team to standardize— meaning agree and align—on what it means to operate in daily interactions in a manner necessary for success. This, of course, is not typical in most organizations.

"Our deliverables are all standardized," a portfolio project manager in the entertainment industry told us. Quality standards? Not negotiable. Safety standards? Don't even think about questioning established processes. Timelines, customer care, and budgets? We rarely budge, the manager said.

But what about how teammates behave? Treat each other? Their conduct when under pressure? "Entirely negotiable. Nothing is standardized," the manager answered. "And that's exactly why we're insanely busy but getting nothing important accomplished."

As with the thousands of teams we've partnered with, we're deeply honored to deliver this to you. Here's why: The DBT Framework doesn't require any of us to change who we are. Instead, it activates and amplifies the brilliance we already possess. Don't buy the lie that your team doesn't have what it takes. **We all have the wisdom within us and the ability to create the whole heart necessary to overcome the obstacles in front of us. The work of doing big things does not require *doing* more; it is a method to *being* more.**

This wisdom is one of the primary reasons why the DBT Framework is so powerful: Its mechanics are always turned on, and always available to us. What's necessary is to make the complex, simple; the mundane, inspiring; and that which seems to take forever, achieved quickly. The vision for the team becomes the reality now.

The DBT Framework from 30,000 Feet

Although we'll be getting to the specifics of each of the steps starting in Chapter 3, to build necessary awareness we want to provide a high-altitude flyover so the big picture is clear (Figure 1.1).

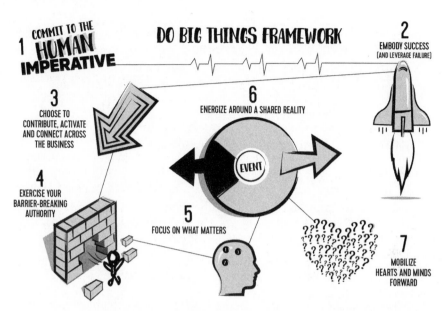

Figure 1.1 The Do Big Things Framework: Seven Replicable Steps Teams That Achieve Extraordinary Success Use

Here are the seven steps of the DBT Framework.

1. *Commit* to the human imperative. Identify and align as team members to the human thinking and actions essential for delivering the business imperative. Often born from a sense of caring for one another, this is the transformative manner in how team members perceive each other that sets the stage for values to be put into action.

2. *Embody* success (and leverage failure). Team members personify the spirit of the success they seek while they pursue their lofty objectives. When excellence is who we are (rather than what we will be someday), then even the hardships we encounter make us better and stronger as a team.

3. *Choose* to make three decisions: Contribute, Activate, and Connect across the business. Each team member decides to bring their best to every situation and bring out the best in those with whom they interact. Then, together, they choose to partner across the business to deliver shared objectives.

4. *Exercise* your barrier-breaking authority. The team determines what stands between them and success—both real and perceived. Then, by controlling what they can control, team members act upon their inherent authority to choose their response in daily situations.

5. *Focus* on what matters. The team uses the *3 Mind Factors* to concentrate on and deliver what causes big things to be achieved: the relationships and teamwork necessary to succeed.

6. *Energize* around a shared reality. Team members use the *Energy Map* to address issues with a similar frame of mind, enable people to better tell the truth, and function with authenticity. The Energy Map is used to guide the focus and common language necessary to elevate how team members interact with one another. This step facilitates the needed skills of adaptability and accountability required to do big things.

7. *Mobilize* hearts and minds forward. Empower the team to own their role in delivering a stronger future. Use *Questions That Trigger Hearts and Minds* so everyone internalizes and delivers the team's business imperative.

The italicized words that begin each step form an acronym that spells *cecefem*, which in Latin means "to come together quickly as a team and do big things." Wait. Um, actually, it doesn't mean that. We just made that up. In fact, the acronym doesn't spell or mean anything.

And that's good news: To be successful you're not going to have to memorize yet another acronym. The reason is because the italicized words are merely labels—just like trust, collaboration, and the other values that are labels for actions. We are going to focus our attention where teams that do big things concentrate their attention: on the thinking and actions that occur to succeed at each step.

What's critical is that the team members together are shaping the team's future, instead of one person doing it. Jim Kouzes, coauthor of the timeless book *The Leadership Challenge*, during a discussion about what's necessary for teams to succeed, told us, "We need to reinforce that leadership is not hierarchical. The role isn't just a position. Therefore, it's the context of leadership we need to change—not just the content. As a team

member, we are not just followers. Leadership is everyone's responsibility."[12]

The DBT Framework is how each team member can be accountable to that responsibility.

What Success Looks Like

Raise your hand if you like power. (Okay, that's nearly everyone.) As people, we behave in curious ways when we believe someone is taking power away from us—or attempting to have power over us. This was especially apparent in one of our consulting projects.*

To say these individuals weren't operating as one team would be to make a gross understatement: The R&D folks and those representing the commercial side of this specialty goods business came into the room in a power struggle with their boxing gloves on. A recent restructure of teams—designed for greater speed and efficiencies—had changed the processes for getting their work done. And it immediately revealed and amplified a serious disability: The people who had to work together were only demonstrating proficiency in finger-pointing and sabotaging the best efforts of others.

Collectively, they were moving toward their Grand Canyon, the one big thing they had to deliver: Momentum had to be regained in sales. Once a titan in their industry, they were losing market share. They had to get back to growth. And the members of ops and commercial were at the center of delivering this one big thing.

Each person in the room agreed: The new structure they were in, on paper, would allow them to move more effectively in delivering on their objectives. But (and it was a big but) *how* they were operating as humans was rendering their structure and improved process nearly worthless.

We asked one of the senior leaders, "Why haven't you elevated this barrier to your boss?"

---

*All the stories we share are based on actual experiences. In some cases, throughout the book we've changed contextual specifics to conceal identities. But the pertinent facts remain.

His answer impressed: "Because we all agree that we can and should resolve this ourselves. We want to communicate to the organization that we're fully capable."

Specifically, this meant that if they were going to accelerate their ability to get innovative products to the market, they had to collectively identify and agree on how they would make decisions faster together. Specifically, who would decide—and how and when—which solution would be given the green light and which would be scrapped? These are difficult decisions—especially because everyone has their favorite pet projects.

Freeze! The story must be stopped here. Do you recognize this moment? It's the point in time so many professionals know because they often experience it in their own work: A new structure, new process, new objective, or a new team (read: they don't have a history of relationships necessary for trust) must perform with excellence when the stakes are high.

The last thing most of these professionals need is training on trust, collaboration, or communication or any other desired behavior. (This is why they so often cancel and postpone or, if they do go, do so kicking and screaming the entire way.) They've seen it all; in fact, they *do* intellectualize it all. Yet what will too many of us be subjected to in this situation? **Another forced professional development exercise focused on** *what* **behaviors are needed to succeed—when what we really want is the** *how*. And because the business is demanding results, we want it quickly. (Please, spare us another talk about how important values are, when we already understand our values.)

The DBT Framework is what the R&D/commercial team was seeking: a playbook to create the thinking and actions that create trust and their other targeted values. And in this case, we needed to make haste: It all had to be oriented toward a decision-making process they all could own.

Fast-forward a couple of days: The most junior person in the group raised his hand and said, "I finally feel like we're on the same team. Why did we wait so long to do this?" Then everyone stood. In the left hand of each person was the agreed-upon decision-making model they had codeveloped; they used their right hands to shake the hands of their teammates.

How did they get there so quickly? Because we didn't train them to do something different. That takes more time than the business has to spare. Instead, by facilitating the seven steps of the DBT Framework, we enabled them to more effectively and consistently demonstrate what they already possess. Once equipped to do so, they ran with the DBT Framework.

Here's what this looked like for the ops/commercial team:

1. They *committed* to the human imperative necessary to increase the sales of innovative products: to function as one team. They began their meetings by focusing on key questions that would advance creative collaboration and innovation. Questions such as:

   ◆ What capabilities do we possess as a collective team that will make it possible for our customers to realize success?

   ◆ What is working in our collaboration?

   ◆ What does it look like to have each other's back when R&D or marketing is being scrutinized by the organization?

2. They gained a clear understanding of what it means to succeed as one team so they could *embody* that specific success. (They also identified how they would respond to failure.) They asked questions like: What does success look like for our customers? For us? The organization? Our talent?

3. They aligned and agreed on what it looks like to *choose* to contribute, activate, and connect with one another, as well as with those beyond the people sitting in the room. An understanding of what it means to be at their best personally, to bring out the best in others, and to partner across the entire organization was established. This team, as an example, determined that transparency in their actions and communications would be critical to success.

4. They began to *exercise* their barrier-breaking authority by identifying and agreeing to focus on the barriers they could control. For example, no longer would the team blame past leadership for decisions they'd made that had created the difficulties the team was now facing. They chose to own how they could influence change by focusing on the customer, internal capabilities to save on resource costs and the monetary outcomes from being first to market with innovative products. They focused on why they needed to remove a barrier as much as they focused on what they were innovating. The barriers that were once formed by the thinking and actions that created silos, were now driven by one team with one agenda.

5. They equipped themselves with a method to ensure that they stayed *focused* on what matters as it related to how they interacted with one another so they could successfully execute their new decision-making model. They made the commitment to speak up to redirect the focus and common purpose when the team was focusing on what was not working or what wouldn't work. They collectively made a choice to stay forward focused, together.

6. They established a means to *energize* around a shared reality so that healthy conflict didn't degrade to relationship conflict. "It's pretty simple, really," said one team member. "When we share the same understanding of how to approach issues that arise, we invest our time seeking out and embracing differing points of view to ensure we bring the most innovative solution to the market for our customers. This fuels our ability to put our passions to work much faster."

7. They determined their plan to *mobilize* the hearts and minds of teammates, including those not in the room, to ensure the new decision-making model was adopted by the entire organization. By cocreating a model that was customer-centric in its design with a compelling story about why it mattered, together, they inspired an organization to rally around what would be a differentiator for the company—something that restored internal pride and confidence, and would be felt by the market. The tools we equipped this team with so they could take these seven steps are examined in Chapters 3 through 9. And each is effective.

"After our time with you," one of the senior leaders reported, "I have observed a different level of trust and communication between leaders in commercial and R&D. Their messages were once passive and tense. Now, they ask each other questions. They share perspectives and ultimately agree to speak with one another to cocreate a shared solution. It is amazing to watch."

We chose to share this story because it highlights the hard work that every team must undertake on their journey to doing big things: Transform the interactions among teammates. Achieving extraordinary outcomes first requires that none of us be ordinary as team members. That's what precipitates improved outcomes, so is, therefore, what success looks like. This R&D/commercial team will tell you that the meetings they now have, spent sharing their power, may not be glamorous, but the improved market share is worth it.

The Important Requirement of *You*

If any of us want to be on a team that does big things, we are required to do something first: be bigger in our character. Our insecurities, our fears, our anger, our jealousies, our discontent, our pettiness—all of this we must transcend if we are to do something significant as a team. We must realize our own potential if the team is to realize its potential. We must go all-in with our hearts if we are to know the reward of being on a team whose whole heart is in it.

It is only when we give ourselves to something greater than us that we realize a greatness within us.

Ultimately, there's no question each of us as professionals is really good at what we do, that we've put in the hours and demonstrated the skill to be on this team. The question is: **Will each of us choose to matter? Will we choose to do something significant, not for ourselves, but for the team?**[13]

The risk of not being significant, of not doing work that matters, is its own quiet terror. Even though we know we shouldn't quit, we see teammates we care about descend into noncaring. It's subtle and gradual, but detectable: One team meeting after another, there's a decay of passion. Their eyes no longer meet ours on the video conference. Smartphones become their conscience. Efforts are minimized. They're protecting themselves from something. Then they travel home in the dark and give their families their leftovers.

And we begin to wonder about our own apathy. We wonder if we've begun to settle, to acquiesce. Then a question enters our mind that, at first, we push away. We don't want to answer it, because doing so may mean a future we don't want to see: Is what I'm doing—all this time committed to this work—worth it? Am I doing the right thing with my life?

The answer should be, can be, will be, *yes*. This existential reckoning, where we judge the merits of our own efforts, is natural. We are not to blame for the experience of stepping from solid ground onto an ever-faster spinning carousel. And we won't be victims, either. The spin of today's workplace, new and dizzying, can be brought under control: A rhythm always forms when we apply a mechanism that better enables us to be who we want to be—to be a part of something significant.

To do big things, we don't have to change our world, the entire company, or even the community. To be bigger than whatever is in front of us, we simply need to do what we *can* do: *commit* to leveraging the power of humanity, *embody* success, *choose* to make a meaningful difference, *exercise* our natural barrier-breaking authority, *focus* on what the business needs most, *energize* ourselves around a shared reality, and *mobilize* our hearts and minds forward. **By using the DBT Framework, we move beyond talk about what behaviors are important—and get busy with the how. We get better at being who we already are.**

We can do this thing; the team is within our sphere of influence; success is within our control. This is our greatest opportunity to matter.

Big Ideas in This Chapter and 3 Recommended Actions

- The question this book answers: How do you equip the team to deliver the thinking and actions to do big things?

- When your team members have heart collectively, then the team's "whole heart is in it." **Recommended Action**: Determine your answers to these questions with your team:
    - What difference does it make when our whole heart is in it?
    - Is this dynamic important to us, and if so, why?
    - How do we know if our team's whole heart is in it?

- It's not enough to train the team in the basics of "high-performing teams." To do big things today requires more. **Recommended Action:** Assess whether or not your team uses the Antiquated Change Model. If so, do you have a proven plan to utilize a different model?

- Knowing what values and behaviors are important for success is only part of the solution. Understanding how to demonstrate targeted values and behaviors is the key to being able to do big things.

- This ability for any group of people to quickly unite and operate with a shared, energized focus that brings out the best in all of us is the defining need of our time.

- Teams that achieve extraordinary success and have an epic impact on their business use a replicable, seven-step process called the Do Big Things (DBT) Framework. **Recommended Action:** Ask your team to assess which steps of the DBT Framework they are already demonstrating. Then determine which additional steps are important to better master to improve the team's effectiveness.

2 Teams That Flatline

There is no greater agony than bearing an untold story inside you.

—Maya Angelou

O ver the past few years we've asked hundreds of people, both younger and more senior than ourselves, as well as those in and out of management roles, this question: How many great teams have you been on in your career? (We intentionally don't define "great," allowing them to determine the criteria.)

Upon consideration, the clear majority of those responding answer that they have been a part of two to three great teams. Very rarely does anyone answer zero, nor five or above. And when asked why they qualified those teams as great, the plurality of answers cited two things, in relative terms: (1) the team achieved something significant and (2) they worked (choose your favorite superlative) together.

Is it good enough to get to the end of a career and claim that the number of great teams one has been a part of can be counted on one hand? It isn't according to most of the inspired people we know. Although there are variables unaccounted for when considering the responses to this question, the fact is the answers reveal perceptions. And that's a glimpse of the reality for a sizeable sample of people.

This is where things get crazy—and frankly, sad—from our perspective. We've observed a significant number of teams unknowingly be on the verge of delivering the steps outlined in the Do Big Things Framework, only to stumble and fall away. You may, for example, recall a team you were on that had tremendous promise. Armed with the DBT Framework now, you might look back, assess, and say something like, "We embodied success (step 2). We broke through certain barriers and functioned from the same reality (steps 4 and 6). But then something went wrong."

In these cases, teams that once had their whole heart in it, where everyone was fully committed, begin to experience the opposite: flatlining. Just like the medical monitor that measures the functioning of a patient's most vital organ, these teams arrive for the big show in arrest. Unable to shape the thinking and actions necessary to do big things, the team succumbs to the weight of the pressure they're under. Progress stagnates. And the potential the team once possessed falls away as too many members of the team become disheartened and demonstrate behaviors even they are not proud of.

From our experience, we believe there are two primary reasons why teams flatline. **First, the members of the team simply don't know how to equip themselves with the ability to operate in a way that enables them to put their whole heart in it and do big things.** Hence, the reasons for Chapters 3 through 9 of this book.

Second, teams too often unwittingly function from outdated methods, or even false beliefs, about how to best develop their team. As a result, left unaddressed, at best their resources are wasted, and at worst they destroy the potential the team possessed.

That's why this chapter is so important: In order for the DBT Framework to enable your team to truly make an epic impact on the business, it's critical that beliefs about how to best develop teams are checked. (The emperor who wore no clothes due to false beliefs serves as a friendly reminder.)

To set the stage, we'll revisit Powell's band of explorers in the early stages of their journey to do big things. The false beliefs they began with almost cost them their lives.

A Team in Trouble

They were in trouble, and they knew it. As Powell's team of explorers descended deeper into the chasms approaching the Grand Canyon, they found themselves ill-prepared for the raging river they rode. Innocently, they had prepared to do the big thing in front of them with the thinking and behaviors that had enabled them to succeed on prior excursions. They had assumed that the actions that had proved vital in Civil War battles and previous treks into the frontier would deliver success in the future. Such an inaccurate belief was particularly poignant in one illustration: They felt secure in deploying the finest boats they could obtain. History would prove them wrong—dead wrong.

The boats Powell's explorers used were built for the lakes and placid rivers of eastern North America. Engineered for efficiency and speed, the crafts were long and narrow, with a rounded body. Those who boat down the rivers of the west today, courageous folks known as "river runners," would consider such vessels suicidal, and for good reason.

In their natural state, rivers in the west drop toward the ocean, and thus the speed and volume of the water generally increases—creating a force and torrent of water greater than a line of bulldozers lined up for miles. Adding to this dangerous environment, semihidden rocks, some the size of small cars or even houses, form obstacles. At many of these points, the water becomes furious. White water rapids form waves bigger than buses that crash in all directions, many of which could swallow a boat whole. It didn't take long for the expedition to learn their trip on this river would be unlike any other boat ride they'd ever been on.

Doing big things successfully often means being able to do things differently than they've been done before. Major Powell's team soon discovered that the boats they'd chosen, and skills they'd developed for efficiency and speed on waters in the east, were not what they needed now. What they had to have to succeed—survive—were vessels and capabilities that would enable them to adapt to the ever-changing conditions of the river.

Specifically, successfully running a river's rapids requires determining the safest route through the rocks and hydraulics. Rarely is this path a straight line; a zigzag is a better description. The boats Powell's men had were built for speed, however. They required time to turn—time the men didn't have amidst the turbulent and chaotic rapids. They could barely deviate from a straight course—until they smashed into an obstacle. (Think of a steel ball caroming down a pinball machine, and you can get an idea of what this team faced each time it encountered rapids.)

As it is today, so it was 150 years ago: The consequences for preparing a team to do a project the same way former jobs have been done can be severe. Just days into their first canyon, three crew members found their boat bearing down on a massive rock. They had neither the skill nor the means to adapt their course.

The rock blasted a hole in their boat. The three men leapt from the vessel and swam for shore, narrowly escaping with their lives. Powell would later memorialize this location of the river as "Disaster Falls."[1]

The End of Teamwork (As We Know It)

Consider: What does your team believe is the best way to develop the thinking and actions necessary to do big things? For certain, the end of teamwork (as we all know it) is at hand. Actually, it's been over for quite some time. How we teamed together before isn't effective in the turbulent times of today.

Our observations tell us these teams rarely flatline and fail because they lack technical skills. Far more often the catastrophe that occurs can be traced to outdated beliefs about what's required to develop the team's ability to effectively work together.

What follows are the four most common flatlining beliefs that cause teams to lose themselves in the crashing rapids ahead. We'll also identify the new beliefs that our research shows are required for a team to do big things.

Flatlining Belief #1: If you develop the leader you develop the team. (False!)

Imagine this: A CEO sits in his office meeting with two team members when the discussion is interrupted. After a knock on the door, three workers in overalls enter the room. *Fish Tank Cleaners* are the words on their uniforms, and the smiles on their faces told everyone they love their job. Setting out their brushes and pads they began preparing for serious work.

The CEO says to his colleagues, "Excuse me," then leaves the table at which they're seated, approaches the workers, and begins pointing at select fish moving about in the wall-sized fish tank. "This one . . . that one . . . and definitely all of those with stripes . . . and the big bottom feeder there," the CEO says.

The fish tank cleaners take careful notes. The two colleagues, still sitting at the table, however, are surprised that the cleaners could even see the fish: The water is filthy. Yellowish-gray scum floats in water that seems to glow. "Why would the CEO wait so long to clean the fish tank?" they wondered.

The CEO returns to the table, but his teammates keep their eyes on the fish tank. With tremendous care, the cleaners use micro nets to catch the fish the CEO identified. Because there are a lot of fish in the tank the job takes time as they swoop and scoop. Occasionally, they catch the wrong fish, shake their heads, drop the fish back into the grimy water, and then dip their net again in pursuit of their targets.

What happens next stops the two observing teammates. When the cleaners catch one of the CEO's identified fish, it is removed and placed in a small glass container just bigger than the fish itself. Then, small brushes with tiny bristles are used with great care to clean the fish.

At this point the CEO's colleagues aren't listening to what he's saying. They pretend to take notes as they watch the cleaners repeat the exercise of removing certain fish, bathing them, and then placing them back into the murky water of the large tank.

After an hour of work the cleaners begin to pack their belongings. The one with a clipboard approaches the table where the meeting is held. In his hand is a plastic bag filled with water and one of the fish the CEO had pointed at—the bottom feeder.

"Excuse me, sir," he says to the CEO. "We've nearly finished cleaning your tank. To complete the job, we recommend you remove this bottom feeder."

"Okay," the CEO says. "I never liked that guy anyway."

"We also recommend that you add several of our new X-Fish," the cleaner states.

The CEO looks up from the papers spread on the table. "What's an X-Fish?" he asks.

"They're fast and agile," the cleaner answers. "Their presentation and swimming style brighten every tank. They're innovative little guys, as well. They find resourceful ways to extend their body energy—which is a cost savings for you because they require less food."

"Great!" says the CEO. "Get me a bunch of those."

The cleaner smiles, nods, and then returns to his coworkers. They pack their little brushes and mini-holding tanks, wipe up the water that spilled, wave at those sitting at the table, and leave the room.

The room is silent for a while, until the two teammates can no longer contain their curiosity. "What did they just do?" they ask the CEO.

"What?" he responds, a bit perturbed that they would ask a question that seemingly had an obvious answer.

"The cleaners, the guys handling your fish . . . what were they attempting to accomplish?"

The CEO takes off his glasses, tilts his head, and squints at the other two. "Haven't you ever seen a fish tank get cleaned before?"

The Dirty Fish Tank Training Model

Despite overwhelming evidence that it's ineffective, the standard for developing leaders and teams today involves extracting employees away from the people and teams (their culture) with which they do their work. Isolated, they are trained with the expectation that they will change their thinking and behaviors. Then they are reimmersed back into unchanged dynamics. The result: little or no change is accomplished in the individual or the group. We call this the Dirty Fish Tank Training Model (Figure 2.1).

LEADERSHIP
TRAINING

Figure 2.1 Dirty Fish Tank Training Model

There is no doubt that the talent of the team leader affects the results of the team. We're not suggesting that teams don't gain some benefit from leaders and individuals being sent away to trainings. We're saying that teams don't benefit enough. It's not even close. A growing body of research makes this clear. American Society of Training and Development (now known as the Association of Talent Development), in their state of the industry report of 2013, reported the United States alone spent $164.2 billion on learning and development programs.[2] *Forbes* found that $12 billion annually is specifically spent on leadership development. Yet both organizations report that only 20 percent of these dollars result in a transfer of learning or directly impact the company's bottom line.[3]

We believe the waste and poor outcomes are grossly underestimated. These numbers only reflect the money spent on training that doesn't work. What must be included as well are the exponential costs of disillusioned team members who see their bosses and teammates leave for development, only to return and demonstrate little or no improvements. (You didn't change last time. Why would anyone expect you to change this time?) Employees who roll their cynical eyes can hardly be blamed for succumbing to the belief that there's no hope for the team and then disengaging.

The costs don't stop here. When organizations don't see the thinking and behaviors of a team change, the blame often settles on the leader. (Hey! You're in charge and were sent to training!) Consequently, untold costs mount as leaders are removed, sent to other teams, or swapped for others. A churn-and-burn approach to talent ensues. **Just as the fish who gets a bath and then is put back in the dirty tank can't be blamed for failure to clean the water, nor can an isolated leader bear the entire burden of failure when their team doesn't improve.**

There's little mystery why the Dirty Fish Tank Training Model doesn't work. It is irresponsible to attempt to change the thinking and actions of a person outside the cultural system of their natural habitat and then expect them to make changes of any significance. It is a false and misguided belief to think that the team will improve by merely developing the leader.

Do Big Things Belief #1: To develop the team, you must develop the *whole* team. (True!)

What's needed to replace the Dirty Fish Tank Training Model is a process for successfully shifting and elevating the thinking and behaviors of the individuals of the team in concert with one another. **Culture change occurs as the members of the team, armed with greater shared awareness and consciousness, move through daily interactions repeating and reinforcing their new skills. Natural accountability to elevated norms takes places as individuals can sense that everyone else is changing.** This often results in accelerated improvement as every interaction drives stronger behaviors. This is another reason why the DBT Framework is so effective: It provides a holistic method for accomplishing systemic change among the team.

Flatlining Belief #2: To succeed, you must primarily develop the team for speed and efficiency. (False!)

Today, business as usual means plans are developed within organizations from an increasingly outdated paradigm: Identify what needs to be done, that is, what resources are needed, who are the stakeholders, building communication and contingency plans; then build a course of action to achieve the objective as efficiently and effectively as possible. This is what Powell's team did as they prepared to go downriver; it's what many team leaders still do as they prepare to launch a big initiative.

Speed and efficiency remain important. But today, the moment plans are made, conditions and circumstances shift. The rapidly changing world doesn't only drown a team because they're moving too slow. It devours them because team members can't adapt to the new world together.

Too often, companies attempt to solve this team-adaptability issue by changing personnel or restructuring. While such efforts can deliver incremental improvements, they usually mask what needs to be done to do big things. Where a person is placed in the organization still doesn't solve how they need to better think and act as an individual in relationship to others.

Do Big Things Belief #2: In order to succeed, speed and efficiency must be combined with team members' collective skill of adaptability. (True!)

The planning required to do big things is more critical than ever, and it must include steps to equip those executing the plan with the ability to adapt to conditions that are unpredictable when the plan is conceived. And what's necessary for a team to be able to adapt? Organizations are rightly focusing on empowerment, the buzz word of this era. However, **empowerment is only a part of what's necessary for teams to adapt.**

We see this a lot: People in the workforce are empowered to make decisions—but they still don't. That's because the empowerment necessary to adapt to rapidly changing conditions requires something additional: developing the emotional and cognitive flexibility of team members in concert with one another. For example, in many companies, it takes remarkable emotional courage to speak up in a meeting and say, "Um, boss, I just want you to know that when the customer told us their requirements, the data was much different than we discussed when we had our planning meeting with you. Therefore, to honor their request and still meet our objective, I made a decision that was different than the one we originally agreed to with you last week."

As you may recall from the fish tank analogy, in too many companies such a statement would subject you to circling piranhas.

When team members develop greater emotional and cognitive plasticity together (and every step in the DBT Framework supports in accomplishing this), they build the capability to adapt in a way that sticks. Increasingly, the team then stays focused on the overall plan or objective (get safely down the river) while also being able to adjust or modify their thinking and actions in that plan when they make discoveries. Now, these rapids of crisis, for example, are diminished as threats: a primary supplier can't make a deadline, the costs of materials suddenly skyrockets, or a product recall is announced (their Disaster Falls).

Flatlining Belief #3: Plans for growth automatically motivate the team to a higher level of performance. (False!)

As authors, we gain our greatest wisdom as gifts from the leaders and teams we serve. This particular client team meeting was no exception as we gained a deeper insight into what's necessary to advance a team.

"We've got to be careful," John, the senior vice president, said. "Our company has had a tough couple of years. Our division is the bright spot of our organization. We need to capitalize on the momentum we have. But we need to reconsider how we do that."

The general manager and others on the phone were silent. The engineering company was facing a critical juncture: Could the strength of their teams meet the rising demands of their customers?

"We've added new people, moved people to new locations, all while our customers continue to up their game," John said. "Every day it seems there are more requirements. And I'm starting to hear people say, 'Schedule and cost are now more important than what we were once known for: quality.'

"To tell the truth, all our focus on growth doesn't mean what it used to. Now, when we talk about growth, employees go, 'No thanks!' It means 90-hour workweeks, with a faster pace, and fewer resources."

No one disagreed. The silence on the phone reflected the depth of the team's fatigue. Then John finished by saying, "Growth for growth's sake doesn't work. It only matters when each team member feels personally rewarded."

The human spirit is built for expansion. Achieving professionals want to live large. They want to seize opportunities that take them closer to realizing their potential. This is why the rallying cry of "Growth!" as John's team experienced, once motivated teams to new levels of performance, just like sugar can provide a spike in energy.

Too much sugar provided too often, however, sends all of us plummeting into fatigue. The constant chant of "Grow! Grow!" increasingly has a numbing or demotivating effect on teams and the culture.

It doesn't have to be this way. This outdated and inaccurate belief must be replaced by thinking that authentically activates the heart of many.

> ## Do Big Things Belief #3: Growth is caused by teams that grow stronger. (True!)
>
> It's inconsistent to think that we can do something more if we aren't more as people. All of us are economical: As humans, we want the greatest return for minimal effort. Therefore, it's no surprise that within the teams we see that do big things there's a motivation that is even bigger than the motivation to grow the company. Instead, **team members shift from compliance to greater commitment when their hearts are rewarded for giving the greater effort**.
>
> When team members are intrinsically motivated, and know they will be better and stronger as individuals and as a team when they reach their finish line, inspiration occurs more frequently. This causes the team to grow, which means the organization will do the same.

Flatlining Belief #4: *Team* is defined by the group of people who have the same functional responsibilities. (False!)

A key moment in Powell's crew's journey occurred where the Green and Colorado Rivers merged. It was a beautiful location, inviting an extended rest.

In addition, Powell wanted to explore. You may recall his priority: notoriety as a scientist. But a new risk to the team had developed: starvation. Their food supply was being reduced to little more than soggy, moldy flour, yet they had weeks remaining in their journey.

At this moment, pretend that all members of the crew have a cell phone. Powell picks up his phone and calls his boss in Washington, D.C., and asks, "Do we stay here or move downstream?"

The boss laughs. That's the easiest question he's been asked all day! "Stay and get your job done," he shouts. "Explore. Do serious science stuff! That's what we're paying you to do."

In the meantime, two crew members, who were hired as hunters for the trip, grab their phones and text their supervisor in Denver. They ask: "Should we stay or go?"

Their boss also laughs. "Stay! Hunt!" he texts in response. "That's how your performance is being evaluated."

Meanwhile, the men responsible for rowing safely down the river have a different discussion with their manager. As you'd likely predict, they received a clear command: "Get downriver now!"

After the phone calls and texts, the 10 crew members convene to discuss their next steps. An argument ensues as members point fingers and ask heatedly, "Wait, who's in charge? Where did you get the authority? And how come we were never informed of their decision before now?"

At this point the team doesn't need roaring rapids or external force to rip a boat apart. Competing priorities within the team have the same effect: The team, along with its chances of success, is doomed.

Too often, cross-functional teams are really just two groups responsible for different aspects of the business sharing the same conference number to conduct business. Serious gaps in execution occur when anyone moves from reporting to one boss to having other leaders to answer to because accountability drops. When we are responsible to everyone, we're ineffective at delivering to anyone.

Worse, when team members choose to be loyal to a person (for example, the boss who conducts their performance review) instead of loyal to the mission of the larger team, no amount of rhetoric will make a difference. In fact, it's not uncommon to see people begin to despise others, despite the fact that they all have the same logo on their shirts. Left unprepared to overcome these dynamics, team members retreat to minimalist thinking: I'm okay if my function wins and the cross-functional team fails.

Do Big Things Belief #4: Big things can be achieved when team members are equipped to connect outside their function and utilize a more holistic, one-team approach. (True!)

The common solution for cross-functional teams to succeed is to have team members align on the priority objective everyone shares (the one big thing that must be done). But if it was that easy, far more cross-functional teams would succeed than currently do.

The reality requires a solution far more psychologically and emotionally sophisticated than that. **Team members must release their functional centeredness and adopt new definitions of what "team" really means—and align on why that evolved definition is important.** Doing so is not for the faint of heart.

Decision-making structures, communication patterns and methods, reward systems, and demanding functional bosses who are eager to position themselves for promotions, can seem to be working against the team's ability to be united as one. Nonetheless, no matter how strong an opposing current can seem, there are ways to proceed safely and effectively.

More than aligning to a shared objective and incentives, what's required is establishing a common language and shared heart for the work that must be done. **Redefining and expanding what it means to be a team requires equipping team members to put emotional courage, transparency, and an enterprise mindset into regular practice.** This is what the DBT Framework does, thereby enabling everyone to act like effective team members all the time, regardless of who's in the room or what functions are represented.

While they had their challenges, Powell's team proved successful in working together despite their different responsibilities. As much as they wanted to rest, and Powell wanted to explore, they modeled the ability to adapt by using critical thinking skills grounded in the emotional aptitude to let go of personal desires in that moment. The team had a new priority: surviving. They would, therefore, pack their boats and go.

WTF (Want the Facts)

- In 85 percent of companies, employee morale sharply declines after their first six months and continues to deteriorate for years afterward.[4]

- Most individuals (75 to 90 percent) employed in companies doing global business are working with virtual teams. In fact, 64 percent are on up to three virtual teams. And 41 percent have never met the colleagues they work with.[5]

- Some 51 percent of HR professionals who say their companies use virtual teams tell us that building team relations is an obstacle that prevents them from being successful.[6]

- 96 percent of executives cite lack of collaboration for workplace failures.[7]

A Big Story to Tell

"Don't believe everything you think."

(BUMPER STICKER SEEN ON A CAR IN DENVER, CO)

The realities of a changing world require an exciting new reality about effective teamwork. Every team can create a powerful heartbeat, a rhythm, a cadence of synergy. But all can be slowed or stopped by choosing to believe what is no longer true about how the team should be developed. Flatlining beliefs diminish the power of who you are as a team, because they reduce who you are innately as a human being.

Flatlining, however, is not a permanent state (at least for teams). You can choose to communicate a grander narrative formed in beliefs that are true and best in today's world.

Your team has a story to tell. And it can be a big one, if allowed. Anything worth achieving often appears unachievable at first. By using the seven steps of the Do Big Things Framework (starting with the first of the seven in Chapter 3) you can turn hearts and talents from doubt to confidence. Doing so means you get the thrill of telling the story your team was meant to tell.

As you begin, be cautioned: You will be watched by others who aren't a part of your story. The cynics will jeer. The jealous may attack. **The skeptics will doubt. And when you arrive where you are determined to go, you'll look at your teammates, nod, and say that you believed all along.**

And the others will wish they had been on your team.

Big Ideas in This Chapter and
3 Recommended Actions

- Teams flatline when their whole heart isn't in it, or in the big thing they must do. **Recommended Action:** As a team, discuss and create a plan of action based upon these three questions:

  - Are we susceptible to flatlining as a team?

  - How do we know? (What conditions, thinking, or behaviors are present?)

  - What will we do immediately to trend toward having more of our whole heart in the work necessary to achieve our objectives?

- The thinking and methods for developing teams that worked before are no longer effective in today's changed world. A new approach is required. **Recommended Action:** Assess the current methods your team uses to develop itself and consider to what extent those actions are effective in today's world.

- The Dirty Fish Tank Training Model involves removing people from the team, training them, and then immersing them back into unchanged dynamics of the team. This approach is costly and rarely effective at changing thinking and behaviors.

- Today, in order for a team to succeed, speed and efficiency must be combined with the team members' collective skill of adaptability. **Recommended Action:** How would you rate your team's ability to quickly and effectively adapt to challenges that arise? What's the rationale for your rating? And what's one thing you'll do to improve your team's ability to adapt?

- To succeed, cross-functional teams must first release their functional-centeredness and redefine team.

- Company growth only occurs when teams grow stronger.

3 Commit to the Human Imperative

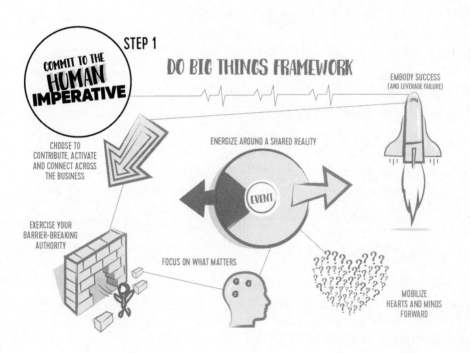

STEP 1

COMMIT TO THE HUMAN IMPERATIVE

DO BIG THINGS FRAMEWORK

EMBODY SUCCESS
(AND LEVERAGE FAILURE)

CHOOSE TO
CONTRIBUTE, ACTIVATE
AND CONNECT ACROSS
THE BUSINESS

ENERGIZE AROUND A SHARED REALITY

EVENT

EXERCISE YOUR
BARRIER-BREAKING
AUTHORITY

FOCUS ON WHAT MATTERS

MOBILIZE
HEARTS AND MINDS
FORWARD

When $60 million is invested in your project, and those in the executive suite have given their personal endorsement, big things are expected. For this project team, there was no shortage of excitement and nerves: Their objective was to totally revolutionize the way the global company gathered, analyzed, and dispensed customer data. If successful, the numerous business units within the company would no longer need to invest in their own research or look to costly outside sources; everything would be done internally, saving the company millions of dollars in efficiency costs.

This was a "we cannot fail" priority project. To succeed, the company did what most organizations do: They created a dream team by putting the brightest minds and the best talent on the job. A clear and definitive charter was established to include alignment among stakeholders, and resources were committed.

Freeze the story! Do you recognize what was missing? (If you do, you already understand the first thing required to do big things.) Despite the ample research findings from brilliant people with impressive initials and titles after their names working at places like MIT[1] that prove it's not how smart the members of your team are that determines success, **organizations keep throwing talented and intelligent people together thinking that somehow talented and intelligent teaming will occur. It's painful to watch.**

While we wish we had been called to equip this dream team with the DBT Framework as they were forming, instead, they enlisted our support after they found themselves stuck in a storming mode for far too long (and an unhealthy one, at that).[2] Their delay is not that uncommon because this fact is easily missed: Teamwork doesn't begin when people are in the right seats on the bus (to use a popular phrase uttered in many workplaces). Nor does it begin just because the same people get invited to a weekly meeting or report to the same boss. The practice of effective teaming begins with identifying, aligning, and equipping team members with the ability to model the thinking and actions essential to success for that unique team. That's why committing to the human imperative is the first step in the Do Big Things Framework.

Defined, the human imperative is this: Team members identify and align to the specific thinking and the inherent behaviors necessary to deliver their business imperative. This is

the act of bringing the best of humanity into the work you do. In other words, has your team answered this question: Who do we need to be as people—together—to succeed as a team?

Committing to the human imperative means the team incorporates into their business plan how they will be accountable for putting those behaviors into practice. Here's a specific example of a team's human imperative: "When, as a team, we are 'all-in early' by being committed to always giving our best—regardless of the situation—then we will succeed in operationalizing our strategy. We will take measurable steps each week to consistently develop our ability to be 'all-in early.'" We'll share more examples later in this chapter, including how to establish your team's human imperative.

The well-resourced project dream team, however, didn't invest a moment up front to determine its human imperative. Consequently, the organization had to wait 18 months to realize the impact to business they envisioned the team would accomplish in a much shorter time. Here's why.

The seven people on the team came from rich and diverse backgrounds. Two of them, seriously-smart-and-purpose-driven millennials, were considered future stars in the organization. And the more seasoned team members had a track record of innovation that distinguished them even further than the framed and distinguished diplomas on their office walls.

Their intellectual superpowers, however, were negated by a certain kryptonite: the inability to work together effectively. Who could have predicted that one of the company's most accomplished and technically respected employees transforms himself into a bully when he feels threatened by people who have as much talent as he does? And how could leadership have known that the most savvy project managers would be distracted by their own brilliance and would stray (and stray again) from the team charter?

This is a key point any team that aspires to do big things must grasp: No one can predict human behaviors until the team determines which human behaviors are a priority. Repeatedly we see teams assume that professionals will do the right thing. Yet, who decides the definition of *right*? And even if everyone has the same definition, assuming that everyone has the ability to model the right thing with each other when under pressure is fraught with risk. In many cases, the chances for success are only slightly higher than randomly pulling five people from a line at a bus stop and expecting them to form a top 40 rock band. **Until your team's human imperative has been defined and committed to, you can predict that the thinking and behaviors of your team will be unpredictable.** Any behavior can and should be expected.

Because this dream team didn't build the human imperative into their plan, they did impact the business—but not in the way the company planned:

- The project stalled, because the people on the team stalled in their efforts to work together. Specifically, certain members of the team were made to feel less important by being excluded from critical discussions, as well as regularly having their work criticized by those who had appointed themselves as judges.

- After months of frustration, the people on the team began doing what most humans do: protecting themselves by playing it safe, or worse, leaving the organization.

- Rumors spread across the company as the team became infamous. This resulted in increased resistance to the team's objectives.

Emotions were high on and around this team, and not the type conducive to a team with its whole heart in it. Despite the fact that everyone wanted to succeed (these are really good people with good intentions), they were flatlining. Regardless of knowing *what* needed to be done, they didn't know *how* to think and act as a team to succeed.

The good news: Until the customer (or your sponsoring executive) tells you it's too late, every team in this situation can resuscitate itself, and get its whole heart back in it. Once equipped with the DBT Framework, this dream team had its awareness piqued.

Somewhat surprisingly, it was the team bully who went first. He made a decision to show up differently. "I've made some mistakes as well," he told the team. "I haven't been the teammate I know I can be. For whatever reasons, I've got the need to control too much."

This was the spark the team needed. Almost instantly, the youngest member on the team spoke up and said, "No worries, man. We've got your back. We'll figure this out." There was some nervous laughter, which naturally turned to a comfortable chatter. Then, a discussion blossomed that was full of confidence.

If they were to do the big thing in front of them, they declared that they had to "have each other's back." It was their way of communicating that they were as committed to each other's success as they were their own.

Predictably, by committing to this human imperative they established an ownership for their own behavioral norms. Immediately, the behaviors on the team began to change. Because they saw and experienced each other differently, teammates began to do something they hadn't before: trust each other, and themselves. As they moved deeper into the Do Big Things Framework, their human skills advanced. Project updates were increasingly transparent. Emails were replied to quicker. Questions were asked and received in spaces once filled with demands. Combined with their technical prowess, this meant it wasn't long before the organization began seeing the outcomes they envisioned long before.

Has your team committed to the human imperative by defining and aligning to the specific thinking and actions necessary to deliver your big business imperative? Like this team, the moment you make this commitment, you put your organization on a schedule to realize your team's epic impact sooner.

Respect Is Not Enough

Here's a big question: Do your teammates care enough about achieving success to care about each other?

We've done the work of equipping teams to do big things long enough to know that, with few exceptions, for teams to achieve their full potential teammates must care about one another. Should you be on a team where this isn't the case, there's no need to fret. You don't have to convince your teammates they have to start elevating their humanity. (That can be a tough sell.) You simply need to begin a specific discussion.

- First, ask the big questions that began this section.
- Then, state and ask: We've emphasized the need to respect each other. Is respect enough to enable us to achieve the big objective we have in front of us?

Be prepared: It's likely some will initially answer "yes." Then, without trying to convince anyone, invite them to explore the difference between respect and caring. It might sound like this:

If we respect each other, it means:

- We listen to what others say, though we may not do anything with what we hear.
- We acknowledge others have unique skills and different ideas, but do little to develop them further.
- We may respect each other so much that we fear each other, and disengage to protect ourselves.

If we care about each other, it means:

- We listen to what others have to say, and seek to incorporate their insights and needs into our efforts moving forward.
- We regard the skills and ideas of others, and find ways to leverage their strengths to accomplish our shared objective.
- We trust one another, and have the confidence to engage with each other further.

The truth is, respect alone is not enough to do big things. It is merely a first step to being an effective team. To do meaningful work together requires that team members be meaningful in their interactions with one another. And besides, **even if you could succeed without caring for your teammates, would the work fulfill you?**

Because human beings are wired to want to be a part of a community, and do good deeds, these outlined discussions build critical awareness, which immediately impacts behaviors and the expectations team members have for themselves and one another.

Frankly, teams have also used these discussions to discover who they no longer want to have on the team, as well. **That's because caring is hard work that not everyone is up for. Caring requires that all of us listen more, accept where people are at in their thinking instead of criticizing them, and defend them even when they're not in the room with us. This also means including them even though they may look different and we may not agree with them. Not everyone has the inner intelligence, or the heart, to do these things.**

The excuses we hear often, albeit disguised in other words, is, "I don't have time for this touchy-feely stuff and to engage with people this way." In the mad dash of today's world, it may be easy to rationalize such thoughts. Yet, should we find ourselves thinking this, it says a lot about us, doesn't it?

The fact of the matter is, everyone's brain is wired for, and already executing, what cynics claim is "the touchy-feely stuff." As one simple example, every five seconds the prefrontal cortex within each of our brains is scanning our surroundings assessing if others are a threat to us. Our history with others, their body language, and the look on their face, among other things, are all being considered to determine one thing: Can I trust this person? Teams that do big things maximize their time by caring about trusting one another.

This is one of the primary reasons why so many teams can only achieve small things. The members of these teams come together and postpone their care for others on the team—until they have proof that their teammates care about them. But the prefrontal cortex isn't resting. You can see the no-win situation: With everyone sitting around waiting for people to care about them before they emotionally invest in others, no one's brain gets the signal that others can be fully trusted. So, no one trusts each other, and the team waits to be a team.

No team can do big things by being passive with the human qualities we all know are essential for success. **You can dramatically speed the development of the trust your team needs by going first: Be the one who cares even more.** To be certain, caring doesn't mean you're lowering expectations of their performance. And it certainly doesn't mean you withhold essential, constructive criticism. In fact, caring means the opposite. You care so much about your teammate that you have to tell them the truth. Now, however, you're telling the truth in a way that can be far better received by teammates.

It's important to note that caring for a teammate doesn't mean you have to be friends with them. For example, a teammate may have a personality style, political bent, or other quality that doesn't resonate with you. No matter. Caring means you still believe each teammate has worth as a person, and therefore, it's valuable to protect and amplify their value.

In this way, the human imperative is a moral imperative. As teammates care about one another more, the resulting behaviors

transform the team. That's because of what we call the amplifier effect. One act, in this case, caring about a teammate, automatically and reflexively models multiple other values in high degrees of distinction. In other words, the behavior basics on the list in Chapter 1, such as trust, collaboration, and transparency, all occur at higher rates when people care.

Our work with teams reveals a unique and important phenomenon as it relates to the effect of caring within a team. **When a team lacks the commitment to a human imperative, the business imperative becomes just one more thing to do on a long list of objectives.** Chronic fatigue sets in. Teammates operate with glazed eyes. Interactions among team members become transactional and diminished in meaning. Distractions of high drama replace the team's high potential as the team descends to flatlining.

Conversely, by committing to the human imperative, teams experience increased confidence. And with it, they see their business objectives differently. They become more energized. They take more smart risks and think more innovatively. They begin to believe they will succeed.

How does your team feel about the big thing that must get done? The answer is largely influenced by how team members think and feel about one another.

What It Means to Make an Epic Impact

When team members change the way they look at each other, they change the way they see their business objectives. This changes how they feel about those objectives.[3] And that increases the likelihood the team will deliver an epic impact on the business. We saw the power of this truth while supporting a team in the baby care industry. Their site once held the premier reputation in the global company. They were known as the best; others benchmarked against them. But over the past couple of years, their results had fallen. The pressure was on to regain lost glory.

During a strategy discussion concerning objectives, it was clear among the team of managers that they knew what had to be done. It wasn't until one of them had the emotional courage to stand up and share her truth that the team identified what was necessary to succeed.

"We've lost sight of who we really are," the manager said. "As a child growing up, I always knew I wanted to work here. My parents did, and so did I. It wasn't as much what they did but how my parents felt about this place that attracted me. It was special. *They* were special. I knew there was no other place for me.

"Now, when I talk to my daughter, she tells me she's not sure she wants to work here—and it's not because of the type of work but who she sees her mom becoming." The manager was quiet for a moment. "That doesn't work for me. It shouldn't work for any of us."

She told her colleagues, **"I remember who we were. I remember how we believed we could do anything. And we did. The reason we were number one was because our hearts were in it."** Then she looked at the team and said, "We're not going to do it the way we've been doing it anymore. We're going back to being people with hearts first. That's what will deliver our objective. And that's what will make my daughter rethink where she wants to work someday."

In 30 seconds, a team that was flatlining had the pulse of passion. Their business imperative hadn't changed, but how they saw and felt about that objective did. Now, a more noble cause had been identified. They reestablished a human narrative by identifying the human imperative—in this case, being people with hearts. They could now see what needed to be done from an elevated perspective. This team took the first and critical step in the DBT Framework by identifying the human imperative necessary to deliver their big thing. Just months after that strategic team meeting, the numbers at that site began to shift. The organization got its pulse back.

Are you interested in achieving big business success while being on a team that doesn't have a pulse? For most of us, the thought of giving our all, but not enjoying the process, is a buzzkill. Rapidly, the world is seeing a growing employee base that will not tolerate such a scenario. And why not? It makes little sense to commit serious time (our life) to activities that don't develop us or drive our own fulfillment.

Therefore, making an epic impact as a team includes a critical component that is balanced with delivering big numbers for the business. (Do any of us need to hear more stories about people delivering blockbuster results, becoming rich and famous, and filling their shelves with trophies and awards—only to feel deficient, destitute, or lost? Likely, not. We all know we have a greater purpose.)

Epic, in this case, means looking at a photo of the team you were on that did big things for the organization and smiling again as you look at the faces of those standing next to you. Yes, the team did something none other had achieved—and you're rightfully proud of that. The richness of the relationships, however, means more to you than the year-end bonus that you spent long ago. The team delivered on a significant objective because the hearts and minds of the team were mobilized. Because of those who stood next to you, your life was enriched.

This is what it means to make an epic impact: The team delivers big for the business and for people.

WTF (Want the Facts)

- Senior executives who don't work as a team and haven't acknowledged necessary changes in their behavior is the number-two barrier to organizational success.[4]

- Unclear objectives are consistently identified as a primary cause of failure in change initiatives.[5] (Author note: Objectives that don't inspire an emotional connection are almost always unclear.)

- 55 percent of change management initiatives meet the employer's objectives.[6]

- 25 percent of employers say they are able to sustain gains from their change management initiatives over the long term.[7]

- Learned skills have a half-life of five years, while human skills last forever.[8]

What the Human Imperative Sounds Like

Diffused or fragmented energy accomplishes little; big things are only accomplished when the team can discern their objective and then direct all their power toward accomplishing it.

"We have to change from being a software company to a business solutions company," a president told us in our initial discussion with him.

"So, that's your one big thing, your business imperative," we responded. Then we asked, "In order to accomplish that outcome, describe the thinking and actions you must see from your leadership team to accomplish your business transformation."

Without pausing, he said the following, by emphasizing every word: "We. Must. Own. The. Plan." The line was quiet. A stake had been driven into the ground. A nonnegotiable was established. "Every person on the team must fully make the plan theirs so that when things get crazy—and they will get crazy," he said adding a laugh, "then we will all know where we must go together and why."

Determining and committing to your human imperative is not a prescriptive exercise. Organizations typically mandate business imperatives to their teams, but they break a human code followed by achievers when they mandate that employees think or act certain ways. This is one reason why identifying the human imperative can be transformative for a team. It's not HQ telling your team how they should act. **The imperative is uniquely yours: It's how the team members see themselves doing something significant.** The human imperative is how they see themselves being significant.

While the human imperative may often include the labels known as the corporate values (trust, collaboration, communication, as an example), often it captures the essence of those values while transcending them in specificity. The human imperative is what jolts the heart and activates the inner strength a team needs to see themselves through their Grand Canyon. **By delivering on the human imperative, the team now says, "I believe. I can see it. We can. We will."**

Figure 3.1 shows several examples of how we've seen teams line up their human imperative to drive their business imperative.

We function in a cause-and-effect world. The human imperative drives the business imperative. These narratives changed the trajectory of the business these teams were responsible for delivering. These statements are not platitudes or rallying cries. Instead and importantly, they provide the disciplined focus the team members will need as they move through the other steps in the DBT Framework.

Importantly, the president and his team responsible for moving the business from a software to a solutions company didn't forfeit trust, alignment, collaboration, or other values. In fact, they made those values come to life.

WHEN, AS A TEAM, WE COLLABORATE CROSS-FUNCTIONALLY ...
...THEN WE WILL SUCCEED IN REMOTELY DESIGNING
AND ENGINEERING OUR PLANTS IN EMERGING MARKETS.

WHEN, AS A TEAM, WE ARE "ALL IN EARLY" BY
BEING COMMITTED TO OUR ROLES AND RESPONSIBILITIES...
...THEN WE WILL SUCCEED IN OPERATIONALIZING
OUR LEAN PRINCIPLES, STRATEGIES, AND TACTICS.

WHEN, AS A TEAM, WE LISTEN WITH CARE...
...THEN WE WILL TRANSFORM THE CUSTOMER EXPERIENCE AND GROW MARKET SHARE.

WHEN, AS A TEAM, WE TAKE INITIATIVE AND CONNECT
ACROSS OUR BUSINESS WITH AN ENTERPRISE MINDSET...
...THEN WE WILL FILL OUR DEVELOPMENT PIPELINE
AND DIFFERENTIATE WITH INNOVATIVE PRODUCTS FOR THE MARKET.

WHEN, AS A TEAM, WE ARE INSPIRED EVERY DAY...
...THEN WE WILL ACCOMPLISH ENTERPRISE-WIDE USER-ADOPTION OF OUR NEW SOFTWARE.

WHEN, AS A TEAM, WE
FUNCTION WITH A ONE-TEAM APPROACH...
...THEN WE WILL SUCCESSFULLY RESTRUCTURE OPERATIONS
WHILE EXECUTING ON CRITICAL KEY PERFORMANCE INDICATORS.

Figure 3.1 Sample Human Imperative Choices

"Look," he said. "We've got really good people here. They care a lot about success. In their natural state, they're trusting and collaborative and everything else they need to be. We just need to make sure they don't do what's normal when we get under pressure." This means they must be equipped to do what they naturally want to do: play bigger.

"The ticket," the president finished, "is to ensure they own the plan. Then, the rest will come."

How to Determine the Team's Human Imperative

Imagine this: Your team has just finished watching a webcast of the division president announcing and defining the big thing the company must do to be successful. As you turn off the computer, you turn to the team. Several team members sit with wide eyes. Others are rolling their eyes. Some are lost in their smartphones, shaking their heads.

What do you do? How do you prepare the team? We can tell you what has minimum impact: spending hours creating fancy slides and graphics, then giving rehearsed presentations and speeches, stating "We're going to . . . !" and "Then you will . . . !" followed by "Success will be ours!" (Cue inspirational music.)

Good salespeople have a saying, "People don't like to be sold. They like to buy." With a twist, the same wisdom holds true when enlisting team members in any effort. Persuading people what they should do with their hands while failing to activate their hearts and minds means there's little hope that the "We've got this!" conviction necessary to do big things will be created. What must occur is for the team to develop shared psychological and emotional ownership of the objective. (Special emphasis on the word *shared*.)

When your team commits to a unique human imperative that they identify, the team is reinforcing a reason to believe they will succeed. Here's how effective teams do this, and so can you.

After you turn off the computer, facilitate a discussion with the team using questions from three specific categories. These questions are proven to work when people are sitting in the same room with each other—or on opposite sides of an ocean. And they're effective when some team members represent each generation. The questions work because they tap into something that matters to us all.

1. **Thinking** of the human imperative:
   - How do we want to operate as a team that can do big things?
   - What behaviors as a team do we want to represent us to the rest of the organization?

- What one word will be said by others about how we are operating as a team as we go about achieving this big thing?
- What does it look like to partner seamlessly with other teams, across boundaries or cultures?

2. **Feeling** and experiencing the human imperative:

- What has been your experience on teams that function with tremendous confidence even though the job in front of you is huge?
- How would you describe the experience when we are in sync as a team and optimizing our collective talent?
- What's the greatest intrinsic reward for us when we function with excellence?
- What does it feel like when you know the team you're on is winning? Succeeding?

3. **Doing** and delivering the human imperative:

- What specifically does the teamwork necessary to do our big thing look like in action?
- How will we know we're functioning in a way that will strongly impact the business?
- How must we function now so that we're even stronger as a team when we finish this?

Let's acknowledge that these questions aren't normal in most workplaces, despite the preponderance of research that says they're critical to elevating the consciousness for anyone to do big things. Given this, it may be best for you to position authentically why you're asking the team these questions. (Additionally, you could simply buy them this book and let us support your voice.)

After the team has answered these and other questions you're inspired to ask, narrow their answers to a common theme. What sort of thinking or action rises to the top of the team's awareness as a narrative? The answer is the team's human imperative. (Tip: Resist the temptation to overthink this by coming up with the perfect words or phrase. It's important to remember that it's far less important what words are contained in your defined human imperative—and far more important how the team feels and experiences the identified words.)

The team is going to feel really good at this point because they're finally getting a chance to articulate the story they want to tell by being real about what it's going to take to get the big job done. They are, however, only halfway in this exercise.

Committing to the human imperative is far more than talking about the thinking and behaviors required for success. What's equally important: equipping team members to operationalize the action they identified. That's precisely what steps 2 through 7 of the DBT Framework accomplish and where we're going in Chapter 4.

When the Big Things of Two Different Teams Collide

Stephen Covey, author of *The 7 Habits of Highly Effective People*, famously told all of us, "The main thing is to keep the main thing the main thing."[9] Once the team knows the big thing it must do and is aligned on the human imperative, Covey's catchy quote is a good reminder: **The main thing is to keep the human imperative the human imperative.**

At no other time is this more important than when two different teams with different objectives must work together. The collision can be explosive and destructive. For example, consider these scenarios:

- A team from R&D, whose big thing is to create new products, collides with a team from manufacturing whose big thing is to eliminate costs. The R&D folks must succeed in changing what is manufactured while those making the products want to simplify and make processes predictable. Who wins?

- A team from corporate finance with an initiative to standardize accounting procedures collides with various regional teams who have identified autonomy and empowerment as their priority. Finance wants to scale procedures so the company can grow more efficiently; the regions want to be nimble and respond to customer needs on the spot. Who wins?

- A sales team insists they could sell more if they had stronger marketing materials they could review with the client during their sales calls so the product sells itself. This belief collides with a team from marketing that says the obvious solution is for salespeople to develop the skill of understanding what the prospect really needs before they share anything about the product. Who wins?

If any two teams aren't equipped with a common language or shared human imperative, no one will win. In addition to the business suffering, the collision results in almost certain flatlining for both teams. From a third-party perspective, this we-must-win-and-they-must-lose approach seems ludicrous. Aren't they on the same team if they're in the same organization?

They are, but it's not the company name or logo that determines the main thing. Rather, it's personal motivations that drive every person involved. This is when human behavior (beautiful or ugly) becomes nearly predictable.

Here's what we all know doesn't work in these situations: one team mandating to other teams their main thing. Knowing that such acts quickly create an oil-and-water outcome, what can two teams do in this classic cross-functional situation?

Leaning on Maslow's hierarchy of needs, consider the Hierarchy of Team Purpose (see Figure 3.2).[10] Numerous times we've equipped cross-functional teams with the hierarchy and encouraged them to take a few minutes at the beginning of their work to transform the pending collision into a partnership. By transparently discussing and assessing what it is everyone is attempting to accomplish, and their motives for doing so, the team can better identify—together—their shared one big thing and the human imperative necessary to achieve it.

As you reflect on the hierarchy of team purpose, here are some questions proven to elevate thinking and actions among any team:

- At what level as a team are we operating on the hierarchy? (Encourage participants to share their rationale.)
- What is your experience as you (attempt to) collaborate with others?
- What's the correlation between our assessment of where we're at on the hierarchy and the results we're delivering?
- Where do we want to be on the hierarchy? And why?
- What sort of thinking and actions will be necessary to get us where we need to be on the hierarchy? (Note: The answer to this question can be considered your human imperative.)
- What's our plan to put those behaviors into action?

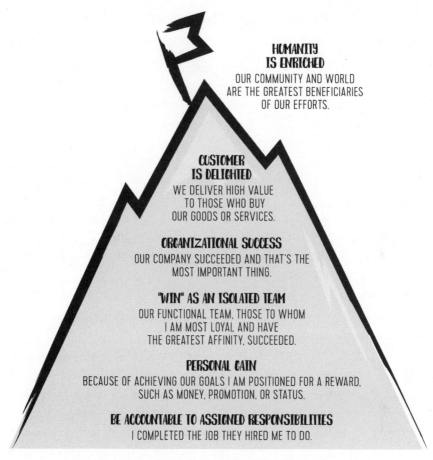

HUMANITY
IS ENRICHED
OUR COMMUNITY AND WORLD
ARE THE GREATEST BENEFICIARIES
OF OUR EFFORTS.

CUSTOMER
IS DELIGHTED
WE DELIVER HIGH VALUE
TO THOSE WHO BUY
OUR GOODS OR SERVICES.

ORGANIZATIONAL SUCCESS
OUR COMPANY SUCCEEDED AND THAT'S THE
MOST IMPORTANT THING.

"WIN" AS AN ISOLATED TEAM
OUR FUNCTIONAL TEAM, THOSE TO WHOM
I AM MOST LOYAL AND HAVE
THE GREATEST AFFINITY, SUCCEEDED.

PERSONAL GAIN
BECAUSE OF ACHIEVING OUR GOALS I AM POSITIONED FOR A REWARD,
SUCH AS MONEY, PROMOTION, OR STATUS.

BE ACCOUNTABLE TO ASSIGNED RESPONSIBILITIES
I COMPLETED THE JOB THEY HIRED ME TO DO.

Figure 3.2   Six Elements Form the Hierarchy of Team Purpose

A former director at a health care company told us after he was lured away by a competing company that he wished he'd had the Hierarchy of Team Purpose to ignite important discussions at his previous company. "I originally chose to work at that company because of what it does and the difference it makes in the world," he told us. "But the way business was done didn't allow me to fully contribute or maximize my skills. That made my decision to leave easy."

Committing to the human imperative and doing big things better frees people to optimize their strengths. Team members are elevated beyond personal motives, and the entire team gains a nearly unstoppable power, in no small part because their top talent stays on the team.

When We Are Exponentially More Effective

We speculate that Powell's team exploring the Grand Canyon had an unspoken human imperative. And it wasn't "every man for himself." After all, the team had nobody and nothing else but themselves and each other to rely on to succeed (survive!). They knew when they started that they needed each person acting with the crew's best interest.

Powell's team didn't deliver entirely on their human imperative, and that brought striking outcomes. Nearly halfway through the epic journey, at a point where the terrain momentarily leveled out and the men knew there was a nearby settlement, a crew member made it his imperative to quit. He walked away and lived out his life in Salt Lake City, Utah. The merits of his decision can be debated: At that point the expedition was already running low on supplies, so one fewer team member relieved some stress. Quitting, however, is quitting. This meant one fewer person to support the team in achieving its objective.

Stark in contrast is what happened to the three men who chose to leave the team just days before the expedition succeeded in navigating the length of the Grand Canyon. They were battered and nearly broken. Nourishment had been reduced to cakes made of moldy flour, and there was precious little of that left. At this point, they found themselves facing their most severe test yet: what has become known as Separation Rapids. It was a stretch of crashing, churning water unlike any they'd seen previously. Certain members of Powell's crew were convinced that to proceed meant certain death.

What happened here is debated. Powell tells a story of three men choosing to leave the party because of fear. The departing members took advantage of a rare opening in the canyon wall, scrambled up the side, and away from the Grand Canyon.[11,12]

But others who have written the team's history, including Robert Stanton (who led a third expedition through the Grand Canyon and disliked Powell), relate a different account. After interviewing members of Powell's team, Stanton wrote in his book, *Colorado River Controversies*, that it was dissension among the team that provoked the men to abandon their team. Particularly, of note, Stanton reports that it was conflict between the expedition's leader and these three that caused the break.[13]

Regardless of the cause, there is no debating the outcome: The three men were never heard from again. It's presumed they were killed by Indians or rogue settlers in the area. In a bitter twist of fate, the remaining six members of Powell's crew rowed ahead, survived the rapids, and safely exited the Grand Canyon two days later.

Many variables play into the decisions people make, and history holds many secrets. The fate of Powell's team, including death and achievement, demonstrates the importance of the first step in the DBT Framework. **Committing to a human imperative is an act of promising to demonstrate a belief that any of us are stronger when we work well together.** United, we are exponentially more effective at doing extraordinary things.

Big Ideas in This Chapter and 3 Recommended Actions

- You cannot safely predict how your team will think and act, especially under pressure, until your team has committed to their unique human imperative.

- The human imperative is the unique thinking and actions your team believes are necessary for the team to achieve its business imperative. **Recommended Action:** If your team has not committed to a human imperative, prioritize and schedule the exercise. (Two tips: Keep it simple and remember that rather than a one-time event, it's a process.)

- Committing to the human imperative means building accountability for delivering the human imperative into the team's business plan.

- When a team lacks a commitment to the human imperative, the business imperative often just becomes one more thing in a long list of priorities that must get done.

- Making an epic impact means delivering big for the business and for the people doing the delivering. **Recommended Action:** Assess your team's effectiveness at enriching team members' lives as they work to deliver the business imperative. What's one change in thinking or actions that would result in increased fulfillment for team members and greater productivity?

- Respect is not enough to do big things. At the core of the human imperative is the wisdom that when teammates care about one another they achieve more together.

- The amplifier effect occurs when your team delivers the human imperative and thereby increasingly and naturally models desired values and morals.

- The human imperative is a moral imperative.

- The hierarchy of team purpose is a model that elevates the awareness team members need to change thinking and actions. **Recommended Action:** Ask your team at which level of the hierarchy do they mostly function. Then, together, identify what steps you'll take to elevate how you function.

4 Embody Success (and Leverage Failure)

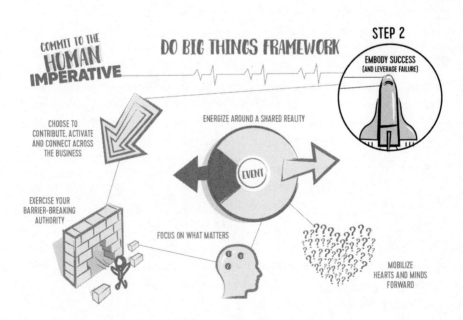

COMMIT TO THE **HUMAN IMPERATIVE**

DO BIG THINGS FRAMEWORK

STEP 2

EMBODY SUCCESS (AND LEVERAGE FAILURE)

CHOOSE TO CONTRIBUTE, ACTIVATE AND CONNECT ACROSS THE BUSINESS

ENERGIZE AROUND A SHARED REALITY

EVENT

EXERCISE YOUR BARRIER-BREAKING AUTHORITY

FOCUS ON WHAT MATTERS

MOBILIZE HEARTS AND MINDS FORWARD

N ot everyone gets to commute to work on a space shuttle. Astronaut
Mike Bloomfield did, though. Imagine joining him for a ride: You take
your seat in the cockpit of a craft that weighs 4.5 million pounds as it sits on
the launch pad. As you put your head back and face the sky, you feel the
engines roar.

Power—massive energy—begins to lift you off of Earth. And then you
get to experience what few people ever have. For the next eight minutes,
your craft burns a ton of fuel every second. (Think about that for a
moment.) You go from zero miles per hour (mph) to 17,500 mph, which
means you're traveling five miles a second. (You laugh as you think of your
business colleagues who are traveling from Los Angeles to New York; it will
take them over five hours traveling in a plane going 500 mph. You're
traveling that same distance in 10 minutes.) Every 90 minutes, you make
another trip around Earth.

There's no being late for meetings now. The last two minutes of your
ascent you're increasing your speed by 1,000 mph every 15 seconds. Three
Gs of acceleration has your back pinned squarely into your seat. Then, as
you arrive at your destination, you float: Instead of weighing 4.5 million
pounds, your craft now only weighs 220,000 pounds.

Just another day on the job.

"Space flight is really, really hard," Mike told us. "The mechanics and
physics of the operation are mind-boggling. NASA makes it look easy.
Private companies, loaded with talented people, are struggling to put
people into space. They struggle not because their employees aren't
competent or hard working, but because the challenge of human space
flight is very, very hard."

Mike was the pilot of the *Atlantis* mission in 1997, as well as on the
Endeavor in 2000. In 2002, he was the commander on the *Atlantis*. Their
big thing: Equip the international space station to do more complex and
advanced work.

Mike is a granite of a man with a humble heart, full of passion for team
excellence. He was the captain of the football team at the U.S. Air Force
Academy and an F-15 fighter pilot. When you meet him, or look at photos
of the teams he's been on, one thing is clear: success. He embodies a
confidence that communicates achievement is imminent.

We asked him, "Mike, were you ever nervous going into space? Come on: A ton of fuel burning every second? Traveling at 17,500 mph? What if something went wrong? How did you remain so confident?"

"Faith in the process," Mike answered. "In everything I've ever done, the first step is to identify the progression of steps that will deliver success—and then you work that process.

"When you have a process of success that covers all scenarios, you're not afraid of one 'gotcha,' or something unplanned happening," he said. "You're prepared to achieve.

"And it's important to remember that success means different things at different times," Mike added. "Take Apollo 13, for example. Some might say that mission wasn't successful because the crew didn't make it to the moon," Mike said as his words picked up their tempo. "But I say it was very successful. The circumstances changed—dramatically—and they had to ask: What is success now? Getting safely back to Earth was the answer. So, they worked their process of success."

A few years ago, Mike the astronaut became Mike the successful business leader. He's a part of an engineering team that develops space suits and other gear for extreme conditions. "In every business," he said, "All the bosses want to know: 'What's your strategy to deliver the business objective?' My strategy is to develop the process of success, one that adapts to the circumstances and environment as we move to our destination.

"People need to be careful that they are not always talking about the business deliverable. Success is a process. It's executing the steps needed to get to the business deliverable," Mike said. "When you do that, you can be relatively certain you'll get where you need to go."

Your Team Either Has Confidence—or It Doesn't

Every team must decide what sort of team it's going to be. Teams that do big things do not team casually. Regardless if a team may have been formed in seemingly spontaneous fashion, those who think their work together can be improvised as they go along make a grave error: When the unexpected occurs (and you can expect it will), winging it or relying on your wits to effectively relate and communicate with other team members means certain disaster. Even teams whose team members have intentionally paired personalities to maximize synergies require a way for those personalities to work together.

Teams that possess confidence that they can achieve big things feel that way because, like Mike the astronaut, they utilize a process to team effectively. That's what the Do Big Things Framework is: a step-by-step approach to thinking and actions designed to enable the team to do big things in all circumstances. Such teams are not afraid of "gotchas" or unexpected events because they know that whatever happens, they have a process to follow that will lead them to success. This results in a move from amateur status to a professional team embodying the certainty of success.

For team members to operate day after day without the confidence that the team can succeed is a neglect of duty. Here then, is a question that stops some teams: Do we have confidence that the team will succeed? As you facilitate your team's response to this question, we encourage you to hold the team accountable to yes or no answers. Our experience shows that ambiguous responses can creep in, such as "sort of," "maybe," and "only if."

These statements, however, reflect one thing: The team isn't confident, at least not enough to do big things. (Uh, Houston, we have a problem.) The team either believes they'll succeed or they don't. There's no gray here, no waffling back and forth, and no room for conditions. ("We'll succeed if we get more resources.")

For certain, knowing the team isn't confident is a good thing to understand—and the earlier the better. Confidence, or the lack of it, is your canary as you descend into your Grand Canyon: If the bird dies, it's an important indicator that the team had better get busy taking the actions necessary for the team to believe.

Teams that do big things don't wait for success to act like a success. They act like a success first because they have or quickly create a reliable teaming process to give them the confidence they need. Just like Mike.

Preparing for Success

While in the field working with a team of information technology (IT) professionals who were launching an internal crowdsourcing initiative, we saw their ability to embody success take shape.

This team had every reason to bring a halfhearted effort. They had just completed the integration phase of a merger: two companies were now one—or trying to become one. For nearly eight months, they'd worked hours that required far more cups of coffee than their bodies should be subjected to. Several people had to move their families to a new city. And on top of all that, now there were people on their team who they had once viewed as the enemy.

As we supported the team, we saw them transform from a collection of individuals seemingly randomly chosen to group together, to a team in the truest sense of the word. Here's what the early part of their discussion and planning looked like:

Before they even applied the Do Big Things Framework, with simplicity they clearly defined their Grand Canyon, their one big objective so they could all see it: *Enable every person in the company to crowdsource information freely, so they could truly be a learning organization.*

Then, they took the initial step in the DBT Framework by defining and committing to equip themselves to deliver their human imperative: *Function with an all-the-time and everywhere service-oriented mindset— especially with each other.*

Next, they determined how they would embody success and leverage failure. This is the second step of the Do Big Things Framework.

Who's in Control of Your Team's Confidence?

More likely than not, at some point in your career you've found yourself on a team with someone who is like Mike the astronaut: They came to work each day with a conviction and determination to succeed that never seemed to break. As well, there were other people on the team who sat right next to Mike, yet their confidence always seemed to get replaced by anger, apathy, or anxiety every time a new challenge surfaced.

When you were on such teams, what did you do? As authors, to tell our truth, 30 years ago, before we had discovered the Do Big Things Framework, we did two things when we found ourselves in these situations: (1) We gave countless motivational speeches, and (2) We pleaded with our boss to swap out the players on the team that were dragging the rest of us down.

Now, after studying teams that do big things, we know clearly there's a better option: Develop within the members of the team a greater locus of control. When you started this book, you likely didn't know you'd learn to speak Latin, too. Consider this a bonus: In Latin, the word *locus* means place or location.[1] Therefore, those with an inner locus of control believe they can influence and determine results; those with an external locus of control are more likely to believe they're powerless.

This is important Latin to know, too, because on teams that do big things team members consistently demonstrate a greater ability to take responsibility for their team's failures and successes. **This is distinctly different than teams that don't achieve much, where external forces determine their level of confidence.**

To learn how likely your team is to embody success then, it's useful to ask the team this question: What are our primary motivations for succeeding that are top of mind for us? When a team is predominantly exposed to extrinsic motivators, team members are conditioned to develop an external locus of control. If this is the case for your team, act quickly.

Certainly, extrinsic motivations such as bonuses, promotions, and awards are all necessary parts of a healthy organization. But mountains of research make it clear, including what author Daniel Pink messages in his timeless book, *Drive*: If external motivations are the only reasons being used to energize us to do big things, we'll be in an unhealthy organization quickly.[2]

Here's why: If we as a team commit to doing something really big, it means we're going to have to make sacrifices. Just like the IT team that came together after their companies merged, success required time away from families. It meant hours and hours in seemingly endless meetings with digitally disjointed images on monitors of teammates they didn't personally know. It obligated them to stare with blurry eyes into computer screens late into the night at home, with children yelling in the background, "Aaaggghhh! Why is Daddy's head spinning?"

If you want anyone to sign up for that experience, then the list of external motivations is going to have to get longer. In fact, the list of rewards will never be long enough. That's because if it's merely an external motivations game that's going to be used to keep and motivate team members, then those team members will play the game, too: They're going to be far more motivated to shop their talent around to other companies and compare the competitor's list of engagement tricks to your company's list.

That game doesn't cause people to embody the success required for a team to achieve. It merely prioritizes personal or self-serving motivations, which is a proven method for causing a team to flatline quickly.

People want their heart to be activated. We all long to be a part of something significant. Daniel Pink provides evidence that we don't want to be bribed away from our greater character. That's why putting intrinsic motivations into play is so critical. Because all of us want to prove we have within us what it takes to do big things.

How to Put Intrinsic Motivations into Action

Pardon the stereotyping here. (We've got wonderful friends and family in IT.) We continue our earlier example merely to support a critical understanding: The IT team wasn't too comfortable sharing their intrinsic motivations. After all, such information is personal.

This is precisely the point. For each of us, our individual motivations are personal. And so is the decision to take responsibility for the results we deliver. Once the team embraced this wisdom, they saw an immediate elevation in their collective confidence.

What this means: **Teams that do big things are made of team members that are accountable to identifying and consistently fueling their personal and key motivators. And as a team, they actively support each other in this endeavor.** To quickly put this knowledge to work for your team, try the following exercise:

Invite each team member to review and consider the motivations listed on the extrinsic and intrinsic (E&I) top motivations scale in Figure 4.1. As they do so, ask each person to identify their top one, three, or five (no more) greatest motivators in total. It's important that the number is odd as the scale of priority motivations is rarely balanced. Lastly, remind the team to be as honest as possible, as there are no right or wrong answers.

As you debrief insights with your team, consider these questions:

- What does the scale of motivations look like for individuals? For the team as a whole?

TOP MOTIVATION SCALE

EXTRINSIC MOTIVATIONS	INTRINSIC MOTIVATIONS
EARN A BONUS	STRETCH BEYOND MY COMFORT ZONE
KEEP LEADERSHIP'S FOCUS ON SOMEONE ELSE	PROVE I AM CAPABLE
BE CONSIDERED THE BEST BY OTHERS	REALIZE PERSONAL POTENTIAL
GET PROMOTED	MAKE A DIFFERENCE IN THE WORLD
KEEP MY JOB	LEARN SOMETHING NEW
PAY THE BILLS	PROVIDE FOR PEOPLE I LOVE
LIVE UP TO WHAT OTHERS EXPECT OF ME	DO WHAT I LOVE TO DO
REACH A SIX-FIGURE SALARY	BE PART OF SOMETHING GREATER THAN MYSELF
KEEP UP WITH MY FRIENDS	BE AN ACHIEVER

Figure 4.1   Extrinsic and Intrinsic Top Motivations Scale

- What is the relationship between the motivators identified and the thinking and actions the team is currently demonstrating?
- Are motivations proportionally distributed in a manner you believe is necessary to do big things?
- What processes, systems, or other aspects of the culture support creating these motivational dynamics?
- Where can the team evolve and better leverage E&I motivations to better enable a more productive locus of control?
- What's the reward to each person for leveraging their intrinsic motivations even more?

As the IT team candidly discussed their primary motivations with one another, several team members surprised even themselves. There were some real "Hey, look, this is what matters most to me" moments.

There was also an agreement: The more fatigued they were (and exhausted is how they described themselves), the more their motivations were weighted toward the extrinsic. The room was silent for a bit as they contemplated: Are we willing to go through the challenging days ahead relying on external forces to motivate us?

The answer was an emphatic *no*. The next step was to identify the intrinsic motivations that would balance the scale or weight it in favor of the motivations the team members could control. And this is the moment when things got even more interesting.

Few exercises develop a team's ability to put their whole heart in it like identifying why the effort required to do big things is worth it. Marketing guru Simon Sinek says, "People don't buy what you do. They buy why you do it."[3] The same holds true for the energy team members will need to do big things: It's not what you have to do together that engages teammates in the effort; it's why you do it that calls everyone to a higher expression of themselves.

Now, as each of us takes greater control of what we can control, confidence surges. We experience successes more today, which gives us greater evidence that we can and will be a success tomorrow.

WTF (Want the Facts)

- Roughly 25 percent of business leaders have an employee engagement strategy.[4]
- In the workplace, performance-based rewards can be "alienating" and "dehumanizing."[5]
- Although paying more can get work done faster, it has not been shown to get work done better.[6]
- People with an internal locus of control are more likely to be more motivated and success-oriented.[7]
- Only 19 percent of executives at firms with over $1 billion in revenue reported being very confident that their employees could accurately communicate the company's business strategy to others.[8]
- 57 percent of American workers reported they "would perform better at their jobs if they better understood the company's direction."[9]

How to Leverage Failure

Big objectives are big for a reason: They're complex, almost always entail significant amounts of change, and test a team's strength in ways that are often underestimated at the beginning. Things rarely go as planned. **Therefore, the best time to measure a team's ability to embody success is to observe their response to failure. When you embody success, even in times of trouble, you look like everything is going according to plan.**

A search on the Internet for "failure quotes" provides a long stream of what successful people say about the topic. When you're asked to speak at the company's annual meeting (or you're writing a book), it's enjoyable to include failure quotes, because they often make people feel warm and fuzzy. The human spirit needs the reminder to pick itself up off the ground, again and again, in order to prevail.

But business is rarely warm and fuzzy. The business of doing big things is hard. If you're an engineering team located in Paris trying to build a plant in India, and you find out that your people on the ground there misinterpreted government regulations, positive quotes about how failure is only failure when you don't learn from it, won't do. If your team is responsible for hitting volume targets in an emerging country, and the employees there decide to go on strike, words Steve Jobs uttered when he was down and out aren't going to get your product off the shelf. You need a team that is accountable, adapts, and focuses on the job at hand.

When your team misses a targeted delivery date, errs in delivering the product to agreed-upon specs, or comes in over budget, is the response one you're proud of? The teams we repeatedly see do big things don't blink, retreat, or assume a defensive posture. They possess an accountability reflex: an ability to quickly adapt to unplanned situations, respond effectively, and leverage the failure.

The key discovery: The magic of this reflex isn't created when failure occurs. What makes the difference, and determines the type of response your team demonstrates, is what the team did early on, long before any failure was experienced. Specifically, development steps are accomplished that create the conditions for team members to be transparent, demonstrate ownership of their responsibilities, stay focused on solutions, and mobilize themselves and others forward.

How these conditions are created is outlined in each of the seven steps of the DBT Framework. As we've equipped teams to do big things, this is a profound and important shift in thinking: The seven steps necessary for teams to do big things apply to any situation—bad or good.

To give you further confidence in this approach, imagine any failure your team could possibly experience. Then, revisit the steps of the DBT Framework, and there it is: Exactly what successful teams do all the time—before, during, and after failure. This means business as usual becomes success as usual.

For now, take this accountability reflex assessment with your team to determine your current strengths and opportunities in response to failure moments. Then use the insights generated to further leverage the steps within the DBT Framework.

Accountability Reflex Assessment

Have team members use this scale to answer each of the five questions:

1 = always untrue, 2 = untrue most of the time, 3 = sometimes true and sometimes not, 4 = true most of the time, and 5 = true all the time.

Then compile the scores, and use the guide after the assessment to determine your team's strength in being able to effectively respond to unplanned, and often negative, situations. Note: We encourage you to use these questions as a discussion guide, having team members share the rationale for their answers aloud. If the team, however, is not ready for this level of transparency, the assessment can be done anonymously.

1. When failure occurs, team members don't get defensive or emotionally upset. SCORE: _____

2. When mistakes are made, team members can take responsibility for failure without fearing negative repercussions. SCORE: _____

3. We can talk openly and speak candidly about what we think happened when the failure occurred. SCORE: _____

4. In times of extreme challenges, team members ask for help in a timely manner. SCORE: _____

5. When something bad happens, we don't point fingers of blame at others. SCORE: _____

Scoring guide for determining the strength of your team's accountability reflex

20 to 25 points: Your team has the collective emotional muscles to do big things, especially in times of difficulty. ACTION: As a team, identify how you've created these dynamics, celebrate, and share with others what you're learning.

15 to 19 points: Your team is at moderate risk of delaying the achievement of success when they encounter difficulties. ACTION: As you move through the DBT Framework, determine which specific step your team should focus on to rapidly develop necessary skills.

10 to 14 points: Your team is highly vulnerable to severe dysfunction when unplanned problems occur. ACTION: Call a time-out to operations soon and equip the team with the DBT Framework. Determine your sustainable plan to consistently strengthen the team's accountability reflex moving forward.

0 to 9 points: You likely already know this: Your team is well on its way to flatlining. It's likely your team has already gotten the attention of others in the organization; support—and changes—should be on the way. ACTION: Have the team collectively determine what sort of character they want to model to the rest of the organization as the intervention occurs. Then make certain you establish a plan to use the entire DBT Framework moving forward. Consider an internal or external neutral resource to provide support and facilitation.

Final note: The consequences of a failed plan are never as severe to the business as the consequences of a team that lacks an accountability reflex. What are you doing with your team today to prepare it for the response it must give to the crisis of tomorrow?

Staying Inspired When the Team Misses Their Target

The IT team was tested—in some cases, severely. Despite their best efforts to address potential rejections of stakeholders prior to making changes, they still had to deal with resistance. One business unit was dismissive of their efforts, saying their objective of implementing an internal social platform was void of value. Others criticized their plan for not including features that were more user-friendly, thus impacting user adoption. And the only attention they got from senior leadership was when they missed a deadline or went over budget.

The team, however, stayed the course by demonstrating their accountability reflex each time they encountered trouble. They had their moments of frustrations, of vigorous debates, of stepping outside for some fresh air (really, attempts to get away from each other for a moment). Interestingly, every teammate experienced some level of difficulty and doubt along the way. But because they had a process for success, like Mike the astronaut, and stayed true to their commitment to apply it, they were never frustrated as a team or doubted at the same time. Therefore, levels of confidence and emotional courage remained far higher across the team than they would have been in the past. They kept their whole heart in it.

As humans, we tether our emotions to our intrinsic motivations. When we get what we want, just as when we don't, our emotions communicate to the world our personal agendas. Intrinsically motivated teams won't be seen succumbing to fits of rage, defeatism, blame, or other self-defense tactics. Instead, their emotions center on trust, particularly of the most important sort: trust of self and each other.

A VP of product supply told us, in referring to his team, "The way work gets done today requires that you get put into countless and different groups of people every day.

"What's your anchor? You'd better know yourself. Your team better know itself," he said. "You have to be able to trust yourself. But you can't if you don't know what it is you're here to do and why you want to do it."

Most teams possess the technical or functional skills to do good work. The teams that succeed in going beyond basic expectations are those that foster and sustain a remarkable will, a determination fueled by intrinsic motivations. They weather the storm and stay the course as employees join midstream or leave unexpectedly (or even expectedly).

The IT team in our example in this chapter ended their year celebrating what they knew would happen: They had successfully achieved their one big thing. And they were stronger and more fulfilled for doing so. That sort of outcome qualifies as making an epic impact.

As we debriefed the experience with them, a funny thing happened: Given the power of celebration, we encouraged them to find ways to acknowledge their tremendous success. They asked us what that could look like, so we gave them some examples. What they decided to do surprised us.

They did very little. Why? Their response: Because they had known all along they were going to succeed, the end felt a bit anticlimactic.

Go figure. (We could only smile.)

How to Know If You're on a Team That Embodies Success

Before your team takes the next step in the DBT Framework, we encourage caution on a specific point: Beware of being deceived by the words of well-meaning teammates. It's not uncommon to hear teammates at a business kick-off meeting nearly shouting, "We're confident!" In moments like this, it's natural to think that the team is ready and able to embody success.

Words of confidence, however, are different than actions of confidence. **What actions will give you the evidence that your team is acting like a success because they're using a process for success?**

In our assessment of teams that embody success, we found these three additional and distinctive qualities:

1. The team looks beyond itself. Just as selfish motives limit a person, a team is limited by a vision of success that only serves the team. When the team sees its larger role in the organization, as a team to support other teams in succeeding, then it embodies success and brings other teams along on the journey by equipping them to also do big things.

2. Teams that embody success transcend traditional measurements of success. Beyond the numbers, getting the sale, innovating a new product, or other efforts to impact the business, they take stock of their character. How they achieve success matters. There is no room for debate on this. They expect their hands to be hardened for the effort, but not their hearts and minds.

3. When successful people want to join your team, you know you embody success. Humans are drawn to the energy of those who know they can do the extraordinary. It's uncommon and most of us crave it.

When the Future Becomes Now

Sting, the famous musician and lead singer for the band Police, recounts the early days of the band long before anyone outside of their families even knew they existed. While recording their first album together, band members would moonlight in a rent-by-the-hour studio; they could only afford the rates charged of artists when everyone else was sleeping.

After their recording sessions, Sting would drive his old, beat-up car back to London singing lyrics loudly while "in a state of euphoria." He was doing what he always wanted to do. He was part of a team that embodied success. Their vision of the future was so clear that they collapsed the future into those early days as a band. Sting said, "We were insane in our optimism, and we were never happier."[10]

Big Ideas in This Chapter and
3 Recommended Actions

- To embody success is to think and act confidently, as though achievement is certain even before the outcome is realized. **Recommended Action:** To what extent does your team embody success? Take immediate action to either reinforce the team's understanding of why they're able to embody success, or identify what they must do to develop their confidence.

- Any team that wants to do big things needs to have a process for success that enables the team to adapt its thinking and actions to new circumstances and environments. The DBT Framework is that process.

- Extrinsic motivations must be relatively balanced by intrinsic motivations to enable the team to embody success during challenging times.

- Every team can control its level of confidence; it's negligent to not do so.

- Teams that have an accountability reflex have developed the ability to adapt to unplanned situations and outcomes, and can leverage failure to deliver future successes. **Recommended Action:** How did your team score on the Accountability Reflex Assessment? Establish a plan with the team to follow through with the recommendations outlined in this chapter. As well, set a date in the future when the team will reassess its accountability reflex (we recommend every six months).

- Teams that embody success think beyond the boundaries of their own team and attract successful people to the team. **Recommended Action:** Discuss the following questions with your team. Would other teams in our organization say we embody success? What steps will we take to improve that perception?

5 Choose to Contribute, Activate, and Connect Across the Business

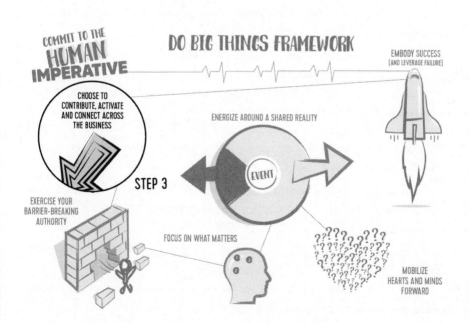

Can a team choose to be great? Yes: unequivocally. (If a teammate disagrees, be concerned.) The Chicago Cubs were a team that made that decision. On the night of November 2, 2016, they became bigger than baseball. They modeled for the rest of us that when we are deliberate and focused on making certain decisions, we can win. And win big. After 108 years of losing, the Chicago Cubs became the champions of baseball.

Game Seven will be remembered as one of the greatest games ever played in any sport. After seven months, 177 games, over 1,593 innings, and approximately 25,842 pitches, the Holy Grail of baseball—the World Series Championship—would be decided in extra innings of the last game.

The drama was thick. The Cubs had been down three games to one in the best of seven series, but had scrapped and clawed their way back to tie the series at three games apiece and force a deciding game seven. Then, in the winner-takes-all game, it appeared an entire city and the legion of fans around the world would be doomed again to their century-old heartache.

In that monumental game, the Cubs pulled ahead, 6–3, only to see their opponent, the Cleveland Indians, come back to tie the game in the eighth inning. The ninth inning went scoreless.

That's when time stopped. Before the game could go into the tenth inning, it began to rain. The teams retreated into their respective club-houses. And the sporting world held its breath.

This was precisely the moment the Cubs refocused on the three decisions that differentiated them as champions. Behind closed doors, team veteran Jason Heyward called the team together and contributed a per-spective to his peers that activated their hearts. "I told them to remember how good they were—how good we are," Heyward said after the game. "I wanted them to know how proud of them I was and that I loved them. And that I mean it from the bottom of my heart."[1]

Heyward said each of them had played a part in bringing the Cubs to this moment in time. And that they had everything they needed to win, as long as they believed in each other and played for one another.

Teammate David Ross provided more details of Heyward's efforts to activate the team. He said, "[Heyward] told us, 'We're the best team in baseball for a reason. Continue to play our game, support one another. These are your brothers here, fight for your brothers, lift them up, continue to stay positive. We've been doing this all year so continue to be us.'"

The Cubs knew their role in history. As players, they were connected to the 108 other Cubs teams that came before them, who had failed in achieving this big thing. Entire generations of die-hard fans had lived their whole lives without seeing their beloved team receive the ultimate recognition. These circumstances create a pressure few teams will ever know.

But Heyward would have none of it. He equipped the team to focus on a decision they could control.

He encouraged teammates to be the Cubs team they've been all season rather than trying too hard to do something new in the last game. Shortstop Addison Russell reported, "We reached new levels. Grown men talking about that stuff, it doesn't happen. The fact we did it here in the World Series, I really respect everyone for that."

What took place in the clubhouse was more than a motivational discussion. It was a decision-making process. During that brief and now historic 17-minute rain delay, Heyward brought the team back to the important decisions they'd been making all year. The formula for success didn't need to be changed now. As a result, the mood changed back to confidence. The team possessed a renewed determination.

"We didn't know what was going to happen, but I knew we were ready to do what we did," Heyward said.

As the team was preparing to go back onto the field, hearts were pounding—not from nerves, but from the belief that they could control their fate. Catcher Willson Contreras later said that in that moment, he was thinking, "Now we are here and we can do this. We've got this."[2]

Indeed, they did. The Cubs scored two runs in the top of the tenth; the Indians could only manage one. The Cubs, when it mattered most, chose to be great. And they were.

Teams That Do Big Things Make Three Big Decisions

There's no doubt: The Cubs had great talent. They had proven leadership, too. But history is full of teams, in all professions, that had those two qualities and never made it to the pinnacle in their work. Every profession has seen such teams flatline and slide away forgotten. Equally true, the past is full of remarkable teams, again in all arenas, that didn't have exceptional talent or leadership, yet still found a way to succeed in big ways.

What's the common denominator? What is it those teams do, regardless of talent and leadership levels, that enables them to do big things? Nearly every team that we've studied that's achieved something extraordinary had team members that made three specific decisions. And in doing so, they amplified the leadership and talent they had, which put them in a far better position to succeed.

Those decisions are the 3 Do Big Things Decisions (DBT Decisions). We've captured them here so every team can deliver on their decision to be great.

3 Do Big Things Decisions

- **The Contributor Decision:** I choose to bring my best to this situation.

- **The Activator Decision:** I choose to bring out the best in others in this situation.

- **The Connector Decision:** We choose to partner across the business to deliver our shared objective.

To win the World Series Championship, the members of the Chicago Cubs baseball team made the 3 DBT Decisions. As members of the team testified, each person on the team contributed to their success. The rain delay in game seven of the championship provided a prime moment in which we all got a glimpse of how the team activated the best in each other. And the roster of 25 players is merely a small portion of the roughly 250 employees (and millions of fans) connected within and across the organization. It took all their efforts working in unison to win.

Can you imagine your team achieving the big thing in front of you without every teammate making these critical decisions? Here's a fact: Your team's leadership and talent is only as good as its team members' ability to make the 3 DBT Decisions. This is what's remarkable and key: The choices to bring the best to a situation, bring out the best in others, and partner across the business—or not—are already being made by every person on every team in the company all the time. The game-changing question is this: Is every teammate making the choice of "I will" instead of "I won't" so the team and company can prevail?

The good news is, we've collected enough evidence that clearly proves: There's a high probability your team members want to make these decisions more frequently. They just need to be equipped to do so.

The 3 DBT Decisions enable team members to cut through the noise and do what's right and best for the team. And in most workplaces, there's a lot of noise. If your teammates are like most, experts say they make roughly 35,000 decisions a day.[3] **Once enabled to make the 3 DBT Decisions, our experience shows that a large volume of those decisions are made more effectively, quickly, and in ways that improve a person's ability to do what they want to do: demonstrate the greatness they have within them.**

The Contributor Decision

Choosing to bring your best to the situation you're in is making the choice to give of yourself. It's selflessness in action, knowing you're a part of something bigger than you. For many, this decision is the act of determining you won't compromise your values—that you will be true to yourself and live authentically. This is when you resolve to be who you know you are, where you put your whole heart into the matter at hand.

There's no doubt that when the team has quality strategies, plans, and processes, team members are more apt to make the Contributor Decision. It's also equally true that a team can have quality strategies, plans, and processes and team members still don't bring their best. What have you experienced with your team?

Those we've observed who make the Contributor Decision more consistently than others, and who we have subsequently interviewed, report feeling a sense of freedom for having made the decision. They say they are less likely to let the circumstances or others determine their actions. By letting go of what others think they should do or think is best for them, they are more effective at making decisions for themselves that are aligned with their values.

This decision to bring your best often has a transformative effect, because as humans we function in systems that increasingly connect all of us. In this regard, by making the decision, the energy you exert in your behaviors has a ripple effect. As others experience your better you, they are often inspired to do the same. And the ripple often becomes a wave of energy across the team. This means that each time you make the Contributor Decision, you are likely being a better teammate (or mother, father, husband, wife, friend, and so on). Your contribution to the team's ability to do big things increases, as does personal fulfillment.

Here are some examples of the Contributor Decision in action:

- Instead of staying quiet about my concern about our plan, I'm going to share my perspective.
- I'm going home now, and leaving my laptop in the office.
- In the project review meeting, instead of endlessly focusing on where we're failing, I'm going to celebrate and acknowledge this team for their diligent work.

We often hear from those teams we serve that this decision is easy to make, because it's a choice they recognize they've made before—or missed before. What's insightful for all is how profound the outcomes are as the decision is more consistently demonstrated. The power comes in developing the self-awareness and the skill (which we'll discuss later in this chapter and throughout the remainder of the DBT Framework) to make the conscious decision to contribute more fully and more often.

The Activator Decision

Choosing to bring out the best in others means you're making the choice to activate their greater potential. It's a decision that begins with an understanding that others have stored or unrealized greatness. This sort of belief is in high demand in workplaces today, as it is a powerful mechanism to ensure the team becomes far greater than the sum of the people on the team.

The choice to bring out the best in others is a declaration. Others are informed through your actions that you care enough about the person or people you're interacting with to focus or adapt your behaviors. This means that the decision to activate the best in others is not a manipulative maneuver for selfish gain; rather, it is founded in the understanding that by bringing out the best in others, something far greater can be developed than could possibly be realized by you alone.

Here are some examples of what the Activator Decision looks like in action:

- Rather than giving advice, I'm going to ask my colleague a question, and then allow their answer to stand without adding to their wisdom.
- I'm going to resist the temptation of telling everyone how I contributed, and instead let my teammate be the hero.
- On my drive home, I'm not going to dwell on what went wrong today; instead, I'm going to prepare myself to be present with my family.

Those who make the Activator Decision do not discriminate in its application. Beyond their teammates, they bring out the best in those who lead them as well as those whose roles hold stereotypes as being undervalued. Because the person who makes the Activator Decision believes each of their teammates' value can be realized, they work to bring that value forth, so these teammates become even more valuable to the team.

The Connector Decision

The choice to partner across the business is the collective decision by the team to form a broader team that delivers a shared goal. It's a decision that communicates to others certain beliefs: We are confident in who we are as a team. We won't play a zero-sum game. We are stronger together.

This decision requires an enterprise mindset, where the team can see its role in the larger organization. There are no fences to throw work over, no misguided positioning for budget dollars, and no beliefs that other functions are mischievously plotting to make things more difficult for all. There's only one team with a shared objective.

Here are some examples of what the Connector Decision looks like in action:

- Before we further build out our plans, let's seek input from operations and see how they might improve upon the idea.

- Instead of complaining about how the work in finance is slowing us down, let's take the initiative and meet with them to see how we can improve this for everyone.

- As we innovate the engineering of our product, let's include the sales team because they're closest to the customer.

The teams that make the Connector Decision believe the intelligence of the larger group holds the potential to transform what the organization can achieve and do in the market. Therefore, members of these teams have redefined the psychological boundaries those with more traditional views hold. As a result, they require less time to develop trust in those with whom they have little history, seek collaborative opportunities, and function with the understanding that when the larger whole benefits, so will they.

Your Most Important Role

What's the most important role you play at work? "I'm an individual contributor." "I'm a manager." "I'm an executive." "I'm the finance go-to." "I'm a project management guy." "I'm HR." Should you find yourself on a team that provides such answers, pull up your boots, take a deep breath, and self-inspire because you've got important work to do.

These responses come from well-intentioned employees who have been taught and conditioned by their organization to be responsible for their own careers. Such an approach drives wonderful individual accountability yet can also embed the negative consequences of placing a premium on individual performance, rather than putting the focus on the team. There's no doubt we all want self-guided teammates with fires in their bellies. But if we are to do significant work as a team, we also need something else.

The most critical role you play is teammate. When a majority of team members embrace this mindset, the research shows that the team sets the conditions for optimizing its collective talents. Team members impact the business far more, and they elevate their personal contributions (and, ironically, usually elevate their careers, too).

To be certain then, the 3 DBT Decisions are not roles. They're decisions. Delivering on your functional role is the responsibility of your job. Yet, it is the duty of each teammate, regardless of role, to use their power to bring their best, bring out the best in others, and ensure the team is connected to the whole.[4]

Here's an example of this in action. While supporting a senior director within a global manufacturing company, we asked him: What's the secret to your rapid career growth?

He smiled, looked over each shoulder for effect, as if he was going to tell us a big secret. Then he leaned across the table and said, "Well, let me tell you it isn't because my resume looks great. I haven't dusted that off and revised it for 18 years." He laughed.

"Seriously, though," he added, "My formula is pretty simple. I've always concentrated on being a great team player first—at giving my best and being there for others. That's it.

"Right out of school, it didn't take me long to figure out that the leaders of this organization crave this approach. When my first boss got promoted, she took me with her. And then I'd find myself on a cross-functional team. I'd use my formula, and sure enough I'd find myself being recruited or recommended to other teams. One team led to another. And here I am." He paused, then shrugged his shoulders. "Pretty simple, huh?"

Simple, perhaps—and yet, profound. So much so, it's worth asking: Of two different roles, which one do the members of your team identify with most:

- Their individual functional role?
- The team they are a part of?

The answer allows you to determine, with relative accuracy, how prepared the team is to make the decisions necessary for the team to do big things. Those who prioritize being exceptional teammates, while bringing accountability to their functional role with them, are the people the rest of us want on our team.

WTF (Want the Facts)

- Four out of five employees do not reach their full potential.[5]
- Worldwide, 13 percent of employees are engaged; 63 percent are not engaged; and an additional 24 percent are actively disengaged, meaning they are so unhappy they are likely to spread negativity to the rest of the team. These percentages translate to 900 million of the world's working population not engaged and 340 million actively disengaged.[6]
- Only 22 percent of U.S. employees are engaged and thriving.[7]
- Nearly half—48 percent—of employees believe that their company's level of engagement matches that of their competitors (in other words, they believe we're all in the same boat).[8]
- Slightly more than half of employees say their leaders inspire them.[9]
- Fully engaged employees return 120 percent of salary in value; engaged return 100 percent; somewhat disengaged return 80 percent; disengaged are at 60 percent.[10]
- 80 percent of managers make decisions that avoid risk.[11]
- 87 percent of managers are not making intuitive decisions (based on wisdom and prior experience).[12]

Doing Big Things Is an All-the-Time Thing

Each of us always has freedom of choice, but we never have freedom from the consequences of our choices. **Every decision a teammate makes, therefore, takes the team further from realizing the team's potential—or closer to being able to do big things.** This is why doing big things is not a sometimes thing. Teammates who approach daily interactions with a casualness or laziness are on a team that will lose to teams where every interaction matters. That's because doing big things is an all-the-time thing.[13] This wisdom forms a standard of conduct on teams that do big things.

No one expects perfection. And it's not about infusing stress and tension into daily routines. It's about the direction the team is going and its ability to advance the organization's health. And your direction is determined by your ability to make the 3 DBT Decisions.

The Contributor Decision: A Closer Look

The phone call was disturbing. "I'm in an organization that has flatlined. And now I'm flatlining, too."

The voice belonged to Roy. We'd met him years before at a different organization, one with its whole heart in it. He left because he thought he'd have more career opportunities elsewhere. His voice was filled with regret. "Bring my best here? That's not realistic," he said. "Not when the rewards encourage everyone to compete—for visibility, advancement, bonuses.

"It's cutthroat around here. It's not safe to give your best because that means exposing yourself. If you fail, and it's public, the consequences are going to be severe," he said. "Anything you say can and will be used against you. Unless, of course, it's exactly what they want to hear up on the top floor," he said. It was quiet for a moment. "I submitted my resignation. I'm out of here," he finished.

On the surface this first DBT Decision can look easy, but most of us know it's not. The brutal truth is that, in some organizations, bringing your best can appear to be career limiting. Yet, an additional truth must also be examined: We as humans are very good at rationalizing why external circumstances should determine the choices we make in our attitudes and actions.

No one is judging Roy. We've all been in situations where we need to set boundaries and take care of ourselves. Roy will continue his search for a team and company that fits his needs. (We'll continue to support him, too, in his journey to self-actualization.) For those of us who don't have, or won't make, the option to leave, we must set a different course.

Ultimately, making the Contributor Decision means choosing what to do at the intersection of our personal needs, the needs of the team, and the business. Consider these examples:

- There will be times when I need to say what needs to be said—while other moments will require that I listen for greater understanding.
- There will be meetings where I must mandate what must be done— and other meetings where I must start a collaborative discussion.
- There are moments when I must be willing to be wrong in the interest of advancing ideas—and other times when I must be perfectly accurate in my contributions.

How a team member decides to be at their best and contribute can't be prescriptive; the intersection of personal, team, and business needs is a perspective unique to each teammate. With that in mind, to what extent does your team practice these examples of successful decision-making? And how will it advance the teamwork you're seeking if everyone more effectively makes such decisions?

Our conservative estimate is that on average, people are making the Contributor Decision, deciding to bring their best to the situations with team members, 30 to 40 percent of the time. On teams that do big things, that number soars to over 80 percent. This single, simple decision provides the genesis (an ignition) that accelerates rapid thinking and behavioral change across a team.

How to Make the Contributor Decision More Consistently

Here are three key questions for you:

1. Do you believe you're bringing your best to daily situations?
2. How do you know?
3. Do your teammates believe you're bringing your best as you interact with them?

Perceptions form reality, though not always the complete or accurate reality—or the reality the team needs to do big things. Therefore, the personal (and life-long) pursuit of knowing how to bring your best, understanding when you are, and ensuring your teammates can trust you to do so, identifies you as one who has potential to be a big-time teammate. This means you likely have strong self-awareness, the personal integrity to stay true to yourself, and are inclined to model the emotional courage necessary to be honest with yourself and others. Couple these skills with the technical mastery required to do your job well, and you are a big-time teammate.

The Contributor Decision leverages the wisdom that rather than learning about values, it's far faster and more effective to focus on demonstrating the values you inherently possess, and grow those values through the experience of application.

To go further in strengthening your ability to make the Contributor Decision, use these five questions to build even greater self-awareness, focus, and a plan for doing so:

1. In what situations would those close to you confirm that you are bringing your best?
2. How do you manage to bring your best in those situations?
3. What is the next situation in which you want to be more effective at bringing your best—and would significantly elevate the team's effectiveness?
4. Why is it important to you to gain greater mastery in this area?
5. What is your measurable plan to accomplish your objective identified in step 3?

Ultimately, if we don't choose to bring our best to any situation, then we are choosing to diminish who we are. There's no middle ground here. No room for excuses. To be on a team that does big things, each of us must transcend the desire to be cautious, to be less of ourselves. If we succumb to temptations to wait, to measure what others think of us, or to step back to see how those who go before us fare, we will surely fail. The measure of a successful team is in direct correlation to the team members' levels of self-awareness, emotional courage, and personal integrity—the ability to make the Contributor Decision.

You can do this. You already are.

The Activator Decision: A Closer Look

The death of a trauma surgeon is not typically required to make the second of the 3 DBT Decisions (the choice to bring out the best in others). In Dr. O's case, though, that's what was necessary.

Before anyone calls the police, we're not talking about an actual murder. In this case, it was Dr. O's determination to transcend the part of his ego that caused him to think of himself far more often than he thought of others. "I had to bring to an end the way I was engaging with others," Dr. O said. "Because what I was doing was wrong."

In Dr. O's previous career, he was recognized as one of the world's leading surgeons. Because he was aware of his status, and felt entitled because of it, his wish was his command; others were always at the ready to do as he instructed. He agreed, however, to be recruited from his work as a surgeon to the commercial world of business, because he wanted to do something even bigger: He longed to see patients in hospitals receive the nutrition he knew could save thousands of lives every year.

Dr. O saw something big that others didn't see: If hospitals would shift the formula in the nutrition patients were receiving during their recovery from a diet heavy in sugar to one with more concentrated protein, the body would regain and sustain levels of health more quickly. His motivation was to save lives.

It didn't take long for Dr. O to fail. Even though he knew the breakthrough solution the company needed to achieve their growth goals, and he had the research to prove it, he was playing the role of teammate in a way that meant the team would certainly flatline. Specifically, while Dr. O was showing up inspired, his actions weren't inspiring others. In fact, he was deactivating teammates.

His attitude and actions had people around him pulling back, and taking their hearts with them. "He talks down to us. And that immediately disengages me," said one teammate. Another added, "He's compelled to talk forever, and always has to have the last word. He has to make it obvious he's the smartest person in the room."

Dr. O was desperate for influence. And all he knew was the approach that worked for him as a famous doctor. The results were devastating.

Chances are, over the course of your career you've known someone like Dr. O. They're brilliant and have big ideas. But they don't yet have the skill to bring out the best in others. Consequently, their big idea to save the world might as well be a small one. Because nothing significant gets done.

Our conservative estimate is that, on the average team, people are making the Activator Decision roughly 20 to 30 percent of the time. Of note, this is highly conditional: The decision is made far more frequently among people with whom teammates have a history of trust. This creates a challenge for many workplaces today, of course, because often, people are joining and leaving teams with increased frequency, not allowing for such relationships to be established.

Additionally, there is heightened emphasis on individual visibility for recognition and promotion, creating competition among teammates. This diminishes motives to bring out the best in others. **Teams that do big things overcome these conditions and make the Activator Decision with their teammates nearly 80 percent of the time.**

There is something you should know about Dr. O. As his self-awareness grew through questions like those used to support the Contributor Decision, he discovered something: He cared more about getting his big idea into the world than he did about receiving fame and glory. With this insight, his self-awareness went to levels where he could see things he couldn't see before. Specifically, he began to have greater empathy for the others on the team.

"My gosh," Dr. O told us, "I'm in the business of saving lives, yet the way I was treating others in the process of delivering on my objective was diminishing the lives of others. Truly, the biggest thing for me now is I really want the people around me to win. It's not about me."

Like most of us, Dr. O cares deeply about people. When he moved from seeing his peers as employees who existed to make his will be done, and began to see them as people, he could more successfully make the Activator Decision. Not surprisingly, people began to respond differently to him. With each interaction, he earned from them the right to influence them more.

With this new and different power, Dr. O could contribute to the team more by activating greater responses from his peers. This meant greater progress toward achieving their life-changing objective. Today, the team has come to life, demonstrating a greater ability to put their whole heart into making the big idea a reality. Their new product has found its way to the market and is now being celebrated. The flagship study the team completed was recognized as the best research done in the industry for the year. And, in control groups, the team is seeing their dream become a reality: readmission rates of patients have been cut by one-third, they're seeing lower rates of infections, and patients sustain their health longer.

"What's cool," Dr. O said, "Is that not only are we succeeding in delivering something the world needs, but we feel much better about how we're getting the job done." That's making an epic impact.

How to Make the Activator Decision More Consistently

Dr. O's transformation was, frankly, even faster than we typically experience with clients. He was deeply and intrinsically motivated to transform the big idea into a big product and channeled that energy into being a person who could effectively bring out the best in others. No surprise: When a person takes the attention off themselves and puts it on others, empathy increases and they become stronger teammates. Similar to the series of five questions we previously provided so you can model the Contributor Decision more consistently, the questions we asked Dr. O came from a place of believing that he already possessed the ability to bring out the best in others. Dr. O didn't need to be fixed; he wasn't broken. He simply needed to get even better at doing what he wanted to do. Here are the steps and questions we used:

1. Tell us a story of when you brought the best out of others with whom you were teamed.
   a. What did it feel like to bring out their best?
   b. What were you thinking when you did this?
2. What did you specifically do to bring out their best?
3. What is a situation with your teammates in the coming week where you want to bring out their best?
4. Remind us: Why is it important to you to gain greater mastery at making the Activator Decision?

5. What are the measurable actions you want to take to accomplish the objective identified in step 3? (Note: We created a list with Dr. O of all the things he knew were effective at bringing out the best in others, including asking questions, listening without adding his ideas on top of others' wisdom, including them in decision-making, and more.)

The Activator Decision is a game changer for the teams that have team members practicing it regularly. Among other things, transactional inter-actions where people come together only to get business done are replaced with meaningful exchanges, where the message from teammate to teammate is clear: I value you.

The Connector Decision: A Closer Look

For six years, this team of incredibly talented people had devoted them-selves to their one big thing. But results weren't coming. A joint venture between two companies, a global consumer goods corporation and a specialty container company, was created to deliver an innovative new product to the customer. While everyone was passionate about the vision, the daily work it took to deliver on it felt like a tangled mess of interactions. The facts didn't lie. Despite their passionate efforts, they were losing market share in their space. The vision was not becoming a reality.

It was easy to cluster the multiple teams working on this effort into three groups: (1) those who got their paycheck from the established and powerful culture of the global consumer goods company; (2) the team members who were part of the equally strong ethos of the established specialty container company; and then (3) the employees who were caught in between in a newly forming culture—an amorphous mix of the original two.

Instead of a partnership across the business to deliver a shared objective (the Connector Decision), the three groups were experiencing a collision. What made this pileup especially painful is this was not only a crash of business ideas, perspectives, and competing objectives. It went beyond that. On a daily basis, due to unhealthy conflict, they saw their whole-heart-in-it approach disintegrate as teammates became disheartened.

At the root of the struggle was the belief (and therefore, approach) that proprietary information could not be shared. Meetings were regularly held with a "what's ours is ours and what's yours is yours" mindset. Predictably, the absence of information drove deep distrust and breaks in communication.

"We weren't a team," said one person. "We were a group of teams, each representing our respective companies. Looking back, it's a miracle we got anything done at all up to that point."

The breakthrough came quickly. Establishing a human imperative together (the team's unique thinking and action necessary to succeed) enabled them to recalibrate where they had established psychological boundaries.[14] **"The idea—the reminder, really—that everyone wants to be great changed everything for us," said one of the R&D members. "Instead of listening to others seeking evidence on why we shouldn't trust them, we flipped the paradigm. Now we listened with the lens of why we can trust them."**

Another added, "It seems simple, looking back at it. But that's the moment we no longer assumed that when information wasn't shared it wasn't because they didn't want to share it. It's because they couldn't. Basically, we stopped speculating that those people were jerks."

Next, the team understood that in order to operate at its best, they needed to do away with the competing team identities and cultures. In its place, a singular identity and team narrative was formed that was built upon the best of both worlds. The teams became one by transcending the limits of operating as separate teams with three competing cultures. This unity brought a renewed sense of ownership.

By equipping each person to connect effectively outside originally perceived boundaries, this newly constituted team quickly impacted the business. A 400 percent improvement was made in their innovation process that revolutionized food storage and recaptured market share.

"Beyond the obvious business outcomes," one of the leaders reflected, "I must say that it's immensely gratifying to see members of the original team still meet with one another. Many of them share that this was the best assignment they ever had."

Doing business together successfully requires connecting as humans effectively, and specifically beyond traditional boundaries. The Connector Decision, the choice to partner across the business, is the DBT Decision that the team must make together. A team can't make an epic impact if only a portion of the team chooses to partner beyond those with whom they interact the most. Therefore, the Connector Decision requires the individuals of the team to first make the Contributor and Activator Decisions. When this occurs, a team improves on its ability to deliver on its responsibilities to the larger organization.

When we consider the average team and its ability to successfully and consistently make the Connector Decision, we conservatively estimate it occurs 10 to 20 percent of the time. Teams that achieve big things succeed in making this powerful decision do so at a rate that's consistent with the earlier two decisions: over 80 percent of the time.

At what rate of success will your team need to make the Connector Decision do big things?

How to Make the Connector Decision More Consistently

As humans, we are prone to judging other groups by their worst actions, while we judge ourselves by our best intentions.[15,16] This sentiment is too often a default truth for many teams within the same organization. Left unchecked, it suppresses and suffocates the company's ability to adapt and grow. Rush to save your company's life the next time you hear this around the workplace:

- "Just do our part, then throw it over the fence . . ."
- "Why do they keep making us do all of this extra work?"
- "We can't let them know the details of our plan because they'll take credit."

This isn't teamwork. It's a fast approach to flatlining.

Change the arc of history in such cases by equipping your team to connect and partner beyond the perceived and psychological boundaries that surely limit their ability to do big things. Here are five key questions we used to support the joint venture team so they could more effectively partner across the business:

1. Do the actions of other teams determine your level of integrity and the behaviors necessary to deliver your business imperative?

2. Where are you already modeling a partnership approach with others? And how did you accomplish that?

3. Where in your daily business do you see an opportunity to more effectively partner across the business to deliver a shared objective?

   a. Are you willing to model the thinking and behaviors of a one-team approach before the "other" team does?

4. Is it important to the members of the team that everyone gives their best and brings out the best in those who may not even be on our team (as it's currently defined)? And if so, why?

5. What steps will we take to hold ourselves accountable to connect and partner across the business?

Michael Fullan, in his wonderful book *Leadership and Sustainability: System Thinkers in Action*, says, "**We need a system laced with leaders who are trained to think in bigger terms and to act in ways that affect larger parts of the system as a whole.**"[17] We certainly agree with Fullan, and based upon our experience, encourage you to go further. Much more can be achieved not only when the leader is trained to think this way but when the entire team is equipped to partner across the business.

For any of us to act in a way that betrays another team is to betray ourselves. We must not allow uncertainty about others to translate into an uncertainty about our future. When the doubts or fears of another convince us to isolate or shun others, we isolate and diminish ourselves. Much is lost: We are left to do and achieve meaningless work. Then, we risk becoming meaningless.

By making the Connector Decision, we acknowledge the connections that already exist among us. By leveraging our contacts and interactions within our daily work, we bring more value to all involved—and more meaning to ourselves.

Do-or-Die Teamwork

The Powell expedition remains a perfect example of the DBT Framework. There is evidence in Powell's journals that the team occasionally failed in making the 3 DBT Decisions. In other words, the members of the team didn't bring their best, didn't bring out the best in their teammates, and certainly couldn't see their work in relationship to anything beyond themselves.[18]

For example, there's the time when the team finally found a camp with enough trees and brush to provide a much-needed respite from the sun that had been baking them for months. Sadly, the cook, a man named Hawkins, built a fire that got out of control and sent the men running for their boats, some of them with clothes on fire. Precious supplies were lost, and trust was damaged. Powell's journal makes it clear that grudges were held against Hawkins the remainder of the trip. Sides were taken to either defend him or regularly press charges against him. Cooperation among the men suffered.

Yet, ultimately, Powell's team members made the 3 DBT Decisions often enough to achieve their big thing. This includes the Connector Decision, as well. While journeying through the arid western region of the United States, Powell proved he was seeing the team's work as part of something bigger than the river.

Years after his exploring days were over, Powell served as director of the U.S. Geological Survey and routinely worked to educate the public. As a civilization, we couldn't move west and treat the land like we did in the East; this was his message from his lessons learned during the exploration of the region around and including the Grand Canyon. The West required different thinking and actions. He and his team saw the bigger picture.

In the work most of us do, we don't face the do-or-die consequences of our teamwork like Powell's team did. But it can still feel like it. Each of us has heeded therapists' advice by not "making our work our life." Yet, we do insist on being fulfilled in whatever it is we choose to do. And often, achieving—doing important things—is what fulfills us. That's why we commit hours away from loved ones; we sit behind desks when we should be exercising; and we feel our heart's temptation to harden when we see others act irresponsibly. The stakes may not be death by waterfalls, but the pressure feels the same.

That's why the 3 DBT Decisions are so important. When we make them, we get our control back. We do what matters most to us: We show that we are, in fact, good people who are capable of doing big things.

Big Ideas in This Chapter and
3 Recommended Actions

- Some teams have top talent and leadership and still lose. Others don't have the best talent and leadership, yet win. The determining success factor: the ability of team members to effectively make the 3 Do Big Things (DBT) Decisions. **Recommended Action:** Facilitate an important discussion with your team. To what extent are we maximizing the talent and leadership of our team? Why is it important to us to do so? What are one or two things we can do to better maximize our talent and leadership?

- The 3 DBT Decisions are:

  - The Contributor Decision: I choose to bring my best to this situation.

  - The Activator Decision: I choose to bring out the best in others in this situation.

  - The Connector Decision: We choose to partner across the business to deliver our shared objective.

- Making the Contributor Decision is a choice to be selfless. Because people and team are highly connected, this decision has a transformative, ripple effect on the thinking and actions of others.

- Making the Activator Decision is the choice to activate and bring out the greater potential in others. Making this decision is a declaration that you care enough about other people to focus and adapt your behaviors.

- Making the Connector Decision is a collective choice to form a broader team across the organization. An enterprise mindset communicates to others: We are stronger together.

- The 3 DBT Decisions are choices, not roles.

- Your most important role is being a great teammate on the team you're on. **Recommended Action:** Make plans with your team to reinforce or establish how you will measure each person's ability to deliver on their role as teammate.

- The 3 DBT Decisions leverage the wisdom that rather than learning about values, it's far faster and more effective to focus on demonstrating the values you inherently possess, and strengthen them through the experience of application. **Recommended Action:** As a team, answer this question: Does what we communicate about the importance of our values match how we prioritize them in our daily interactions? Then create or reinforce your plan to strengthen the team's ability to model its values.

6 Exercise Your Barrier-Breaking Authority

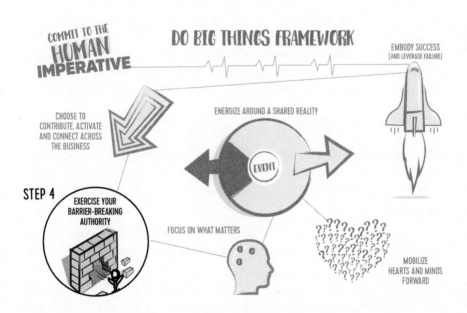

COMMIT TO THE **HUMAN** IMPERATIVE

DO BIG THINGS FRAMEWORK

EMBODY SUCCESS
(AND LEVERAGE FAILURE)

CHOOSE TO
CONTRIBUTE, ACTIVATE
AND CONNECT ACROSS
THE BUSINESS

ENERGIZE AROUND A SHARED REALITY

EVENT

STEP 4

EXERCISE YOUR
BARRIER-BREAKING
AUTHORITY

FOCUS ON WHAT MATTERS

MOBILIZE
HEARTS AND MINDS
FORWARD

On August 2nd and 6th of 1869, John Wesley Powell's journal entries foreshadowed imminent doom for the crew in their journey into the Grand Canyon. Had his predictions come true, history would forever have been changed.

> 2, Aug, '69 . . . We have now gone 28 days without seeing a rabbit or deer. Our food rations have been reduced to flour, moldy bacon, and the two containers of beans we found at the bottom of Sumner's ruck sack. No one told me there'd be no game to shoot in this canyon of death! I'm tired of the fellos constant complaining of my poor planning . . . I'm forever determined to hang the shop owner back in Missouri who insisted I bring two hunters instead of one. He fooled me . . .
>
> . . . had to carry the boats around another rocky rapid. The 3rd one today. We're losing precious time—time that in its stead I could be using to better map this ugly world.
>
> 6, Aug, '69 . . . Lewis and Clark are lucky they are deceased. If they were not, my first errand upon getting off this river of Hades would be to show them the sharper end of my knife. Who were they to tell such lies about the abundance of the west? We must endure conditions far more severe than they, yet their legends only grow . . . the spirit we had when we launched is now broken.

If you're thinking, "No way! The team was falling apart like that?" then trust your instincts. Because you're right. These two journal entries are entirely, 100 percent fabricated.

We included this piece of absurd fiction to prove a point: The false narrative conflicts with what you likely understand is a description or story essential for teams that do big things. Teams that do big things function with a sense of integrity that shows up in the form of acute responsibility. This enables them to stay focused on what they can control and influence.

You likely knew this—and that's the point. Step 4 in the Do Big Things Framework—exercise your barrier-breaking authority—is powerful because it quickly translates into action what so many teams know in their guts. **When a team is disciplined in identifying what stands between them and success, and concentrates solely on what it can control rather than what it can't, success comes faster.** And it's a far more fulfilling process for all involved.

The truth, in contrast to the fiction shared at the opening of this chapter, now becomes even more powerful as it demonstrates how the explorers broke through barriers:

- Powell and his men did go long stretches without seeing deer or other big game they thought they could hunt during their journey. It was a miscalculation to which, despite its severe consequences of near starvation, the expedition adapted. They got serious about hunting the scrawny geese that would occasionally fly over; they honored a system of rationing food among crew members; and they sought ways to supplement their rations with plant life.

- While there were certainly arguments and complaints among team members, per Powell's actual journals, such distractions were kept to a minimum. They stayed committed to their unspoken human imperative, the thinking and actions that would best enable success. Even Powell adapted; he knew he was floating through a geologist's heaven. Even though several disasters in the rapids (including losing a boat) cost him some of the equipment he needed to do his job, he seemed to waste little time lamenting the misfortune. As time went on, he chose to forfeit opportunities to explore and focused instead on getting the team through the Canyon to safety.[1]

- The Lewis and Clark reference was an over-the-top attempt at demonstrating a team becoming disempowered by comparing itself unfavorably to other teams, which they can't control.

Ultimately, Powell's team did what they had to do: They exercised their ability to focus on what they could control. It was a key step in their success.

The Barriers to Success

Your team will break through barriers much faster when they can see and understand them. Therefore, teams that do big things ask important questions, such as: Are we focused on what the business most needs us to influence? Can we clearly identify what's between us and success? And, are all team members equipped to take effective action?

Try this: Read the following statement and determine what's getting in the way of success. *Because there are too many competing priorities pulling on the same resources, we can't execute our plan effectively.*

Did you find the barriers? There are three. Sharpening your team's ability to identify and differentiate these barriers is necessary in order to break them. Here are the three barriers articulated in the statement above:

1. **Real Barriers:** The company doesn't have the resources to do everything people want to do. That's a fact.

2. **Perceived Barriers:** The real barrier, however, doesn't necessarily mean that the team can't execute its plan effectively. That's a perception, and a limiting one.

3. **Symptomatic Barriers:** In this case, competing priorities is a symptom that hides a real barrier; something is occurring within the larger system of the culture that's causing unproductive thinking and behaviors. Symptomatic barriers are often unspoken (or only whispered). For instance, in this example, competing priorities may be caused by leadership not being aligned on a common purpose, strategy, or plan.

Nearly all teams come up against these three types of barriers to varying degrees. Until the team can name them, and focus on those that are real, they're at greater risk of staying blocked in their progress.

Here are three steps we've equipped teams to take to begin breaking through the barriers they face:

1. Name the barrier. Discuss whether a barrier is real, perceived, or symptomatic. By naming it, the team better understands a shared reality and is enabled to focus on what matters.

2. Address real barriers as a team by identifying the **thinking** and **actions** themed across all of the barriers (e.g., stories such as, "I believe there will be consequences if I speak up *[thinking]* so as a result, I stay silent *[actions]*.")

3. Focus on what you can control and rewrite the team's narrative. Identify the necessary thinking and actions to do big things. Partner with others in the organization who can support your team in influencing processes and decision-making.

Regardless of the type of barrier, in order to succeed in these three steps, the members of the team must then exercise their barrier-breaking authority.

Authority: Take It or Leave It

Is there anything achievers (professionals who get serious stuff done) detest more than not being able to determine their own destiny? We don't think so. To want to do things that are significant, but not have the authority to act, is professional prison. To be certain, top talent won't settle for sitting around in prison. They flee. And fast. Leaving entire teams comprised of people who will tolerate being disempowered.

This is a big deal. Organizations know they need to attract the best talent and deliver a great employee experience. Remarkable champions, who deeply care about making their organization the best place to work, devote intense and extraordinary energy to this effort.

In most cases, leadership is put in the spotlight to deliver the sort of cultural experience employees will relish. While their role is key, the rest of us as team members have responsibility, too. Is the way you are thinking and acting as a member of the team attracting and retaining the type of teammates who want to do big things? How you respond to the barriers you face is a good place to start.

The inspired Denis Waitley, author of the best seller *The Psychology of Winning*, said, "There are two primary choices in life: To accept conditions as they exist, or accept the responsibility for changing them."[2] Every person and team possesses the authority to make this decision. Exercising this authority is fundamental to doing big things.

As teams work toward their business objective, conditions and circumstances appear that present themselves as barriers: obstacles that restrain or obstruct the team from progress. This is when teams that do big things model this truth: Each person on the team possesses and exercises their barrier-breaking authority.

This isn't, of course, the authority to make strategy, planning, budgetary, or other decisions. That's largely determined by roles people have on the team. **The barrier-breaking authority we speak of is formed in the wisdom that we are all autonomous beings and therefore can make the human decision to do our best, regardless of our circumstances.**

This isn't child's play; it's an authority that can be difficult to master. Yet, when you can improve your skill even incrementally, it impacts outcomes exponentially. Specifically, the authority drives an empowerment that enables the team to focus on where they can have the greatest influence. This level of responsibility has the power to change the world we all live in.

When facing barriers, does your team forfeit its authority? Or seize and act on its authority?

WTF (Want the Facts)

- 35 percent of employees leave their jobs because of internal politics.[3]
- According to research, the most common barriers within organizations include[4]:
  - ◆ Unclear direction on strategy and values, leading to conflicting priorities
  - ◆ Executives who don't work as a team and haven't committed to a plan or acknowledged critical changes in their behavior
  - ◆ A top-down or laissez-faire style by the leader, which stops honest discussions about problems
  - ◆ Employees' fear of telling the senior team about obstacles to the organization's effectiveness.
- 57 percent of employers identify that they want a candidate that works well under pressure.[5]
- A study for the Project Management Institute found performance factors associated with human mindsets and behaviors have the strongest impact on overcoming barriers. When successfully addressed, teams experience:[6]
  - ◆ Improved overall performance
  - ◆ Higher ability to deal with risks and uncertainties
  - ◆ Stronger personal effort
  - ◆ Greater commitment to established objectives and teammates

---

Teams That Forfeit Their Authority

This finance team was going nowhere—fast. Responsible for guiding the fiscal health of their region, the team consisted of 12 people working in seven different countries. Collectively, they were getting tons of pressure: Their region had been underperforming, and a cause had been identified. Despite deploying software for improved data sharing, there was still little connectivity among the different countries. They were sharing numbers without collectively interpreting what those facts meant to their business. These were real barriers.

Our assessment of the interactions the members of the team were having with one another, specifically what they chose to concentrate on and discuss, was telling. Shadowing team members in their virtual meetings, and in interviews asking them about the content of their emails and texts, we found that the team had fallen through an important threshold. They were forfeiting their authority to responsibly address the challenges their business was facing.

Figure 6.1 offers a list of the most common topics members of the team discussed that diverted the team from being able to deliver on their purpose.

DEBATES AND DISAGREEMENTS OVER DECISIONS
THE EXECUTIVE LEADERSHIP TEAM WAS MAKING

THE (POOR) PERFORMANCE AND DISAPPROVAL OF THE
DECISIONS AND ACTIONS OF OTHER FUNCTIONS IN THE BUSINESS

JUDGMENTS OF CONDUCT OF FELLOW TEAMMATES

GLOBAL AND REGIONAL POLITICS

THE REGIONAL ECONOMY AND THE PRICE OF COMMODITIES
(BEYOND STUDYING THE DATA NECESSARY TO MAKE INFORMED DECISIONS)

Figure 6.1 Team Diversions

We made two observations at this point, subtleties we see with great consistency in other teams that are stuck making only incremental progress.

1. Even though nearly every person on this finance team reported that they were flatlining, those same people participated in giving up their authority to make changes. They knew concentrating on issues outside of their control was unproductive and unfulfilling, but since the cultural norm of doing so was strong, and they lacked the personal skill to do otherwise, they still participated in such discussions. In this regard, what cultural norms does your team commit to reinforcing? And are those norms useful in getting the team where it needs to go?

2. There was a difference in what people talked about when they were together as a team versus when they were in smaller, informal groups of two or three. Our observations resulted in the assessment shown in Figure 6.2. The first chart is an analysis of where the team focused in formal meetings. The second chart reveals a shift in their focus when in small groups having informal/unstructured discussions, including

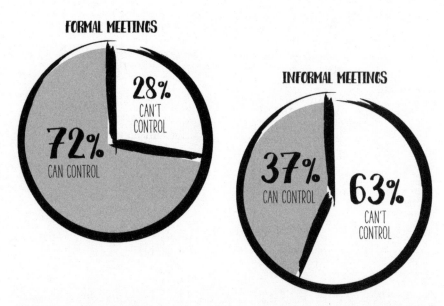

Figure 6.2 Estimated Percentage of Time Spent in Formal and Informal Meetings: What Leaders and Teams Can Control versus the Percentage of Time Spent Focusing on What They Can't Control

small talk occurring among subsets of the team after the formal meeting. Do these data look similar or different from the experience you have with your team?

In a world where nearly every professional reports, "I've got too much to do and not enough time to do it," this data can ignite important wisdom. Is your team fully leveraging the time it has?

Sadly, the story this finance team gets to tell doesn't have a happy ending. (This isn't Hollywood.) Before they could receive the DBT Framework and equip themselves to act upon their authority, an acquisition was announced, and they were the "being acquired" part of the equation. All discretionary spending was frozen. (In companies destined to do small things, this is code for: You cannot invest in the human imperative. It's a numbers game at this point.)

Soon after, the team was disbanded; people were let go or shuffled to other teams. With that, yet another team, composed of brilliant people and good hearts, went down in history as forgettable.

Teams That Exercise Their Authority

"Got milk?" Or in this case, "Got budget?"

Nothing creates a perceived barrier to success like the lack of money. And if you're in the business of making loads of the best cheese and other dairy products in the world, you need a lot of money to buy a lot of milk.

Tillamook is a sizable dairy co-op located in a town of the same name near Portland, Oregon. The company possesses an iconic food brand. In the grocery stores of the northwestern United States, Tillamook's products are as recognizable as Coca-Cola.

Then something happened and Tillamook's world changed. In a moment, their 100-year-plus history of success was suddenly in jeopardy. As the company moved into the early days of 2014, milk costs shot up— way up. Overnight their path to success became blocked.

"We have massive fluctuations in the costs of our raw materials," Patrick Criteser, CEO of Tillamook, told us. "In 2013, we built our budget for 2014 using the futures market to forecast our annual spending on milk." As the costs of business went up due to factors outside of their control, it became clear their calculations were wrong—very wrong.

"We started 2014 in a 40-million-dollar hole," Criteser said. "Our budget was off from the start. Historically, team members would have thrown their hands up. I've worked at other companies where people would have said, 'The year's over.' But we weren't going to go about our business that way."

Freeze the case study right here! It's an important juncture, because teams that do big things don't do what average teams do. Many business books (and there are several good ones) would focus solely on the decisions and actions of leadership. Specifically, what did Criteser and the other executives do to lead the organization past the real budget barrier they encountered?

Leadership, of course, is a prime component in any enduring success. Tillamook's executives did what many leadership teams would do: they raised prices, lowered costs, preserved cash, drove greater process efficiencies, and strengthened decision-making—while still doubling down on their investments in the future. But those actions are only one piece of a two-part equation necessary to bust through barriers. In fact, in a world where leadership often gets most of the credit, Criteser reminds us that the glory really belongs to the team.

"We didn't want to overcome this budget challenge the traditional way," he said. "We knew there was going to be a 2015, 2016, 2017, and so on. We were determined to make sure those years were even stronger."

This meant that Criteser's team also doubled down on their commitment to the human imperative. They equipped the team to function differently by identifying the thinking and actions now needed to persevere. Typical spreadsheet maneuvers wouldn't do.

Culture eats strategy for lunch.[7] Criteser knew this: It wouldn't matter if Tillamook's leadership team made plans to break through barriers if the teams within the organization didn't have the ability to think and take the actions to break through those barriers.

"There's a high level of connection between people—and people to the company," he reports. "Everyone cares. A lot. So we decided to invest in and leverage that."

When the team learned that the budget was in shambles, "There was a belief that we could do something unique, different," Criteser told us. "We knew it was going to be hard to overcome, but this is why people choose to be here."

They successfully took the fourth step in the DBT Framework: They identified the barriers under their control and acted upon their authority to choose their response.

"We were constantly asking ourselves, 'How do we respond? What's under our control? What can we do right now that will have the greatest impact?'" Criteser said.

A consideration of the most common topics members of the teams within Tillamook concentrated on stands in stark contrast to the finance team's list (in the example of a team that forfeited their authority). Figure 6.3 depicts a short overview of a list you might recognize if you're already on a team that does big things.

BRAINSTORMING ACTIONS THEY COULD TAKE TO MAXIMIZE THEIR RESOURCES

IMPLEMENTING INNOVATIONS AND IMPROVEMENTS THAT COULD BE MADE TO EXISTING PROCESSES

IMPROVING THE QUALITY OF THEIR PRODUCTS

ADVANCING AN ENTERPRISE MINDSET

BUILDING A ONE-TEAM APPROACH

Figure 6.3 Actions That Accelerate Teams

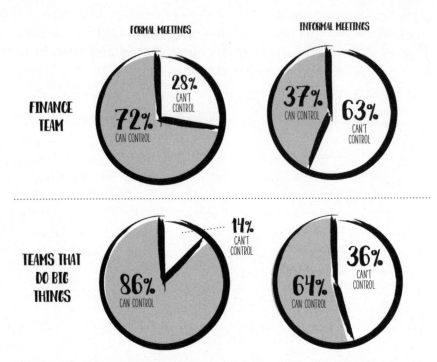

Figure 6.4 The Estimated Percentage of Time the Finance Team versus Teams That Do Big Things Spend in Formal and Informal Meetings Acting on What They Can Control Compared with the Percentage of Time Spent Focusing on What They Can't Control

An assessment of the percentage of time teams like those at Tillamook demonstrate their authority to control what they can control—in both formal and informal meetings—stands in as much contrast to the finance team as the results delivered (see Figure 6.4).

By demonstrating the inherent authority we all possess to choose our response to any given situation, a team can quickly become larger than the obstacles they encounter. Big motivating speeches or obnoxious threats aren't required from leadership—because the team is now more self-empowered to do big things.

"2014 was our breakthrough year. We almost hit budget," Criteser said. "But looking back, the way we handled that budget challenge gave us the confidence we needed to overcome future barriers. Previously, we had been too discount- and volume-oriented. We're more effective risk-takers now."

They were leery of increasing price tags and scaring customers away. However, because Tillamook was able to grow despite raising prices in 2014, Criteser added, "It gave us the conviction that we can be the premium brand we know we can be."

To be certain, Tillamook has grown. In the two years after demonstrating their authority to bust through the budget barrier of 2014, the company saw 20 percent revenue growth; they doubled income and improved the distributions to the owner-farmers of the region by over 35 percent. Additionally, they've gone from 600 to 800 employees. In a town of 4,500 people, that means the company's ability to do big things is also a big thing for the community.

Tillamook's success has its roots in the human imperative. By believing in the potential of people and equipping them to show that potential, they changed the trajectory of the company. "We know that when people can express their values through the work they're doing and the environment they're working in, the business benefits," Criteser said. "The community benefits."

"When we commit to enriching people's lives," he said, "we all get value from that."

Using the Contributor Decision to Break Through Barriers

"Danger! Turn around! Go back to where you came from!" This is the flashing red sign that greets teammates with a victim mentality, as they consider how to respond to the barriers they are facing. Most of us know this, because we've experienced it: The idea of accepting that we have the authority to respond to challenges in a productive way is scary and hard work. Sometimes it means overcoming the reflexes of apathy, anger, the blaming of others, or other defense mechanisms. It means being responsible.

Teammates who choose to forfeit their natural-born authority to choose their response to events, other people, or situations become powerless. And that won't work for teams with great aspirations; the team needs all the power it can get.

When we look closely at the members of the Tillamook team—and others like them who succeed at breaking through barriers—we see people effectively making the Contributor Decision, the choice to bring their best to the situation. To do so, they took a two-phased approach. They *accepted* the perceived barrier and then took *responsibility*. Specifically in the face of daunting barriers, they didn't do—and did—certain things. We're sharing their thinking and actions here, along with a question for your team to consider:

- They didn't fight the fact that they had made the budget they had to live with. They did model integrity and own their role in creating the conditions they now faced. *When a barrier pops up, how quickly does your team accept that the conditions are what they are, and begin demonstrating their ability to respond?*

- They didn't condone the error or mistake. They did ensure accountability by addressing past decision-making. Some teams struggle with this. Team members falsely think that if they don't express their anger over how bad things are that they're condoning what's occurred. *What does effective accountability for past actions look like for your team?*

- They didn't waste time pretending the barrier didn't exist. They did model emotional courage, move fast, and trust their process for success—the DBT Framework. *From your experience, what does it look like when a team pretends barriers don't exist?*

- They didn't argue or point fingers about any *should haves* or *could haves*. Instead, they did model trust in themselves and each other. *To what extent does your team effectively do this?*

- They didn't waste precious time and energy engaging in discussion about how they were drowning in 101 number-one priorities. They did get serious about further developing the skill to prioritize their work and celebrate what they were achieving. *What does it look like for your team to embody success even when it seems getting all the work done is impossible?*

The two phases of *acceptance* and *responsibility* equip every team member to better make the Contributor Decision, which is a decision we all want to—and can—make.

Using the Activator Decision to Break Through Barriers

True or false: If you have power, and you give power to a teammate, that means you have less power. For teams that are destined to do small things, this statement is true. That's because there's a self-centeredness that inserts an unnecessary word into the statement, so it reads: If you have power and you give *your* power to a teammate, that means you have less power.

But who said anything about giving up your power?

Those who make the Activator Decision, the choice to bring out the best in others, don't give up power. Giving others power doesn't mean we become power*less*. The reality is quite the contrary. Effective teams know that when we empower others, we enable them to be even more successful than they already are. Doing so means we become power*ful*.

When we interview the members of teams and ask, "Who are some of the teammates you value the most, and why?" we get telling answers for the reasons why teammates value their peers. Years ago when we started asking this question, we anticipated we'd hear responses that pointed at "friends" or "shared styles." But the replies went beyond that and were inspired: They "believe in me" and "hold me accountable to my values" and "empower/trust me" were some of the most common statements.

In short, teammates value those who bring out their best. Which means, of course, that particularly when a team is facing perceived barriers, when you can activate the best in others, you become more valuable to the team. We haven't lost anything as a teammate; we've only gained.

Using the Connector Decision to Break Through Barriers

Barriers are most commonly addressed in meetings—big ones that have everyone's attention across the business. One person we interviewed for this book reported that their team was, unfortunately, a perfect model for how *not* to address barriers—especially symptomatic barriers.

She was not happy about the company-wide operations meeting she'd just been in earlier that week, and she let us know it.

"Everyone in that meeting was a bunch of bobbleheads," she said.

"What do you mean by that?" we asked.

"The entire time, people sat and nodded in agreement and said things other people wanted to hear," she said. "There's too much fear of disagreement. Some people will agree just so they can end the meeting, but they leave with no intention of supporting what they've agreed to."

She explained, "Then they rush out and have a meeting after the meeting. They find people back in their part of the building who they can align with and make decisions about the company's plan that are different than what we all aligned to in the bigger meeting," she said as she shook her head. "It's a killer. And the dysfunction just soaks deeper into the organization."

This is it: Those who understand that the company only wins big when all teams in the company win (instead of just their team) must trust their instincts and take action. Choosing to partner across the business, the Connector Decision, is not a passive decision. We emphasize this because our experience shows that overwhelmingly employees know when their team is not partnering well with other teams. Yet, too few teams take effective actions to change the behavior.

If this is true for you, never fear. You can break this barrier and here's why. Your instincts reflect an important core feeling or gut reaction. Most of us know humans are meant to connect, and that is how successful business is done. And when it doesn't happen, all of us can feel it.

It's highly likely your company's processes and structure are impacting your team's ability to partner across the business. Until those further improve, here are three proven sets of words and actions we've coached other teams to use and take to connect and break through this symptomatic barrier.

1. Acknowledge what's not working and what you believe are important actions moving forward. It might sound like this: "I don't know what all of you see, but my perspective is that this team must get better at telling our truth in this meeting—instead of after the meeting. It's important to me that we improve in this way because this team sets the tone for the entire business."

2. Successfully model the ability to have vigorous debate. When a teammate challenges the information you've shared or provides constructive feedback in public, it can be tempting to put your hands up, shut up, or provide reasons why you did what you did (which everyone else hears as excuses). Because you don't want your teammates to do these things when you give them feedback, model what it looks like to be on a team that does big things by leaning forward and sincerely saying something like, "I'm grateful

you're bringing this to my attention. Say more about this, please. I can step forward in this area."

3. **Address your fears.** In those moments when you're sensing that team members might be tempted to revert to old habits of having side conversations that belong to the entire team, stop the discussion and say, "It's critical that the conversations we have on this topic are done so as an entire team, so that we can move forward effectively." Then ask: "What else needs to be said here and now so we can make the best decision possible and fully focus forward?"

Does your team hold meetings after the meeting? (Any bobbleheads?) If so, how will you trust your instincts and act so your team can better connect across the business?

The Path to Doing Big Things Is Open

Teams that do big things embrace the wisdom that a path to success does, in fact, exist. They are not trapped or confined by limits in their thinking. If barriers or obstacles appear they know that the response to what they've encountered is theirs to determine. When team members forfeit their authority to choose their response to the difficulties they encounter, the team forfeits its greater role in the future of things. Disempowered, they are merely a group of people with unactivated potential, only capable of doing tasks assigned to them.

Luck does change the fortunes of a team. Teams that do big things, however, are too impatient to wait for chance. By acting on the authority to choose your focus and actions, your team steels itself with a heart of optimism and sets a course of consequences far more spectacular than those teams who choose the absurd belief that they don't have choice.

By exercising your barrier-breaking authority, your team is free to do what you've wanted to do all along: deliver great work. The next step then, is to focus on what matters most.

Big Ideas in This Chapter and 3 Recommended Actions

- Your team will break through barriers much faster when they can see and understand them. **Recommended Action:** Determine as a team your comfort level in openly and constructively talking about the barriers the team faces. Then determine what's necessary to increase that skill and comfort level.

- Teams often face three types of barriers:

  - *Real*—obstacles grounded in facts

  - *Perceived*—Difficulties based on an incomplete interpretation of the facts

  - *Symptomatic*—Challenges that are an indicator of a bigger, sometimes hidden real barrier, occurring with the system or culture

  Recommended Action: As a team, discuss the barriers you're currently facing, finishing by identifying which ones are real.

- Every person and team possesses the natural authority to choose their response to any event or circumstance.

- When a team exercises its barrier-breaking authority, it increases its ability to do big things and make an epic impact on the business.

- Teams that don't exercise their barrier-breaking authority spend significantly more time focusing on and discussing things they can't control in comparison to their counterparts on teams that do big things. **Recommended Action:** Assess the percentage of time your team focuses on what it can control vs. what it can't. Is it a productive ratio? Then determine what you will do to improve your focus as a team.

- Choosing to make the Contributor, Activator, and Connector Decisions empowers a team to better exercise its barrier-breaking authority.

7 Focus on What Matters

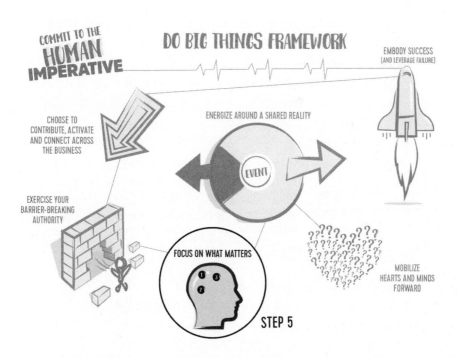

COMMIT TO THE **HUMAN IMPERATIVE**

DO BIG THINGS FRAMEWORK

EMBODY SUCCESS
(AND LEVERAGE FAILURE)

CHOOSE TO
CONTRIBUTE, ACTIVATE
AND CONNECT ACROSS
THE BUSINESS

ENERGIZE AROUND A SHARED REALITY

EVENT

EXERCISE YOUR
BARRIER-BREAKING
AUTHORITY

FOCUS ON WHAT MATTERS

STEP 5

MOBILIZE
HEARTS AND MINDS
FORWARD

Oracle Team USA was in trouble. Big trouble. With tens of millions of dollars in funding, some of the most skilled sailors in the world, and the greatest sailing technology ever used, they were favored to win the prestigious 2013 America's Cup.[1]

Yet, after nine races and an early penalty, they found themselves regularly following Emirates Team New Zealand across the finish line.[2] One more victory for the Kiwis, and the oldest international sports trophy would be New Zealand's. What occurred, however, will likely never be repeated. And the team that achieved it will never be forgotten.

With seemingly insurmountable odds stacked against Team USA, the media pushed for a concession as they interviewed their skipper, Jimmy Spithill. He wouldn't give it to them. "We feel we've got just as good a chance to win this," Spithill said. "[The race] is all about development. It's not about how you begin the competition. It's how you finish the competition."[3]

Then he finished with, "It's not over. It's a long way from being over." Spithill remained focused.

Moving a seven-ton, 72-foot-long vessel across the water, with a 13-story sail and foils that want to pull your craft out of the water while going 50 miles per hour is no easy job. Even with the team's mastery and years of preparation, how could they possibly close such a huge deficit and overcome their evenly matched and equally prepared opponent?

Like all teams that do big things, this yachting crew maintained a focus on what matters most: the human imperative, the specific behavior they needed to succeed as a team. With it, they began to find their way. They took the next race. And the next. And the one after that. By race 19, the deficit that once seemed as big as an ocean was closed. The winner of the next race would take home the trophy.

What had they done to alter the winds of fortune?

It wasn't better equipment they needed. And it wasn't different crew members who were required to succeed. The answer came in how the team utilized what they had. "The biggest change we made with the boat is how we sailed the boat," said Spithill. "The technique we used to trim, sail, and steer the boat came from [members of the team] off the boat," he said. It wasn't just a subset of the team, those on the boat that made the difference. To win, it was the entire team working together that proved to be the difference. "All that support . . . we utilized 100 percent," Spithill reported.[4]

"This ability to come back from such a desperate position," said general manager Grant Simmer, "and not to flinch, not to point fingers at each other, but to just get stronger, that was incredible."[5]

Most teams, in all arenas in life and business, come together for the purpose of doing a job. The teams that do big things, however, are as devoted to excellence in their collective efforts as they are in outcomes. Consequently, these teams become stronger as they move from start to finish.

As Simmer said of Oracle, "They came out fighting every day, and getting better and better."

Focusing on what matters most better enables a team to win. And Oracle Team USA did. As the team crossed the finish line in their come-from-behind win, champagne was served. And the history books added another epic story about the power of teamwork.

After the race, Spithill reinforced what mattered most as he described how the team was able to prevail. "One of our biggest strengths as a team," he said, "is looking after each other as teammates. It doesn't matter what sort of adversity we're facing. Eight to one down, **whatever the issue is, we always look after one another. We're a team. And that's what got the job done.**"[6]

Distracted, Hopelessly Stressed, and Disconnected Teams

Most people know what's necessary to get the job done, but something specific happens to too many teams that blocks their path to success. It can be depressing to observe.

Consider a team we supported on the East Coast in the food industry. Their big thing was to advance and further implement the lean principles the organization held so dearly. This cross-functional team was diverse in age, gender, and nationalities. As we observed them move through their weekly meeting, it wasn't difficult to identify why they were delivering what their leader described as "marginal results"—and why they couldn't achieve big outcomes. The team was in the state we call DSD: *distracted*, hopelessly *stressed*, and *disconnected*. It's a demoralizing phase a team enters just before they flatline. Here's what that looks like.

We saw a couple of people sitting at the conference table seemingly anesthetized, their eyes buggy as they stared at the team's numbers being projected on the screen. Several people had their chins on their chest, looking down at their thumbs, which were getting a workout on smartphones. (Occasionally, a couple of them would quickly glance up and throw a little smile, as if doing so sufficed for communicating, "I respect you!")

Two others slowly shook their heads as they whispered to one another, their eyes moving around the room as if to pierce any compassion that may have remained among their teammates. One lonely person sat at the corner of the table taking notes and smiling. (About what, we do not know. We smiled back, though.)

Finally, on the bottom of the screen, below the team's numbers, were the images of four people moving in jerky fashion. Of the four who were remoting in from other locations, one seemed intent on giving her opinion about every number that was read (it was apparent she was defending the outcomes), while the three others seemed bored by the whole affair.

Distracted, hopelessly stressed, and disconnected is the phase a dying team goes through that's typified by the following traits:

- The inability to collectively sustain a prioritized focus as a team
- Disablement or near paralysis due to overwhelming workloads or circumstances and exceedingly high expectations in performance
- An obvious lack of human connection among team members.

The team's whole heart wasn't in it. They weren't even close to being bigger than the sum of the talents in the room. By staying busy in discussions and endless strings of emails, they were attempting to create the illusion that the team was productive— with little success.

To be certain, teams that have not been equipped to do big things can't be blamed for falling into this state of DSD. The mind has its tendencies and defense mechanisms. Nearly all of us close ourselves off when our brain circuits can no longer effectively process these and other provocations, such as:

- Competing priorities
- Mixed messages resulting from an endless sea of change

- High volumes of relationships to manage with people we don't personally know
- Digital gadgets pulverizing our consciousness
- The constant bombardment of media spewing news that repulses us
- Nonstop emails and texts
- Personal and unspoken worries each teammate is likely facing, such as raising teenage children, eldercare, financial troubles, marital discord, illness, substance abuse, and more.

As humans, when we feel distracted by low-value temptations, hopelessly stressed by the requirement to deliver colossal outcomes with few resources, and disconnected from those in our community, we regress. And in big ways: Suddenly, we fall under the illusion that what matters most is our safety and our ability to make money. (That guy named Maslow knew what he was talking about with his hierarchy of needs.)

Far more often than not, what stops a team from doing big things is not that they lack the technical skills or functional experience to get the job done. It is, rather, that the members of the team succumb to being people they don't want to be. Life is sucked out of the team.

That's what makes this fifth step in the Do Big Things Framework so powerful. Team members gain the skill of a required and certain focus. And rather than having to change who they are, they become more of the amazing people they already are.

WTF (Want the Facts)*

- Employees waste, on average, 759 hours each year due to workplace distractions.[7]
- 82 percent of all interrupted work is resumed on the same day, and it takes an average of 23 minutes and 15 seconds to get back into a deep focus after being distracted.[8]
- The typical level of employee disengagement hovers around 70 percent. Managers who focus on team members' strengths cut employee disengagement to 1 percent. (Not *by* 1 percent, but *to* 1 percent.)[9]

- Groups of people who have five positive interactions to every single negative interface perform strongest.[10]

*All data reflects U.S. population.

What Matters Most

In the long list of things your team needs to do to succeed, at what level does your team prioritize how team members think and act, particularly with one another? While nearly every team we support says this should be a top priority, rarely does it rise above the other priorities of business without a developmental effort occurring. As we've shared, when it comes to teams who achieve big business imperatives, what matters most is the human imperative. It's about you, your teammates, and, most importantly, who you are together in your efforts to do big things. The strength of the connections among people, where humans are being the best human beings they can be together, is what history shows is required to succeed. This is the core of the human imperative we established in step 1 of the DBT Framework.

Captain Spithill, while being interviewed after the Oracle Team USA victory, said their human imperative was, "Whatever the issue, we always look after one another." You don't have to be like Spithill, however, and wait until after you've won the contest to determine how you did it. **The DBT Framework enables your team to identify what matters most _prior_ to your effort. Deciding who you are going to be is always a more powerful act than assessing who you were.**

And a critical reminder (because we've seen too many teams miss this): The human imperative is not to be prioritized over the business imperative. Too many companies filled with big-hearted people on well-intentioned teams have gone out of business. No. **The human imperative is the prioritized strategy to deliver the business imperative.**

Some of the examples of the human imperative, provided in Chapter 3 (step 1) of this book, make clear that this is far more than living our values for the sake of the values or just to score well in performance reviews. This is the business of delivering the business. It's the business of the heart: being bigger as a team than the challenges we face.

Here's a quick snapshot of those examples we offered earlier:

- We must practice creative and collaborative teamwork.
- We are all-in early by being committed to our roles and responsibilities as teammates.
- We take the initiative and connect with an enterprise mindset.

Step 4 of the DBT Framework, Focus on What Matters, is how a team sharpens their concentration on the human imperative, thereby enabling them to place better attention on the business imperative. Because they know they'll be severely tested as they move forward, this is how team members ensure that as a team they don't become distracted, hopelessly stressed and disconnected. Rather, they will build an immunity to the turmoil, chaos, and unrest around them.

This is making sure that none of us are minimized as human beings as we take on the challenges in front of us—but just the opposite: We realize our greatest personal fulfillment by contributing to a team that becomes stronger in this epic work.

How to Focus on What Matters: The 3 Mind Factors

How do we focus on what matters? Oddly enough, the answer is the same answer to the question, "How do we focus on those things that distract, hopelessly stress, and disconnect us?" That sounds strange, but it's true. The solution, therefore, is not for us to change our brains; it is to train our brains to do what we want them to do, instead of what our brains want to do.

Imagine someone sitting in front of you holding his hand up. He can move it anywhere he wants. He can wave it and touch and hold objects with it. (Heck, he can slap his face if he wants to.) It's a tool at his disposal. And because it is, he can use his hand to make a weapon—a fist—to do destructive things. He can also reach his hand toward yours and connect with you by shaking your hand. Or he can use his hand as a tool of service by holding it open and offering assistance. Indeed, the hand is a powerful tool.

The brain is a similar tool in exponentially more powerful ways. Like the hand, your thoughts can be used as a weapon, a tool to partner with

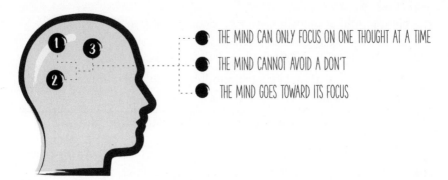

THE MIND CAN ONLY FOCUS ON ONE THOUGHT AT A TIME

THE MIND CANNOT AVOID A DON'T

THE MIND GOES TOWARD ITS FOCUS

Figure 7.1   The 3 Mind Factors: Research-Driven Principles to Support Focus

others, or a device to offer support. To grasp how this is so requires leveraging three basic facts of the brain and how it focuses.

These qualities were first defined by authors and our friends Ed Oakley and Doug Krug, in their groundbreaking book, *Enlightened Leadership*.[11] In this section, we're building upon and refining their work. To do so, we call this tool the 3 Mind Factors (Figure 7.1).

Within each of us, these mind factors are always turned on. We can't *not* use them. It's how we're wired as human beings. Therefore, to better develop our immunity to DSD, we don't have to do something different; instead, we simply have to do something we're already doing—only *better*. This wisdom is the core to speeding the transformation of teams, leaders, and entire work cultures.

Mind Factor #1: The Mind Can Only Focus on One Thought at a Time

Try this, right now: Think of two thoughts at the same time. But don't try very long, because it can't be done. You can do different things at once, such as walk, chew gum, and have a discussion with another person. But facts are facts: As you move through the day, your mind can only focus on one thought at a time.

For some, this is where things get wild, because we're all having a lot of thoughts. And by living in an ever faster world with growing digital intrusions, the menu of things our minds can focus on is growing exponentially.

But don't blame the brain. It's doing what it's made to do to keep us alive. Therefore, the claim that "I can't focus" misses an important point.

It's not that the mind can't focus. It's that the mind focuses so *well* and *so quickly*. And always on one thought at a time.

The now-classic selective attention test by Simons and Chabris (1999) supports this wisdom.[12] In it, hundreds of unsuspecting people were shown a video and instructed to count how many times three players wearing white shirts passed a basketball among themselves. It's important to note that there were an additional three people in the group wearing black clothing and passing a basketball. (A chaotic scene, certainly, just like in real life.)

After some time the experiment seems to come to an end, and the observers were asked, "How many passes did you count?" The correct answer was not important.

What's far more insightful were the responses to the next question Simons and Chabris asked: "Did you see a person dressed in a black gorilla outfit enter into the activity, pound its chest, and then walk off?" Only half reported seeing the gorilla.

As Simons said, "When our attention is focused on one thing, we fail to notice other . . . things around us—including those we might want to see."[13] (Because we genuinely care about everyone's safety, we'll add: This explains why nobody can safely text and drive at the same time.)

Daniel Kahneman, winner of the Nobel Prize in economics and author of the can't-put-it-down book *Thinking, Fast and Slow*, lifts the curtain on what our brain is doing—in our favor or not. Particularly when we are distracted, hopelessly stressed, and disconnected, the part of the brain we use the most focuses so intently that "what you see is all there is."[14] In other words, anything that occurs around us is either ignored or quickly folded into the framework of what we're focusing on. Thus, you don't see the gorilla. You're focusing on something else.

Emotional intelligence expert Daniel Goleman said it this way in his superb book *Focus*, "Instead of splitting [our focus], we actually switch rapidly." We can only have one focus, one thought at a time.[15]

Occasionally, multitaskers debate the validity of Mind Factor #1. "But I can sit in a meeting while answering emails easily!" they argue. What's telling is that as they make this claim, many of their teammates roll their eyes and silently shake their heads. That's because we all know the truth: We may be able to physically do multiple things at once, but we only hold one concentrated thought at a time. And when we continually switch from one focus to another, it saps the attention needed for full and concentrated engagement.[16]

One leader told us: "Multitasking makes us stupid, because nothing gets done well." Experts who study the human's ability to concentrate would agree. They estimate that the time it takes to change our focus and then return back to the original focus and task we had is equivalent to the amount of time it takes you to get your favorite beverage in the morning at the coffee shop—when there's a long line of other customers in front of you. And a really long line at that.[17]

So every ding of an incoming text that a teammate then reads on their smartphone takes them away to lines at coffee shops. They leave behind the work they're doing (say having an important discussion with your direct report? manager? colleague? or completing a project update), and then return their focus many minutes later.

Here's another way to look at it. Imagine you and your teammates are huddled around a bomb and are working to disarm it by carefully cutting delicate wires tangled in a web. Everyone's focus is glued on the task. Then, without warning, a teammate's cell phone rings. Should they answer? (And allow their focus to go get a coffee?) Of course, they likely wouldn't take their focus from the job at hand; no sane teammate would risk detonating the bomb.

The metaphor is intentionally extreme: When well-intentioned teammates allow outside distractions to jar their focus away from discussions they're having with others, they subject themselves to severe and real costs.

For starters, who's got an extra 20 minutes each time one of us receives an interrupting text or phone call to get back to the level of focus we need to truly engage with other teammates? Beyond that, distracted teammates communicate to others, "I don't care enough about you or your thoughts to stay focused on our discussion." The result: Future interactions among team members become predictably explosive.

Mind Factor #2: The Mind Cannot Avoid a *Don't*

"Caution! DON'T LOOK UP!" You couldn't miss the enormous yellow and black sign that greeted visitors to this glass bottle manufacturing plant. The entrance to the older facility was located next to the furnace. With temperatures ranging near 3,000°F, globules of molten glass left the furnace to be poured into molds to make bottles and jars. The spectacle is amazing to behold.

But don't look at it! Glass particles can escape from the top of the furnace and rain down on unsuspecting faces of those who look up. Even when wearing protective goggles, it's best to keep your face down. Could you do so, though?

It's likely each of us already knows the plant had to repeatedly deal with offenders. The sign's unambiguous instructions not only had people looking up, people reportedly twirled their bodies around to get a view of what they were told was forbidden. And no one can blame them for doing so.

Our brains are wired to scan our surroundings for risks. Constantly and often unconsciously, we are searching for threats to our well-being. This wiring, however, comes with an ironic twist: When we identify that which can cause us harm, we focus on it.

To quickly experience this, take this quick test. Read the following four statements and then identify what you are thinking most:

1. We *can't* come in over budget.
2. *Don't* touch the machinery.
3. When you're in the meeting with the boss, *never* talk about "that" subject.
4. *Stop* sending so many emails.

If you're like everyone else (and you are because all our brains use the 3 Mind Factors), you're thinking about *over budget, machinery, that subject,* and *emails.* Which means, of course, if these instructions have dire consequences, you're in big trouble.

The brain can't resist thinking about the don't messages it receives. Harvard psychologist Daniel Wegner tells us why we shouldn't beat ourselves up for thinking about—and quite likely doing—the very things we were instructed not to do. In his paper, *How to Think, Say, or Do Precisely the Worst Thing for Any Occasion,* Wegner likens this quirk in the brain to slapstick comedy.[18] The very thing we don't want to think, say, feel, or do, occurs with a frequency triggered by how distracted and stressed we are. (Which, for most teams, is a lot.) Sadly, the results in our efforts to team together aren't nearly as funny as slapstick.

No one is suggesting teams not use don't messages. (Pun intended.) Top-performing teams that have high expectations know that it's an imperative, at times, to be crystal clear about what is not acceptable. (If the team is heading off a cliff, attention needs to be seized immediately.) Used sparingly, the negative words become even more powerful.

Ultimately, teams that do big things are far more productive because they stay focused on what they want instead of what they don't want. This includes demonstrating an ability to translate what they don't want to occur into what-they-do-want-to-have-happen messages. As an example, consider a team is approaching a critical project deadline. The temptation may be to utter the mantra, "Don't miss the deadline!" Because this consumes the brain in unproductive ways, the message is changed to put the brain to greater use, with something like this, "What will we accomplish in this meeting to ensure we meet our deadline?" Given Mind Factor #3, which we'll cover next, that modification in focus creates entirely different outcomes.

Mind Factor #3: The Mind Goes Toward Its Focus

"Your focus determines your reality," said the Jedi Knight in the movie *Star Wars*.[19]

This is certain: For any of us to survive, our brain must establish and function within a reality, a belief about how the experiences in our world work together. Without a frame through which to see the world, our image of the world doesn't have definition or meaning. As a result, we don't know how to act. To create a frame of the world requires establishing beliefs, what we think is true or not, and right or wrong.

Once such beliefs of how the world works are established, the brain does not like to be wrong. Being wrong means we're at risk. So the brain figures, "Let's not make this more difficult than it needs to be." Left unaffected, this reasoning can set us on a course of living myopic lives.

Since we can only focus on one thought at a time, when the brain receives new information, it checks it against the current beliefs in our frame of reality. "Does this new information fit in my truth?" the brain asks. If no, it has a tendency to quickly yell, "Bull!" and dismiss the new information. Or if the new information validates and reinforces the reality that the brain has established, it breathes a sigh of relief and shouts, "See, I told you! I'm right again." Then it does a little happy dance and moves on to the next thought.

Psychologists, of course, call this confirmation bias. A nation's political parties (teams, certainly) rely on this tendency of our brains by constantly pushing stories and information to their respective teams. They must reinforce and further entrench the beliefs of the team. Heaven forbid, if they allow the belief of the opposing party to creep into their reality and alter it in any way, the survival of the team could be threatened.

Have you ever observed two long-time neighbors standing at their shared fence attempting a political debate? With uncomfortable and cordial smiles, they passionately share their opinions and pretend to listen to each other. Then one of them begins thinking, "How can this guy be such an idiot? I have spent my entire life collecting the evidence that my political party is the correct and virtuous party! Can't he see the obvious data that proves he's wrong about his party?"

The assumption by this neighbor is correct. The person on the other side of the fence *can't* see the same evidence. The human brain can only focus on one thought at a time (remember Mind Factor #1); also, it takes its carrier (you) in the direction of its focus, regularly collecting evidence that's consistent with the beliefs and reality that have been established. (Your brain thinks it's working for you; it wants you to resist anything that doesn't fit in its definition of reality. It wants to stay warm and cozy in a reality of current-state thinking.) As a consequence, both neighbors are right in their beliefs— and blind to the fact that another reality could possibly exist for others.

This scenario is painful for those who believe that the ultimate team eclipses the notion of a particular political party and is instead defined by the entire country. With a broader frame for defining the team the reality shifts, and civil discourse and productive discussions occur because the neighbors now see broader implications and possibilities in their thoughts and actions. Instead of using the 3 Mind Factors to their disadvantage, they apply them for a greater cause.

The example of the political parties is an important one for those teams serious about doing big things. Political parties often use Mind Factor #3 to their party's advantage. Those observing the effects of this narrower focus can see how it limits the ability of the citizens of a nation to do significant things together.

If the neighbors do not check and assess their focus, they soon quit meeting at the fence. (Most human brains don't like conflict.) Because the mind goes toward its focus, the neighbors slide from not caring for the ideas of the person on the other side of the fence to not caring about them as people.

For a bit, they quit concerning themselves about their neighbor, ignoring them as they drive into their garage. Then, with that trend in focus unabated, emotions begin to simmer. This means their focus—and beliefs—become even more set in concrete. Because one person's brain sees their neighbor's beliefs as a threat to their own reality, judgments are made and words are shared at the dinner table, "Our neighbors are nuts! They're completely wacky."

The kids hear the words, and what happens next is both predictable and tragic. Even though they've played with the neighbor kids for years, suddenly the kids adopt the reality their parents hold. (Psychologists call it the horns effect: when a negative impression is made that overrules opposite impressions.)

The point here is not whether employees bring national or local politics into their workplaces. What's at stake is how teams in the business world make missteps in focus on any topic that results in dividing a team, rather than uniting it.

As an example, as authors we've seen several organizations painfully agonizing over their inability to create a more diverse and inclusive work environment. Teams function in a fractured state, as good-intentioned teammates hold steadfast in their beliefs—about the customer, the company's products or services, the direction of the company, and so on—and they doggedly spend their day collecting evidence to support those beliefs.

When these teammates meet another team member (like the neighbors at the fence) who holds different beliefs, perspectives, and experiences, a tragedy occurs: The difference of ideas (which the company desperately needs to succeed) slides to judgments about each other. Sometimes these judgments are based on race, gender, or other demographic differences. And suddenly, really good people with big hearts begin to care less about one another. Trust, collaboration, communication—the behaviors we all know are essential to succeed—disappear.

The implosion all started by allowing the brain to establish a focus, which turned into a belief that the brain collected evidence to reinforce, that then established a reality not shared by others. When the members of a team become small in their thinking, the team can only do small things.

But these teams can get their whole heart back in it. Our experience shows teams committed to the human imperative can do so quickly as long as they're equipped with a method to better master their focus. With the 3 Mind Factors, team members are better enabled to deliver their imperatives rather than letting their brains deliver something far more dreadful: a team that flatlines.

Collecting Evidence to Prove You Can't Succeed

They called themselves the Lightbulb Team. They were a bunch of talented individuals from across the organization thrown together to do something big: Innovate and develop the manufacturing technology needed tomorrow so they could get their product to the customer far faster and without spending all the company's revenues to do so. Given how they were connecting with one another or, more specifically, how they weren't, they could have called themselves something far less honorable.

"I don't get it," one of the team members told us. "Everyone on this team was either recruited or begged to be on it. I mean, we've got bright people here. You'd think that figuring this out wouldn't be so difficult."

As we listened to the members of the team in one-on-one interviews, it was easy to hear how they were using the 3 Mind Factors to their disadvantage and why their whole heart wasn't in it.

A project manager said, "The problem is that no one is following our established process."

The lead engineer told us, "Nothing's going to change until leadership changes." (We noted a tone of resignation, though curiously not laced with pain.)

And the HR lead reported, "I'm trying to talk corporate into giving me four hours to take everyone through our high-performing teams training program. We've got to get back to understanding our reason for being, our charter."

There were other interviews we conducted, of course, yet this sample makes the painful point. The Lightbulb Team was using their focus to dim their potential. They were collecting evidence that proved they couldn't succeed as a team.

It's one of the greatest tragedies in business (if not life). **Most people will say they want teammates around them with hearts activated and brains turned on, but then too many will focus on everything wrong or inadequate about these same people.** Consequently, because what they see is all there is, they shut down and destroy the very attributes they long to see and know the team needs to succeed.

None of us are gods, yet our focus creates the reality we must live with. If team members are going to routinely collect evidence on what they don't like, care about, or respect in their teammates, why not quit as a team now? Why prolong the suffering and inevitable decline to flatlining as a team?

These are ugly, backward-focused words, we know. Yet, the act of creating destructive beliefs about other people is even uglier. It's called the Doofus Principle. And teams that do big things will have nothing to do with it.

The Doofus Principle

With apologies to Merriam-Webster, note the definition shared in Figure 7.2.

Teams that can only do small things get stuck in a toxic culture where people are Doofusing themselves and others. It sounds like this: "All everyone in finance is ever worried about is money. They've got no heart." Or, "Don't invite her to the meeting. Her personality style always derails us." Or, "This company will never be able to innovate."

Doofus: "*doo-fus*," noun: someone who is stupid, bird-brained, mentally dull; a fool.

Doofus Principle: To focus on and collect evidence that reinforces destructive beliefs about people, places, or things. The focus diminishes potential and is specifically destructive to a team's ability to impact the business in a meaningful manner.

Figure 7.2 Definition of Doofus

Teams that intend to elevate their performance must answer this question: Because we will always find the evidence to support any belief we choose about ourselves, our teammates, or other teams, are we choosing the beliefs that are useful to what we need to do to succeed? Or are we merely focusing on and collecting evidence of what we can prove is true? (Because the mind is wired to go toward its focus, it can prove that nearly anything is true.) If we answer yes to the second question, then we must address this: Why would we deliberately choose to believe something about ourselves or others that is destructive?

The act of Doofusing will extract the heart from any team. Those who understand this wisdom, as they join a team, don't hope they get teamed with great people. Instead, they make the people they're teamed with great. They are purposeful in establishing beliefs about themselves and each other that draw them closer and drive the meaningful connections the team will need to succeed. A richness in diverse and inclusive thinking and actions occurs as team members bring the best out of everyone they interact with.

Now, the team can do bigger things in epic fashion.

How to End Doofusing

The experts who study the human mind are clear about this. Where each of us places our focus can be easily concentrated into three domains:

1. An *inward* focus

2. A focus on *others*

3. A focus beyond others, or on the *outer* domain[20]

You deserve a raise in pay if you recognize these distinct areas of focus. (Okay, we can't authorize that. Sorry.) These points of focus align perfectly with the 3 DBT Decisions. Today's business demands that your team be agile in moving between these three domains of focus. The ability to do so is the essence of a team that can adapt to new and unpredictable circumstances. The Contributor, Activator, and Connector Decisions each prove to be an effective method for developing this type of focus agility. Specifically, here's what that looks like.

To make the Contributor Decision, to bring your best to every situation, requires that you focus inwardly first. As you do, your choice to focus on what you do well versus a consistent focus on what you don't do well, will determine your ability to contribute fully.

Because you go toward your focus (Mind Factor #3), any self-chatter such as "I can't speak well in meetings," or "I can never get ahead," only means you'll find more evidence that diminishes your confidence, if not your self-worth.

To put an end to the self-Doofusing, take this challenge: Provide yourself with the opposite type of feedback you've been giving yourself. Specifically, if you're serious about being more consistently at your best, focus on and celebrate those moments when you are demonstrating the behaviors you want to model with greater consistency. Even more than positive affirmations, this focus means you will only find more evidence that you are capable. With growing confidence, you form a healthier and more productive reality. Now, you can contribute even more.

Succeeding in making the Activator Decision, to bring the best out of others in your interactions with them necessitates the need to shift your focus from self to others. Just as giving yourself affirmative feedback works to build the thinking necessary to contribute more, so does giving positive feedback to others bring out their best. Despite the fact that this type of feedback is well documented to transform behaviors, it's woefully underused in most workplaces. Therefore, consider these examples so you can be an even greater model:

- If you have a teammate who others are Doofusing by thinking, "She never does quality work," then you can seek those moments when she does deliver quality and tell her so: "Your quality work on this allowed us to hit the deadline. Thank you."

- If people are Doofusing the team by saying, "We never trust each other around here," you can change that by providing feedback when you see trust in action. For example, "I really appreciate how we trusted each other to deliver on our roles with this project. It allowed us to be far more efficient."

We all go toward our focus; when teammates are guided to concentrate on the important difference they're making, they are far more likely to make a greater difference.

To prevail in delivering on the Connector Decision, to partner across the business and deliver shared objectives, demands an outer focus beyond the team. And, it's entirely natural: When you don't have a relationship with others, the mind is quick to skew to negative thinking. (As the wise have said: Humans fear what we don't understand.) However, teams that do big things refuse to lower or dishonor themselves by Doofusing other teams. Rather than inhibiting their own progress by focusing on the lack of relationships, they instead focus on what matters: creating the evidence that supports the beliefs necessary to accelerate the trust needed between teams.

We encourage you to do what the best teams do when they connect across the business: Give other teams sincere, affirming feedback. It works well for many reasons, including: (1) Entire teams follow a focus (not just a person), and (2) When done genuinely, it builds affinity and relationships quickly. Here are some examples.

- "We know this was our first meeting, yet we just want to acknowledge both teams for being so transparent. That will be a key for us moving forward."

- "Real quick—I know everyone has to run to their next meeting, yet before you go I just wanted to thank you for trusting our team. We just started this work together, and it's apparent by the comments that were made that we believe each team is fully capable."

Here's what the Lightbulb Team did to succeed: Once they were equipped with the DBT Decisions, and the 3 Mind Factors necessary to effectively make those decisions, they chose to end the Doofusing. Instead, they focused on what matters most: strong connections among teammates.

The project manager was challenged on her assumption that *no one* followed established processes. When we provided her with evidence that while the workers in the field hadn't been perfect, they had indeed hit several milestones, she was on her way to an insight: Her focus on failures meant she'd only find more failures, and drive a wedge between herself and others. What would keep wedges out of relationships? She knew the answer: focusing more on where they are following processes rather than where they're not. Then, she'll be more effective when she addresses the deficiencies.

We also challenged the lead engineer on her statement that *nothing* would change until leadership changed. It's true, we told her. The higher someone goes in an organization, the less self-aware they are likely to become.[21] As well, their ability to demonstrate empathy by reading emotions through facial cues often dwindles.[22] Despite all that, we asked her: "Was it possible the leaders she was criticizing might not be aware of the outcomes they were creating?"

"Not aware?" she asked. "How could they not be aware? It's flagrant and abusive."

Perhaps, we replied. Then we asked her to consider as well that while leaders may lose their ability to be empathetic, so is there a decline in reverse empathy: the employees' ability to be empathetic of top leadership. When we asked her how she engaged with and acted around senior leadership, she confessed that she avoided them.

"If this is so," we told her, "and given the research, what would it mean if they were unaware of the effect their actions were having on you, but they *were* aware that you were avoiding them?"

That question transformed thinking and actions for her. At that moment she made a commitment to control what she could control, starting with her thinking and behaviors.

The HR lead seemed perplexed by our question: Why did the team need their directive or charter reinforced through another high-performance training? His answer, in so many words: They're not collaborating, because they're not aligned on what's most important.

We agreed with his observations regarding the lack of collaboration; however, based on our experience, we came to a different conclusion as to the cause. Consider, we said to him, that the focus he sensed the team lacked wasn't related to what they had to achieve, but was a symptom of how they were seeing and interacting with one another.

To pull people from across a business, who have little or no experience with one another, and expect them to start their work at a level of trust necessary for effective collaboration, has as much chance for success as mixing oil and water. It's difficult, given everything we know about how the brain is wired to focus. A leader can spend weeks covering the details of the charter and teaching about collaboration, but until the new teammates are equipped with the ability to focus on the behaviors of others in a way that creates a healthy, shared reality, little productivity will occur.

Figure 7.3 Team Purpose Hierarchy Pyramid Showing Common Beliefs of Teams

To assist, we provided the pyramid (Figure 7.3) to the HR lead, and then asked him: When you consider the beliefs team members have of one another, at what level do they function?

His answer came quickly: "We all see each other as competitors." When we asked him why, his response didn't surprise us, because it's a reality on too many underperforming, cross-functional teams.

"They're excited about building new technology," he said. "But each of them also wants to make sure that whatever they create is of the greatest benefit and lowest risk to their respective functions. This new technology will likely require a lot of resources, and we're always competing against each other for those. As a result, our debates are less about innovating than they are negotiating."

We have a lot of empathy for what the members of teams like this have to endure because they're being asked to overcome incredible, silent forces. They work on the cross-functional team, but they operate and belong to seemingly separate universes. Our assessment work revealed that when the Lightbulb Team went back to their functions, there was serious Doofusing occurring. They were surrounded by other teammates who held beliefs such as, "Everyone from engineering is cold-hearted." "All those project managers are slave drivers." And, "Those people in HR are (fill in the blank)." Such conditions make it nearly irrational to expect productive outcomes.

We've seen it hundreds of times: When teams move beyond nametags and ice-breakers as the method to create identities for teammates, they can create the necessary identity as a team to do big things. That's what the Lightbulb Team was finally able to do. By being equipped to focus on what matters most—the human imperative—their results improved just as you would expect them to: quickly.

The moment teammates realize that collectively they are far bigger than the objective they must accomplish, a team prepares itself to go further than they've ever gone before. **To be bigger as humans begins with what we all want to do anyway: understand and honor the roles and lives our teammates lead and live.**

Perhaps it is Daniel Goleman who summarizes this wisdom best: "The more you care about someone, the more attention you pay. And the more attention you pay, the more you care."[23]

Now we realize our potential not just as a businessperson, but where it matters most—as a human being.

We Need Each Other

Oh sure, some brave or foolhardy individuals had attempted to float the Green and Colorado Rivers prior to Powell's team doing so in 1869. Today, on rocks next to the river, there are carvings of initials of daring trappers and prospectors who explored the area.

Included in the lore is the story of James White. Found by rescuers in late 1867, floating out of the Grand Canyon, he was naked, disoriented, and near death. Chased by Indians, he had made a simple raft and launched himself into the river. For a while, lore had it that he floated through the entire Grand Canyon. But the story was eventually dismissed. Nearly all the legends about these early explorers include calamity, reinforcing the idea that the canyons of these rivers were unpassable.[24]

There is no doubt: Powell's men had their share of conflict and in some cases even despised each other. Stuck with the same people under severe circumstances has this effect on most of us. Many river runners going through the Grand Canyon today know of the infamous Day 10. It's the day when the members of a party, having been cramped in impossible proximity together in small boats and tents, often snap emotionally. (It doesn't have to be on the tenth day of the trip; it could be days sooner or later. Veterans of the river simply know the tension eventually becomes too much.)

Some river runners will go the remainder of the trip, roughly 15 to 20 more days, nearly oblivious to the beauty and excitement around them. Their focus is consumed with what they don't like or respect (in some cases, hate) about those in their party. For those who have a natural mastery of the 3 Mind Factors, they shift their focus and overcome the conflict. Their reward: the trip of a lifetime.

Powell's team, according to his journals, had plenty of Day-10 moments.[25] They, however, unlike the river runners today, didn't have the choice to not work together the rest of the journey. That would have meant certain death. They needed each other.

The members of your team spend a lot of time together. How do they come into the experience? Are teammates merely to be tolerated to meet an end? Or do they seize the opportunity for the trip of a lifetime?

We each need to do big things. What's more, we need each other to discover who we truly are. And that's what matters most.

Big Ideas in This Chapter and
3 Recommended Actions

- A team is at high risk of flatlining when they suffer DSD: distracted from their prioritized objective, hopelessly stressed, and disconnected from each other as teammates. **Recommended Action:** Evaluate the steps your team has taken to build immunity to DSD. What's working? Where do you need to improve? And how quickly do you need to act?

- Often, when teams fail, it's not because they lack the necessary technical expertise or functional experience. Rather, it's the result of team members not being able to think and act as the people they know they can be.

- When it comes to achieving the business imperative, what matters most as a strategy is accomplishing the human imperative.

- The 3 Mind Factors is a tool that enables a team to focus on what matters most, by providing a common language and method to leverage the natural way the brain focuses. **Recommended Action:** As a team answer these questions: Do we have the collective ability to sustain a focus on our priority objective that the business requires? How do we improve that focus?

- The 3 Mind Factors are:

  ◆ The mind can only focus on one thought at a time

  ◆ The mind cannot avoid a don't

  ◆ The mind goes toward its focus

- The Doofus Principle is in action when team members focus on and collect evidence that is destructive to people, partnerships, and performance. It's impossible for a team to do big things this way. **Recommended Action:** Facilitate a discussion with your team by first encouraging transparency and honesty. Then ask: Do we currently believe things about ourselves or others that are destructive in limiting our potential? If so, how will we apply the 3 Mind Factors to shift our focus and transform those beliefs?

- There are three domains to your focus: inner, other (people), and outer (beyond the team). These align with the 3 Do Big Things Decisions: Contribute, Activate, and Connect.

- You eliminate destructive Doofusing by using the 3 Mind Factors to make the 3 DBT Decisions effectively.

- Don't read this bullet.

8 Energize Around a Shared Reality

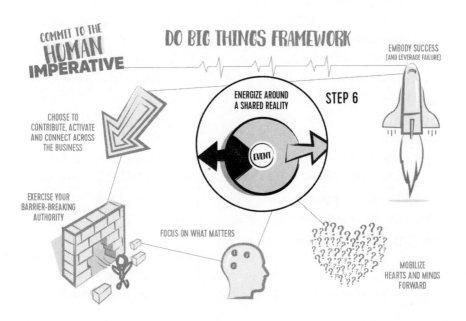

"**O**h, I know what heaven is," the four-year-old girl explained matter-of-factly to the doctor. Then with a broad smile, she said, "I've seen heaven."

The doctor grinned at the young girl, then at her parents. Before the appointment, the adults in the room had made a decision: The little girl's life-threatening illness had worsened. There wasn't much time left. With hearts that only those who've endured such a situation can ever know, they decided to try to talk with the child about what was going to happen. With good intentions, they had asked the girl, "Do you know what heaven is?"

Sometimes, though, even the brightest doctors aren't as smart as children. After being told that she had seen heaven, the doctor said, "Oh you have, have you? What did heaven look like?"

Without fear or doubt, the girl confidently answered, "It's a magical place where they serve ice cream in the morning!" Her smile was so broad and big that it now lives beyond her life—and in the hearts of those who made sure she knew a heaven on earth.

"The child wasn't afraid of dying," said Pam Landwirth, CEO of Give Kids The World. The phone line was quiet for a moment as we all lived in the space of a miracle for a moment. Then Pam added, "That's why we do what we do."

No one takes their business imperative more seriously than the team at Give Kids The World (GKTW). Founded by Henri Landwirth in 1986, the nonprofit resort located in Central Florida provides weeklong, cost-free vacations to children with life-threatening illnesses and their families.

Of the 27,000 children in the United States who are annually diagnosed with a life-threatening illness (and far more around the world), half of them want to visit the collection of theme parks and other attractions of the warm-weather state. The team at GKTW will serve over 8,000 of those families, and they do everything within their power to make sure every single one of them has the trip of a lifetime. They even serve ice cream for breakfast.

"Our guests only get one experience," Pam told us passionately. "So it has to be perfect. And with more families coming every year, that's not easy." The size of their operations is mind-blowing. Nearly 200 full- or part-time team members coordinate the efforts of over 18,000 volunteers. With 1,600 shifts each week, GKTW may be the largest single-source volunteer organization of the nearly 1.5 million charities that exist in the United States.

The team at GKTW is doing huge things. For the rest of us who have ever attempted (and likely struggled) to lead four or five volunteers in our communities, comprehending the effort and excellence needed to lead 18,000 is nearly impossible. How do they do it?

"Everything is about *yes*," answered Pam. "Every wish a child has, every challenge we face as an organization, our entire focus as a team is on how to make it happen."

This type of empowerment requires that every person on the team at GKTW be equipped to make the 3 Do Big Things Decisions. "Our team members all believe that 'once upon a time' begins for our guests *with me*. That means that everyone on the team, whether you're a cook or a housekeeper or whoever, you are empowered to make things happen," Pam said.

When something doesn't go as planned or a problem surfaces, there isn't time for focusing on who's to blame, the myriad of other problems they have, what they don't like or respect about one another as teammates, or all the reasons they can't do something. In every interaction there's a predominant focus on how to deliver with excellence. This concentration creates a stunning energy that elevates the organization to solutions.

"Ninety-seven percent of our guests rate their experience with us as one of highest satisfaction," Pam said. "We're determined to move that up. There's so much at stake. Excellence for everyone is what we're about."

Some may think it would be easy to energize teams who are tasked with fulfilling a child's dream. Such an opinion, however, is a misguided insult to nearly all those who operate in the nonprofit world. The energy of purpose and passion are powerless without focus, structure, and process.

Among the teams we've studied—no matter whether for profit or not, education or government—those that consistently do big things have an undeniable ability to frame a shared reality, and then approach events, issues, or problems in a common and energizing way. In other words, it's less about what these teams do. It's how they do it that makes the difference.

How to Energize the Team Around a Shared Reality: The Energy Map

You know that drive you make to work each morning? Or to the grocery store? You've made the trip so many times you could make it in your sleep, as they say. Your brain has established neural pathways, mechanisms by which information travels, that with repetition become deep grooves of thinking. The result is an autopilot effect: You don't have to think much about what you're doing.

Now imagine you're observing a team through a one-way mirror. Let's say there are 10 people participating in a meeting, six seated at the table and another four via video on the large screen. Each person is operating with their own established neural pathways, and every repeated or similar experience the team has deepens the grooves of how everyone thinks about events, the business—and each other.

As a result, the behaviors of team members become predictable due to the formation and reinforcement of neural pathways in the brain; repeated focus results in replicated thinking, that drives the same behaviors. Just like that drive you take frequently to the grocery store, it may look something like this: One person rolls his eyes every time a certain other teammate says something. When the customer is mentioned two team members sigh, because they think they know more than everyone else about the customer. Every problem the team faces sends certain others into a finger-pointing exercise or a hands-up posture of apathy.

Regardless of how much talent is on a team like this, how clear the business objectives or plans are, these teams will always struggle to achieve much at all. Such teams lack the collective intelligence levels and collaboration skills necessary to succeed. With members of the team defaulting to outdated or destructive neural pathways, the focus—and therefore thinking and actions—drives unhealthy conflict due to always following the same lines of concentration. And to be certain: A team that can't process and exchange information together can't work together.

Unequivocally, what separates the teams that accomplish big things from those that achieve little is this: collectively, team members orient their focus and energy more consistently forward. **Indeed, your team's human forward focused energy is the imperative resource to accomplishing any objective of significance.**

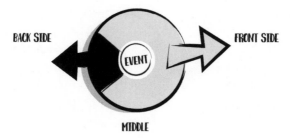

Figure 8.1 The Energy Map

Teams like those at Give Kids The World and others that are high achieving have constructed distinct and powerful norms when it comes to how they process information together. Specifically, they establish similar neural pathways together that are productive and effective at navigating and aligning the team forward far more collaboratively. Collectively, the intelligence of the team, along with its ability to work together, measurably increases.

This is when a phenomenon occurs. As team members focus forward together it translates into the experience of expanding and bigger energy. As a result, rather than developing a narrative or way of thinking that diminishes the team's effectiveness, a team can purposefully stimulate and energize itself in seconds. Now, individually and collectively, people are elevating the best of who they are in a new, shared reality.

The Energy Map (Figure 8.1) captures and makes tangible how a team can effectively align and focus their energy. It is a mental model (a frame everyone can *see* with their mind's eye) that enables a team to quickly—within seconds—construct an effective way to share how they relate to the world they're all operating in. This is accomplished because the Energy Map provides your team with a common language, a method to communicate two things: (1) This is where my or our focus is on the Energy Map, and (2) This is the space on the Energy Map that I or we need to have our focus right now to be productive.

From your experience, how often do you see a team come together and agree on how the members of that team will see, experience, and respond to the thousands of events or issues they will encounter in their work together? It's rare. This is precisely why teams that do big things are rare. This doesn't need to be so, as the teams at Give Kids The World prove.

Figure 8.2 Back Side of the Energy Map

They adapt far more quickly and effectively than average teams do because they function with an orientation toward *yes*.[1]

The Energy Map represents 100 percent of a person's or team's focus, energy, and time.[2,3] Because your brain can only focus on one thought at a time (Mind Factor #1), in any given moment, you can only be in one of three locations on the map: the back side, the middle portion, or the front side. Equally significant: Energy is never static. Because your brain goes toward its focus (Mind Factor #3), you automatically go deeper into that portion of the Energy Map where you've chosen to bring your focus.

For example, as you can see on the Energy Map, if a team is focused on problems (Figure 8.2), it's literally impossible for them to see a solution. As clarified by the brain research presented in Chapter 7, they can only find more problems and increase the chances that they'll experience more of the stress and fatigue associated with doing so. This explains why teams report high incidences of wasted time in meetings; too often, one person starts by stating the problem and—instantly—because people go toward their focus, entire meetings are spent discussing problems. Teammates then hang up the phone or close their computers thinking, "We never get anything done." Or worse: "This team will never do big things."

As we've supported scientists, engineers, and others in the technical community, we've learned of their unique fondness for the Energy Map, too. Often they tell us one of two things occurs for them in meetings: (1) They work with team members who want to rush to identify solutions before the facts of the event or issue are fully understood, or (2) The team gets stuck in neutral, the middle portion of the Energy Map, endlessly analyzing data. No one seems to have the courage to say, "We know enough to make a decision. What's the best solution moving forward?"

With the Energy Map, team members now have a common language because everyone can *see* where their focus is and then collectively decide where it needs to be for the team to be most productive. Teams that aren't ready to move forward, like those in the technical community we identified as an example, can now say, "Wait! Let's spend more time in the middle part of the Energy Map before moving forward." Or, "We've spent enough time collecting and analyzing data. Let's move to the front side of the Energy Map."

When the team does shift their focus forward on the Energy Map, given the research we cited in Chapter 7, their concentration enables them to see more possibilities. At this point, even the bodies of team members get rewarded: A dopamine rush occurs. The chemical, in this case released deep in the middle of the brain in the mesolimbic pathway, tells the other parts of the brain, **"Hey, something good—maybe even awesome—is about to occur. You'd better pay attention!"** And, of course, the body of every teammate responds with an energy most teams are dying for. The whole heart is now in it.[4]

In your meetings, is your team fatigued and sneaking peaks at the clock or are team members bringing their best selves, with an energy that drives improved outcomes? Your answer provides a clue as to where your team likely is spending much of its time on the Energy Map (see Figure 8.3).

No surprise, the teams at GKTW likely experience a dopamine rush more often than teams that do small things. They are deliberate with their focus so they can be of greater service to their team's business imperative. They spend less time focusing on the back side—trying to determine who

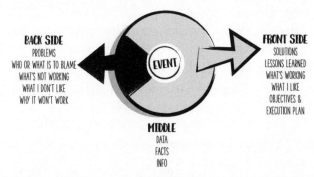

Figure 8.3 The Energy Map with Choices for the Back Side, Middle, and Front Side

or what is to blame, what they don't like or respect about one another, why things can't be done, and so on—and more time in the middle and on the focus points on the front side of the Energy Map.

There are endless choices for your focus within the three portions of the Energy Map. Those identified in the diagram are merely a sampling; they represent the most significant choices in focus teams must be aligned on to do big things.

Noteworthy is the fact that a lightbulb turns on in the brain only after a lightbulb turns on in the heart. Conversely, sitting too long on the back side of the Energy Map creates a dark experience. We don't recommend you try the experiment, because others have: They maintained a focus on all the reasons why their team can't succeed (or other back side focus points). As a result, doubt quickly gave way to pessimism, and ultimately, cynicism.

This sort of thinking and actions are predictable, because focus and emotions are hardwired together. The type of focus you have predicts the type of emotions you experience. What's more (and this is key), it also works in reverse. Left to its own choosing, your brain will select a point of focus based upon what you are most emotional about. In other words, the focus that evokes the strongest emotion often gets the most attention. (Your teammates who incessantly talk about the same things over and over again, and show little ability to move on, provide the perfect example.)

The Energy Map provides you with a mechanism to be purposeful about the focus, energy, and emotions you want your team to experience. And there are certain situations that require a team to go to the back side of the Energy Map before they can effectively focus forward. (We'll be exploring those situations later in this chapter.)

How much time does your team spend focusing on the three parts of the Energy Map? And what sorts of results is the team capable of delivering as that focus is shifted strategically? As we take you through the examples of how teams have leveraged the three parts of the Energy Map, this wisdom is important: Your team can strategically begin its discussion anywhere on the map it chooses. In other words, in the example that follows, the team chose to start on the back side for good reason; you may choose differently. Your choice is determined by the needs of the team and business. Either way, get ready for the type of energy you need to do big things.

Stop Trying to Be So Positive

You could hear the desperation in Carl's voice. Everyone in both companies that formed the partnership effort had their eyes on the project Carl was responsible for leading (a multimillion-dollar marketing campaign featuring your project will cause that to happen).

Halfway through the teleconference, the truth came out: "Listen everyone," Carl said. "This thing is a house of cards right now. If anything unexpected happens, then this whole thing comes tumbling down." Then he cleared his throat, giving everyone the cue that he was raising his hands and asking for help. "I'm doing everything I can to keep people on the team positive. But we're losing it. The stress is unbelievable."

No one said a word; the phone was silent.

Just be positive. That's the solution, right? The positive psychology movement has and continues to take humanity to important places in thinking and actions. Most of us now know that positive thinking is life's magic elixir: We live longer, healthier lives. We have better relationships. We're more productive, and the list goes on.

Yet, in this moment, none of those aspects are on Carl's priority list. He's got one thing on his mind (and we don't blame him). Make bloody sure the project succeeds.

Have you ever tried this experiment? The next time your team is feeling hopelessly stressed and is leaning toward an angry meltdown, smile and say, "Hey! Let's be positive about this!" If you've ever done that, you've likely noticed two things: (1) The rest of the team seems to get angrier, and (2) In the weeks that follow, you discover that you're no longer getting invited to key decision-making meetings.

In our work with teams, we've found an undeniable dynamic: There's a severe gap between what experts in positive psychology are saying is necessary to accomplish a positive mindset and a team's ability to get there. Equally important, it's not because people don't want to be positive. Instead, they're simply not equipped to better facilitate a shift in focus.

This is one simple and profound way the Energy Map has supported thousands of teams. It equips them with a practical and easy way to facilitate a necessary focus that creates more positive outcomes—without having to tell people to be positive. Here's what that looked like as we supported Carl and his team's ability to deliver their big project.

Leveraging the Back Side of the Energy Map to Develop the Team's Ability to Move Forward

Fact: A team can only do big things when the members of that team have an open mind that is receptive to bigger and enhanced thinking. No matter how insanely common the practice is in companies, minds don't open by putting money in someone's wallet. Nor do the number of windows in a person's office correlate to an open mind. There's only one way.

The Dalai Lama XIV said, "An open heart is an open mind."[5] As has been established, emotions rule our day. **When we control the focus that determines our emotions, we become greater masters of our mind.**

It's virtually impossible for any of us to have an open heart—and therefore an open mind—when we're upset (angry, insecure, jealous, frustrated, and other emotions often labeled as negative). Carl's team was becoming distracted, hopelessly stressed, and disconnected. And they had a right to feel that way (see Figure 8.4). The relentless feedback they were receiving from others on where they were failing, what they were doing wrong, and all the problems they had (all focus points on the back side of the Energy Map) was de-energizing them. Plus, their self-chatter about what they disliked about some of their own team members and why the plan they had wouldn't work, had added a dizzying amount of confusion and insecurity.

Worse, some team members were turning everyday debates (the healthy conflict the team needed to find the best way forward) into

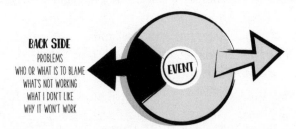

Figure 8.4 The Back Side of the Energy Map Includes Specific Points of Focus

moments of relationship conflict. Ideas weren't being deliberated; people were. Meetings became energy-sucking exercises, leaving the team with an inability to adapt in effective ways.

Carl, and leaders like him, who take on the burden of trying to get their team to "just be positive" under such circumstances might as well try to get through the Grand Canyon by rowing a bathtub. It's an impossible task. Instead, we coached Carl on taking these three steps so he could create more positive outcomes by effectively making the Activator Decision and bringing out the best in others:

1. Draw a picture of the Energy Map and give a three-minute overview of how everyone's brain works: the 3 Mind Factors.

2. Instead of ignoring pain, we coached Carl to meet the team where they were in their focus (and thus their emotions). Carl's ability to acknowledge the team's stress, anxiety, or frustrations would have a significant effect. We told Carl to leverage his emotional courage by sharing a story of how he, too, was frustrated at times.

3. Next, we coached Carl to bring out even more of the back side energy the team was experiencing. After all, if they didn't do it now, they'd carry that dysfunctional focus into future discussions, or into the hallway, cafeteria, parking lot—or worse—home. Instructions had to be given to the team that no one could defend or reply to how team members answered these and similar back side of the Energy Map questions:

   • What are you frustrated with at this point in our project?

   • What circumstances or dynamics anger you about our current situation?

   • How might you be disappointed in the team as a whole at this point?

Freeze! Our experience tells us that some people will say, "No way! We can't discuss these questions as a team. That's too scary." Yet, remarkably, these same people will confess that they devote endless hours to such scary discussions in informal side discussions. These conversations have a high probability of pitting members of the team against each other by driving separate realities. The Energy Map enables the team to bring the veiled barriers they must break through into the meeting in a safe manner. By doing so, everyone on the team can now be real, tell their truth at the same time, and talk about what most people are already aware of, anyway. Now, everyone can process and move forward together.

Here's what the back side of the Energy Map discussion may sound like for Carl's team. Notice that the words center on the team, rather than on individuals.

- "I'm tired of not finding out that we're not on target until people blow up with anger."
- "My perspective is that we have too many side discussions occurring that make our decision-making process irrelevant."
- "It's frustrating doing everything you can to succeed only to have people who are supposed to have your back sabotage your efforts."

No one is suggesting that a team regularly initiates discussions on the back side of the Energy Map. Far from it. Remember Mike the astronaut? We couldn't identify one moment when his space shuttle crews had to spend time on the back side of the Energy Map; experience tells us that most teams don't have to start or go there often. But, just like Mike the astronaut, now, if something goes wrong, you have a proven process for success and can take the team to the back side or middle part of the Energy Map as needed. This enables you to more effectively move forward.

Using the Middle of the Energy Map to Create an Emotionally Neutral Space

William Shakespeare was a big fan of the Energy Map (Figure 8.5). (No, we didn't coach him. The great bard intuited this powerful way for seeing the world around him.) He once said, "Nothing is good or bad, but thinking makes it so."[6] Were he alive today, Shakespeare would make a fine business consultant because he would immediately see what causes so many teams to underperform: peer judgment. In other words, on many teams, there's a whole lot of "he/she's good, bad, right, and wrong" occurring.

Business requires that each team member's performance be assessed by how much value they bring to the team. This, however, has unintended consequences. It's no mystery why so many people on average teams shut

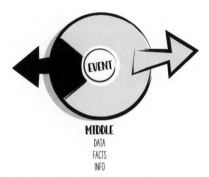

Figure 8.5 The Middle of the Energy Map Includes Specific Points of Focus that Relate to Data, Facts, and Information

up and never speak up. To offer thoughts and ideas freely is to subject oneself to the judgment of, and possible rejection from, others. On too many teams, being vulnerable is far too risky. It's better to be quiet than to be perceived as wrong and risk being Doofused (the act of someone holding a destructive belief about others) by teammates.

This is how the middle of the Energy Map rescues teams from debilitating judgment and unnecessary conflict. Carl's team, for example, had encountered big problems and was desperate for a method to analyze those problems without triggering defensiveness and blame and casting dark clouds over the heads of teammates.

The middle of the Energy Map is emotionally agnostic; it's fact-data-information centric and nothing more. Therefore, its energy is neutralized. It's a space that enables each team member to speak up and state, "This is my understanding of what is." There is no persuasion, no energy of attacking others or defending self. **The middle of the Energy Map is where the team gains a full view of their reality. It is how a team forms a truth together.**

For a team like Carl's, this process sounds something like this: "Here's what we know: We are twelve days from our next milestone, and our supplier can't get us the material we need for seven more days. That gives us a five-day window to do the job." Or, "We've discovered, from our perspective, that if we are to do this job, it will require greater technical skill than we currently possess on the team." Or, "The customer continues to provide us with clear instructions on what they need done."

Albert Einstein said, "It's not that I'm so smart. It's that I stay with problems longer."[7] We presume that the late, great management guru Peter Drucker was a fan of Einstein's, because he added, "The right solution to the wrong problem is more dangerous than . . . the wrong solution to the right problem."[8]

Doing big things as a team requires the patience to invest essential time and truly understand the problem your team is facing. Some teams can't do this, however. Focusing on and discussing problems about the work generates defensiveness among some team members, shuts down others, and builds walls where transparency is needed. It presents team members with three perceived and nasty options: (1) Keep your mouth shut and let someone else speak up; (2) Speak up and risk being wrong, viewed as "negative," and therefore, Doofused; or (3) Speak up, offend someone, and provoke defensiveness and conflict with other teammates.

If these appear to be the only options, a lot of people choose to play it safe. They sit back, hope the customer will understand why the real problem wasn't addressed, and wait for the meeting after the meeting when they can have honest discussions with one or two colleagues who are sympathetic to their perspective. This approach, of course, means that it is far less likely the real problem or issue will be accurately understood by the entire team. Spending more time on issues means people on the team may be exposed; the real truth about what happened or what's necessary to improve is going to come out. And it must if a team is to truly do big things.

No amount of preaching about trust will enable the team now. What's necessary is a mechanism to see the same reality and tell the truth faster. The Energy Map is the tool to do that.

Thousands of teams, like Carl's, love the middle of the Energy Map because it immediately gives them a space to act on their emotional courage and deliver the transparency the team needs to transcend the issues they face. This skill creates these and other important outcomes:

- A focus on problems no longer creates problems with people.
- The removal of emotions from events, issues, facts, and data creates safety for everyone to speak and be their authentic selves.

- Any team member can now apply their preferred process for determining the cause of problems and strengthen connections among team members as they do so.

We equipped Carl to ask questions oriented toward the middle of the Energy Map that enabled the team to reference this same point in reality. Here are some samples:

- What do we know for certain about this most recent event?
- How do we define the issue we're facing?
- What do we believe is the truth about this situation?
- What information do we need to consider before we move this forward?

Because Carl's team knows the Energy Map and understands that it's okay to respond to the neutral questions, it creates psychological safety. Such a dynamic is a requirement for effectively addressing problems, because it creates the conditions for everyone to freely share diverse and different ideas before the team starts to explore solutions.

Every team that does this becomes more effective, because the people on the team are able to operate within their integrity more consistently. Their whole heart is in it.

Using the Front Side of the Energy Map to Put Values into Action

We'll return to Carl's team in a moment. First, though, let's explore the brain trust, a team at Pixar, that harnesses their focus to make sure their film studio consistently delivers top films to the market. As directors and producers, the job of the brain trust is to provide feedback on films that are being developed by other people and teams in the organization.

We've observed teams in some companies where giving feedback can be a career-threatening exercise for people (and, ultimately, life-threatening for the organization). Only a certain type of feedback fans the flames of creativity, greater innovation, and the creation of a future people can't yet conceptualize. Sadly, despite good intentions, some teams kill ideas before they're ever given an opportunity to develop.

Members of these teams dump feedback from the back side of the Energy Map. They utter phrases such as "what I don't like about the idea," "why it won't work," "the problem that wasn't considered," and other nonstarters. These backward focus comments sap the very energy from team members they need to bring new ideas to realization. **Energy that is being used to protect oneself can't simultaneously be used to expand and build the connections necessary for the team to succeed.**

That's why the Pixar brain trust, led by CEO Ed Catmull, uses a front side of the Energy Map approach. Disciplining their focus to concentrate on that which is constructive to the team's purpose enables them to make an epic impact in their industry. According to author Greg Satell, in his *Forbes* article, "The Little Known Secret to Pixar's Creative Success," members of the brain trust at Pixar give creative feedback for one purpose, and that's "to move the project forward. Anything that does not fulfill that purpose—no matter who it comes from—has no place in a feedback session."[9]

The Energy Map enables teams like Carl's to replicate the discipline and practice modeled by Pixar. Here are the steps we equipped Carl to take with his team as they built on the momentum they created in the back and middle portions of the Energy Map:

- Make it clear that "this rocket is about to take off." In other words, we're ready to move forward. Ask: What else does the team need to discuss on the back or middle parts of the Energy Map before we move to solutions?

- Ensure the team has the same reference for reality by sharing what's important regarding the event or issue, and why that's important. For example, Carl could say, "It's critical that we adapt immediately given the feedback we just received, so that we can stay on schedule and on budget."

- Ask these and similar front side of the Energy Map (see Figure 8.6) questions to move forward and improve outcomes:

  - What does it look like for us to succeed in integrating this new data into our work plan? (What the team sees is all there is!)

  - Why else is it important to us that we adapt quickly? (Intrinsic motivations are the fuel to our inspiration.)

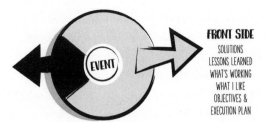

Figure 8.6 The Front Side of the Energy Map Includes Specific Points of Focus for Solutions, Lessons Learned, What's Working, What You Like, and Objectives and Execution Plans

- What do we need to prioritize to execute effectively? (Identifying what we can control is empowering.)
- How will we know we're succeeding with our new plan? (Accountability is a human choice; this question leverages that wisdom.)

No longer does Carl need to tell his project team, "C'mon guys, let's be positive." Instead, because he's strategically using the back and middle parts of the Energy Map, the conditions have been set for his team to focus forward. The positive energy that follows powers the team to do big things.

Psychologist Barbara Fredrickson and other experts who study positivity report that when we shift our concentration to points outlined on the front side of the Energy Map, human perceptions are altered. Positive emotions flow. Seemingly without effort we begin feeling better (and emotions rule), our mindfulness expands, and we transmit a focus and energy that moves us from *me* to *we*.[10,11]

This is the same energy you experience during birthday celebrations, festive holidays, or when you leave a place of worship having spent an hour living in gratitude. In other words, it's the state of mind our brains are in when we're more likely to be modeling our values.

Now, however, Carl's team doesn't have to wait for the end of the project or a date on the calendar or feedback from the customer for his teammates to focus and feel this way. He equips his team with the Energy Map so they can replicate this focus and energy any time they choose. This is how they deliver on their human imperative and live the behaviors necessary to do big things.

It's working. (The Energy Map can't *not* work; it's how everyone's brain operates.) Carl's team used the Energy Map to ensure each person was bringing their best (the Contributor Decision), bringing out the best in others (the Activator Decision), and partnering across the business to deliver the shared objective (the Connector Decision). By enlisting the focus and energy of those on and beyond the team to a greater forward focus, Carl's house of cards project has stabilized and delivered on target and on budget.

"I've been very impressed in terms of how everyone has been engaged," said a senior VP in Carl's organization as he spoke about the team. "We've put aside our old thinking of what company we come from or the function we're responsible to, and have approached this as a true team effort. I think we've done more joint collaboration between the two companies than I ever expected in such a short time."

WTF (Want the Facts)

- 200 studies involving 275,000 people worldwide showed that happiness leads to success in nearly every domain, including work, health, friendship, sociability, creativity, and energy.[12]

- Almost 50 percent of the positivity you experience is the result of the activities you choose to engage in and the way you interpret the world.[13]

- The part of our brain that reacts the quickest in any situation responds more strongly to losses than to gains.[14]

- In 2008, U.S. employers spent approximately $359 billion in paid hours (based on average hourly earnings of $17.95) dealing with employee conflict. This is the equivalent of 385 million work days.[15]

- More than one-third of employees say that conflict has resulted in someone leaving the company.[16]

- Your brain works significantly better when you start at positive rather than waiting for future success: Sales improve 37 percent, productivity goes up by 31 percent, you're 41 percent more likely to receive a promotion, and nearly 10 times more engaged at work.[17]

The Energy Map: The Direction Needed to Successfully Innovate

How fatigued is your team? Do you possess the energy needed to do what you must?

A leadership team, within a global company that relishes making sure you have nutritious food to feed your family, was losing power. Their business imperative was beginning to look unachievable: They needed to successfully adapt and innovate internal operating processes to meet changing consumer needs. When we first met the team, they were adrift and making only painful and slow progress against their goals. Despite the innovation centers and think tanks they had established, they had little to show for their efforts, except evidence that they were thoroughly exhausted. It didn't take long to figure out why.

Focusing on problems wears people out. Nicole Torres, in her *Harvard Business Review* article, "Looking for Problems Makes Us Tired," revealed that researchers have proven that we all feel twice as much mental fatigue when our brains are focused on avoiding risk (*what we don't want to have happen*, a focus on the back side of the Energy Map).[18]

Because the Mind Factor #3 is always turned on (*the mind goes toward its focus*), one observation of the leadership team would give anyone the impression the team was on a treadmill of rumination, repeating a cycle of back side of the Energy Map discussions. Not only does such repeated and reinforced thinking cause team members to disengage, researchers also show that, left unchecked, even depression can occur.[19]

Here's the part of every story about a self-sabotaging team that breaks everyone's hearts: The people on this team are really good human beings. You'd choose them for your neighbors; you'd trust them with your kids. And, like all good people, before they were even introduced to the Energy Map, they knew something was wrong—which, with sick irony, made things worse.

A focus of "why are we failing" only throws people further into despair. "Focusing on what's wrong about what we do activates circuitry for distressing emotions," according to Daniel Goleman.[20] **"Negative focus leads to discouragement and disengagement." The result? Our brains "long to tune out."**

This leadership team was going backward—and picking up speed as they went.

Enter Mary. In our discovery work prior to engaging with the team, we found out that because of Mary's role in operations, she touched nearly every part of the company's internal processes. And when she inserted herself into idea-generating discussions, it had one effect: innovation stalled. That is, unless it was her idea.

Joe Brown, the brilliant portfolio director at IDEO, a famous global design company, makes it clear that Mary's approach dooms organizations to the status quo. He told us, "One of the biggest things that gets in the way of creativity and the innovative process is when people think, 'My idea is better than yours.' To succeed, you must separate the idea generation process from the judging process."[21]

The CEO at the food company could see Mary's caustic effect on the team. "She has a way of de-energizing people," the CEO told us. "Don't get me wrong. She's well respected, knows her job like nobody else, and is a huge technical asset to our organization. But she doesn't bring the best out in others, that's for sure.

"When people go to her, she intimidates them with her intellectual interrogation," the CEO said. "When I told her that she was shutting people down, she replied, 'We don't have time to waste. I can't stand it when others come to me with half-baked ideas that are not well formulated.' That's when I knew exactly why we weren't innovating fast enough."

Experts call the energy between two people relational energy, and it's a big deal if a team wants to do big things. According to Wayne Baker and his fellow researchers at University of Michigan's Ross School of Business, when teammates focus on a positive vision, contribute meaningfully to a conversation, are fully present and attentive, and when we give signals of progress—all things we associate with the front side of the Energy Map—relational energy goes up. No surprise—attention, motivation, absorption in work activities, and improved performance follow.[22]

In short, and likely no surprise to anyone reading this: Being on the front side of the Energy Map generates high-quality connections among team members.

Perhaps you've seen this dynamic before: A bright teammate (like Mary) started her career full of energy and the ability to relate to others.

She climbed the ranks fast. She seemed destined to be a superstar. Then something happened. She stalled. Not because she'd suddenly lost her technical skills. Somehow, she began to lose the ability to connect with others and relate to their environment.

If any of us didn't know about the 3 Mind Factors and the Energy Map, we could easily capitulate to Doofusing (subscribing to a harmful belief about someone) this once bright teammate ("What a loser! She used to be so cool—and now she's a jerk."). But brain researchers would caution us and encourage us to check our own focus. What happens to the rising stars, like Mary, can happen to any of us. Here's how.

When a teammate increasingly focuses solely on metrics, numbers, and problems (which is what a lot of people in roles higher in the organization are required to do), their brain repeatedly stimulates a neural circuit called the task-positive network. This stimulation, in turn, overpowers the default mode network, which is critical to being receptive to new thoughts and concepts, people, and moral issues. This leads to trouble. Teammates with a curbed default mode network have difficulty seeing or having empathy for the people around them.[23] In sum the more the brain focuses on hard numbers, the less the brain can engage at a more human level.

The CEO of the food company had invested a lot of money in assessing personality preferences and styles of team members. While the exercise helped build awareness and empathy, the information gleaned from the effort still didn't predict a person's ability to focus on the Energy Map. (Neither does a person's IQ level.) Despite the fact that the team knew who they were as individuals, they still weren't equipped to connect energetically and transfer knowledge among themselves effectively.

Often this is where teams fall apart, and good people suffer. The space between people where there are no connections are filled with wedges, and divisions become greater. Team members who had hearts filled with optimism begin to deliver a diminished effort. As the team flatlines, headhunters begin to circle like vultures, then drop in and poach talent.

Here's a seven-step sample* of how we supported the CEO in equipping Mary with the Energy Map, so she could more effectively

---

*Note: There are ample opportunities throughout these steps to incorporate value-add coaching points and questions. Trust your experience and instincts.

connect with others in a way that would fuel the energy needed to successfully innovate:

1. The first step was being grounded in the wisdom that nothing is wrong with Mary. She has everything she needs to be great, including a heart the size of the Pacific Ocean.

2. Ask Mary: What sort of focus and energy do you believe are necessary for a team to successfully innovate?

3. Then show Mary this book and equip her with the 3 Mind Factors and the Energy Map.

4. Share with Mary in your authentic way something like this: I have some middle of the Energy Map data for you, Mary. In the interest of sparking new thinking, some of your teammates come to you with ideas that are not fully baked. Their experience is that you respond on the back side of the Energy Map. Whether their experience is the reality or not, if it were, what would you want to do about it?

5. Listen carefully to Mary's response.

6. State clearly to Mary what's important to you—and why—as it relates to focusing more strategically on those parts of the Energy Map that will effectively foster the conditions for innovative thinking.

7. Ask Mary: Is it important to you that you better connect energetically with those around you? And if so, why?

After the CEO had this type of conversation with Mary, we debriefed with her. She informed us that, at first, Mary responded defensively, attempting to explain why she had to lead the way she was. She even folded in the common excuse of "We're here to get results!" This rationalization once provided a free pass for command-and-control managers in many of yesterday's organizations, but not here. The CEO listened and validated, then brought Mary back to the middle and front side of the Energy Map by asking, "What focus and energy is important for the rest of the team to have for us to deliver on our initiatives?"

It took several weeks, yet because the 3 Mind Factors are always turned on, Mary began to shift. Predictably, as Mary changed her focus from judging what her teammates' ideas lacked, and instead concentrated on being curious and exploring, she soon began to respond like the star she is.

Predictably, in time, people began bringing more ideas to Mary. And as they did so, breakthrough thinking and actions followed.

The team was saved. **The talent on the team has stayed, and is attracting people with even greater skills.** (An enjoyable moment included observing team members laughing together, something they rarely did before.) And, as this book went to press, the leadership team had sustained a shift in their focus that was driving a renewed vigor as they pursued their lofty innovation goals.

People want to be great. And being great requires a certain sort of focus and energy. Equipped with the Energy Map, people can prove they are who we believe they are.

The Power of a Shared Reality (Dude, What Planet Did You Come From?)

Try this exercise. When you read the test statement at the end of this paragraph, please determine how it makes you feel by choosing from one of three options: It makes you feel (1) good, (2) bad, or (3) neither (you simply don't care). Ready? Here's the statement: The U.S. women's national soccer team is the most successful team in international women's soccer.

Are you excited about this news? No? Indifferent? It's safe to say that with a large enough sample size of readers, we'll find ample people who respond each of the three ways to the statement about U.S. women's soccer.[24] And consequently, three diverging interpretations of reality will emerge. (We know this is true given our own tests with our friends from Germany, Brazil, and other *futball*-crazy countries.)

Our focus determines how we see our world. That focus, largely established by emotions, comes with personal biases and tendencies. It results in a frame of reality that locks in how we perceive and interpret events or issues around us. And as nearly every expert who's studied human thinking has said: Our brains make their own reality.[25]

It's one thing to be sitting in a sports bar with friends from other countries debating the realities of who has the best national soccer team. That's a low-risk exercise; unless someone's had too much to drink, everyone is usually friends when it ends. Of much greater risk is when you enter a meeting with peers representing other parts of the business, and everyone is framing the reality of your shared business imperative differently:

- Some people are seeing big opportunities to grow market share for the business.

- A couple of other teammates can only see what the initiative is going to cost them (their budgets are already shot and they've got no extra time to give).

- A few others can only see what success or failure will mean for their year-end bonuses.

- And still others are there to support any decision, though they passionately caution the impact of the decision on a team and organization that is already exceedingly stressed and short on resources.

What all too often ensues for teams is a display of human behaviors that is unbecoming of any of us, as people attempt to disguise their reality or convince others their reality is the true reality. It all leaves participants wondering what planet their peers came from.

Forcing others to see, let alone adopt, our reality or truths doesn't work. As a civilization, we have a few thousand years of experience (and counting) to prove that persuading or demanding others to adopt our worldview is an exercise in futility.

Teams destined to do small things function from this harmful belief: If we pump enough data and information out to everyone, they'll *get it* and understand why we have to do things our way. This tactic rarely works, however, because despite the fact that everyone is looking at the same data (and tons of it), they're focusing on it in a manner that only reinforces their frame of reality. (What you see is all there is.)

If data were all anyone needed to get a team across the threshold of working together, the political parties of our nations would already be harmonizing our world (and that's currently not happening).

"We need to reconceptualize what 'team' means. It's far more a lateral exercise now," leadership authority Jim Kouzes told us.

"And what's necessary to succeed?" we asked.

"The skill of the twenty-first century is empathy. If we're going to solve the problems of the world, we'll need to understand diverse points of view—and not just understand, but value those views."[26]

What we've repeatedly observed in teams that do big things is that at some point in the team's maturation, something clicks. They move from pitting realities against one another and leave behind old frames of the way things used to be. And they form, see, and function from a reality they create together. Most often this occurs when there's a frequent focus on a shared objective or motive. This prompts hearts to open, which enables the eyes to see what they previously couldn't. Here's an example.

Mike Taigman is on a team doing big things. Their charter: Establish what the future of emergency medical services (EMS) looks like in the United States. It's a joint and massive undertaking. The National Highway Traffic Safety Administration, Department of Defense, Department of Health and Human Services, and Department of Homeland Security are all sponsors. What this team of the nation's physicians, firefighters, emergency medical personnel, and dozens of other professionals must accomplish isn't easy.[27]

"We need to build a system that is patient-centered and community designed, where all the entities are truly integrated," Taigman said. "The entities and people within health care are quite separated right now. Getting everyone to share an understanding and adapt to changes in the world that aren't even conceived of yet requires remarkable teamwork."

Here's a prediction: Given what this team will accomplish, the odds are that, in the years to come, someone reading this book will know a person whose life was saved because of the success of this team. The stakes are high. Their ability to make an epic impact is directly correlated to their ability to construct a common way to see our world now and in the future.

Taigman is well aware that data will play a significant role in their success. From experience, however, he knows they must go further than just facts and figures if they are to achieve this big task in front of them. The data must evoke a shared meaning. To accomplish this, two questions, among others on the front side of the Energy Map, can transform a team: What is our ultimate purpose or objective as a team? And why is achieving that so important to us?

"These are essential steps," he told us. "If you can't get to a deep sense of shared purpose, your success is imperiled." He told us what that looks like.

"We once facilitated this approach between the emergency medical services team [the people in the loud and fast ambulances] and the hospice care workers."

Until Taigman accomplished a shared emotional connection for everyone involved, things were a mess. Debates raged over who was doing things wrong and why. "Paramedics typically totally disrupt the hospice world. It's not pretty," he said. Sirens and speeding ambulances don't make peaceful moments. "But after we brought everyone together and got a deeper shared purpose running through our system, things changed quickly.

"Everyone involved wants those in hospice care to have their wishes honored and to die with dignity in a place of their choosing. Once we consistently made that our focus, the rest of our work—like budgets and the need for extra steps in the process—those things all took care of themselves," he said.

This wisdom reinforces why teams that do big things can make an epic impact. **They know that changing and elevating behaviors is not an intellectual exercise. It's the business of the heart.** Teams that bring only intellectual energy to their efforts will increasingly struggle in today's data-rich world. It doesn't matter so much what any of us see; it matters more how we experience what we see together. **The more meaning we have in our work, the more energy we have for our work. The more meaning we have when we're together, the more meaningful the impact we make together.**

Big Ideas in This Chapter and 3 Recommended Actions

- Teams that consistently do big things have the ability to frame a shared reality, and then approach events, issues, or problems in a common and energizing way.

- What separates teams that accomplish big things from those that do little is the ability to deliberately focus their thinking and energy forward. **Recommended Action:** Have a frank discussion by asking your team this question. Do we have the skill to shift and sustain a focus as a team that enables us to generate the energy we need to succeed? What could we do even better?

- The Energy Map is a mental frame that makes tangible how team members can effectively align and focus their energy together.

- You can only be in one of the three parts of the Energy Map at a time: the back side, the middle, or front side. And, wherever you are on the Energy Map, the further you will go in that direction; if focused on problems, you'll see more problems. When focused on solutions, you'll find more of those.

- The needs of the team and business determine where you should take your focus on the Energy Map.

- The Energy Map enables the team to *see* a shared reality, eliminate destructive emotions, and create a psychologically safe place for team members to tell their truth faster. **Recommended Action**: Plan with your team when and how you will practice using the Energy Map. Create a visual of the Energy Map everyone can see, then facilitate a discussion about a challenging issue the team is facing.

- The Energy Map is not about being positive; it's about determining where your focus needs to be so you can guide your energy to create more positive outcomes.

- Functioning on the front side of the Energy Map creates a physiological response, including a dopamine release that elevates the energy of the team. **Recommended Action**: With your team assess the level and type of energy on your team and in the organization. What's the correlation between where people are mostly focusing on the Energy Map and the energy they are demonstrating? What, if any, shifts in focus are necessary to create a more energized team?

- Changing behaviors is not an intellectual exercise (numbers and facts don't do the job). It's the business of the heart.

9 Mobilize Hearts and Minds Forward

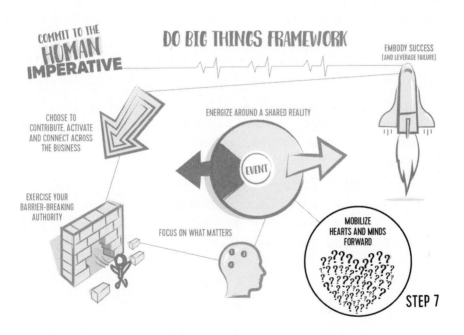

COMMIT TO THE **HUMAN IMPERATIVE**

DO BIG THINGS FRAMEWORK

EMBODY SUCCESS
(AND LEVERAGE FAILURE)

CHOOSE TO CONTRIBUTE, ACTIVATE AND CONNECT ACROSS THE BUSINESS

ENERGIZE AROUND A SHARED REALITY

EVENT

EXERCISE YOUR BARRIER-BREAKING AUTHORITY

FOCUS ON WHAT MATTERS

MOBILIZE HEARTS AND MINDS FORWARD

STEP 7

As Powell's Grand Canyon explorers descended deeper into the unexplored territory, the tales of horrific waterfalls and no-way-out scenarios loomed in their minds. A dark fear rippled under their thoughts every day. What would we do, they wondered, if we came upon a mighty waterfall, with steep walls of rock on both sides (so there's no place to land the boats), and an enormous current of water that doesn't let us retreat?[1]

Would you go forward with your plans to do big things if you found yourself in a similar situation?

Nearly everything about the future for Powell's crew was a mystery. "We have an unknown distance yet to run, an unknown river to explore," Powell wrote. "What falls there are, we know not. What rocks beset the channel, we know not. With some eagerness and some misgiving, we enter the canyon below."[2]

Would you go forward if you couldn't see a clear and certain path in front of you? Would your team put its whole heart in it even if they risked meeting unimaginable calamities at every turn?

Powell's ragtag bunch could only guess at what the exceedingly diverse landscape and conditions held in store for them. The big thing they had to do required that they execute a plan without seeing their challenge in one comprehensible assessment.

"You cannot see the Grand Canyon in one view, as if it were a changeless spectacle from which a curtain might be lifted," Powell recorded.[3]

If your Grand Canyon—the big thing your team must do—is truly significant, it's probably difficult for team members to articulate with certainty what the work ahead looks like exactly from beginning to end. Powell may have spoken for many of us when he wrote, "The wonders of the Grand Canyon cannot be adequately represented in symbols of speech, nor by speech itself. The resources of the graphic art are taxed beyond their powers in attempting to portray its features. Language and illustration combined must fail."

All Powell's team could do to know the future was to move forward—in his words, "to toil from month to month through its labyrinths."[4]

River runners of this era recognize the I-don't-want-to-get-into-the-boat-today fear. When you wake up in the morning next to the river, there can be a strong inclination to stay in your sleeping bag. The evening before, all eyes were on the map that read "big rapids ahead." Stories were told of people who have gone before you only to reach a disastrous fate.

Somehow, you slowly force yourself to stand. Your stomach doesn't welcome its breakfast. Your muscles tighten and you are loath to pack your gear. A certain gravity pulls you to the land. But you get on the boat. You go. Because you know that doing significant things doesn't always mean doing easy things.

Teams that flatline sit on the shore too long. They speculate and watch those in other boats row toward the obstacles ahead. They stall their energy and disengage because they create a false future in their minds that the ego and body choose not to suffer.

Teams with their whole heart in it ultimately succeed because they take great care to manage their focus and the direction of their energy. Therefore, they are compelled to take action and mobilize themselves forward. This means that individually teammates use their self-awareness to summon the emotional courage necessary to actuate their potential. The team then comes together and puts in motion a forward-focused energy that has the power necessary to achieve the significant objective in front of them.

Is your team compelled to take action because of what team members see—and can't see—in the future?

Leave the Abstract and Make an Impression

"I felt really good about my presentation," the vice president of human resources told us. As the new member of the leadership team, he had just delivered to the 15,000-employee organization his vision for the function he was responsible for leading. He shared, "As I walked off stage, our president approached me as if he was irritated and asked, 'What was that?'

"'What do you mean?' I asked him. I thought I'd done exactly what he told me to do—deliver my vision for how the function will support the organization.

"He shook his head, and said, 'You can see it all clearly in your head, can't you? Like an impressionist painting by Monet, you can see the path in the garden. But telling them what you see doesn't mean they can see it. You

Figure 9.1 The Impressionism of a Monet-like Drawing versus the Abstraction of a Kandinsky-like Drawing

just left thousands of our employees seeing nothing but an abstract vision of the future. You have a painting of Monet in your head; they have an abstract painting by Kandinsky in their minds."[5] (See Figure 9.1.)

We see it often as we support organizations: A team begins its work energized, but the power needed to move forward quickly disintegrates because it's not concentrated toward a common vision. If the members of a team all see their business imperative differently or don't share a common path to get there, the chances of impacting the business are minimal.

Teams that do big things aren't attempting to create and share a Rembrandt–type still life where the image of the future is perfectly clear. After all, the team is moving fast. Plus, the richness of diversity in perspectives and ideas are an asset for every successful team. The president's plea for the vice president of HR to share an impression, an image that depicts light and the inclusion of movement like Monet's *Garden Path*, is a must for all teams to succeed.

This is where far too many leadership methodologies fail teams today. The emphasis is on *the need for the team leader to transfer his or her vision to the team*. This approach may have worked back when the leaders had more time on their hands and the team spent endless hours together. But it reflects outdated thinking today.

While the leader must be certain of the direction the team must go, to do big things today, there's no time for the team to sit around on the shore and wait for a constant download or transfer of vision and planning from boss to worker. **The longer a team has to wait for the boss, the greater the likelihood the team will flatline.**

As a friend of ours said, "The notion of a single team leader is over." Because this friend is responsible for developing leaders within a global organization with nearly 340,000 employees, that's saying something. He added, "Distributed leadership must occur so the team is able to flex, person to person, and adapt to each issue or situation they face."

A team's ability to succeed today is directly correlated to a team's ability to cocreate an image of where they're going and how to get there. This chapter is devoted to how teams that do big things move from the abstract of Kandinsky to creating their own Monet—thus generating a shared impression of the future that mobilizes hearts and minds forward.

WTF (Want the Facts)

- Asking questions peaks at age 4–5.[6]

- In the workplace, asking questions results in over 85 percent higher performance than telling people what to do.[7]

- People spend 32 percent more on the company's products when they are asked to focus on what's good about a product they are already using from that company.[8]

- The term *neutral questioning* was first used by Brenda Dervin in 1981, to describe specific communication techniques used to understand from another's point of view—giving them the freedom to tell their own truth.[9]

- According to Self-Determination Theory, autonomy is one of three core psychological needs of humans. Asking questions promotes autonomy by giving choice, allowing volition, and fully endorsing one's own decisions.[10]

End the Suspense: Make the Unknown Future Known

He who has a why to live for can bear almost any how.

–FRIEDRICH NIETZSCHE

What does your team see, and therefore anticipate, is going to happen in the future? Teams that do big things effectively answer this question quickly. Consider this example.

Dan Robinson, the CEO for Longs Peak Hospital in Longmont, Colorado, is taking his team into its own Grand Canyon. As the CEO for hospitals in the past that have earned the prestigious Malcolm Baldrige Award for Healthcare, Top 100 Hospitals award, and been recognized for clinical excellence, among other accolades, Dan has plenty of experience leading teams that do big things. When we interviewed him, the Longs Peak Hospital only existed on paper and as a construction site locals looked curiously upon as they drove by. It would be another six months before an idea that had been in development for years would become tangible.

"It's an incredible challenge building a hospital of the future when you don't know what the future looks like," Dan told us.[11] The difficulties the team faces are rocky and severe. Dan laid out what he called the high-risk challenges:

- "The future of the health-care industry has never been so unclear."
- "We'll serve the fastest growing area of population in the state of Colorado. We have to effectively predict what that will mean for us."
- "We're going to bring the most advanced tele-health services ever. When we pull this off, it will mean that a patient can be in our ICU unit and get full-time access to expertise from around the world. Few hospitals are doing this successfully yet."
- "We also have the ability to bring in advanced services and enable technology in ways that have never been done before." Then he laughed and added, "It's amazing, though, because the technology we were building our plans around a year ago is already outdated."

Despite the challenges of all these unknowns, Dan's team is on plan and on budget as they near the delivery of their business imperative. As they "toil month-to-month through the labyrinths" of their effort, how are they empowering and mobilizing forward? When you listen to Dan, you quickly understand that he's cocreating the image of the future with his team. They anticipate the same future because everyone on the team is contributing to creating it. They see Monet instead of Kandinsky.

"What I'm most motivated by is bringing to life the dreams of our team members," Dan said. "Bringing a new hospital to life is in their heart and soul, not just mine. Together we share a deep understanding of what we want our patients to experience. We know that every hospital says that the patient is the priority, but what we're doing is different. **From the start, our priority is to develop the culture that we know we'll need to succeed, a culture that makes certain when a person leaves our care they'll say, 'Wow. That was truly exceptional.'**

"We've got 5,000 things to do on our checklist before we see our first patient, yet the focus and engagement is easy. When a team believes they can deliver on their dreams, it drives big energy," Dan told us.

If you like suspense, you wouldn't like being on Dan's team. The "will we succeed, or won't we?" nail-biting that makes so many average teams hopelessly stressed doesn't exist as the team grows at Longs Peak Hospital. Instead, there's a certainty. The team embodies success because they anticipate success. This mobilizes their hearts and minds forward.

How to Mobilize Hearts and Minds Forward

Imagine you're in a meeting with two teammates: Chen is participating via video and Ava is sitting at the table across from you. As the meeting nears its end, you realize: We've got to come together and act—now. I've got to mobilize this team forward.

Many people we've observed in similar situations say something like this to their teammates: "So, we're all aligned and ready to go then. Any questions?"

Chen nods his head. (Or was that an interruption in the video feed?) Ava lifts her eyes up from her smartphone and replies, "I'm ready."

To which this common follow-up is offered: "Good then. Thanks for a great meeting. Let me know if you need my help with anything. And let's check progress next week. Okay?"

Chen, however, has already signed off; the screen is black. Ava smiles as she picks up her laptop, then puts her phone to her ear and begins a different conversation as she walks out the door.

Teams that do small things ask questions that aren't intended to solicit answers. Like this imagined one, they merely take repeated small actions. Instead of mobilizing hearts and minds, there's only nudging, prodding, and hoping.

Teams that are serious about achieving their objectives execute brilliantly on the seventh step of the Do Big Things Framework. The fact is there are a lot of ways to mobilize hearts and minds. History is replete with the effective use of these and other methods:

- Fear or threats (Powell's team certainly had a good dose of this.)
- Commands and directives (At certain moments, people look to leaders to tell them what to do.)
- Narrowing people's options ("We can do this or that.")
- Leverage what motivates others ("Why we care is what will get us through this.")
- Tell inspiring stories ("I remember when I was in a similar situation.")
- Appeal to a shared world view ("All of us care, so all of us are responsible.")

There is only one technique, however, that enables you to leverage any of these methods listed and make certain that an intrinsic response is activated within teammates. What do you suppose that technique is?

We just modeled it: We asked you a question. And by doing so, we began your exploration, discovery, and visualization of a more defined future.

It's a fact: The human mind cannot resist a well-timed or well-phrased inquiry. Try it: Ask someone next to you what time it is and watch what immediately happens to their focus. The moment any of us hear or think of a question our focus is concentrated on the thought that was triggered by the question. And, as established with the Energy Map, whatever direction your focus goes, so does your energy.

Experts such as David Cooperrider, Diana Whitney, Kurt Wright, and others pioneered the understanding of how certain types of questions prompt people to certain action. The method is so effective, Peter Drucker even said, "The leader of the past was a person who knew how to tell. The leader of the future will be a person who knows how to ask."[12]

That future is most certainly here, and it's different than even Drucker imagined: **It's not enough for just the leader to ask questions. If teams are going to do big things, then every team member must be equipped to ask the types of questions that mobilize hearts and minds forward.**

If Dan Robinson, in his pursuit of building the hospital of the future, had been in the meeting with Chen and Ava, you would have seen a teammate be far more effective in mobilizing the team forward. The primary reason why: Dan cares enough about people that it affects his behavior. He doesn't see teammates as people that need to be tolerated to get business done; they're human beings with remarkable stories, hearts, lives, and talents. He also understands that it's not *his* heart and mind that will mobilize the team forward; it's the hearts and minds of his teammates that will get the job done. (That distinction is key.)

Therefore, in the meeting with Chen and Ava, Dan would have asked different questions. Specifically, he would have combined his wisdom of the Energy Map with Questions That Trigger Hearts and Minds to strategically guide focus. Doing so enables Dan to take the focus of his teammates to the area of the Energy Map that will best enable them to move forward.

Here's what merging the Energy Map and Questions That Trigger Hearts and Minds looks like to mobilize hearts and minds forward:

Backward Focus Questions: Questions like those shown in Figure 9.2 bring forth an emotional energy that triggers people to drive their focus deeper into the back side of the Energy Map.

Important reminder: Sometimes teams strategically use backward focus questions when the team needs to process and let go of emotions that are holding them back. More often than not, however, we observe unaware teams sprinkle backward focus questions throughout their meetings; the result is a halting effect. Just when the team is ready to move forward, another backward focus question is asked, and energy again moves away from the future.

BACKWARD FOCUS QUESTIONS

WHAT'S FRUSTRATING ABOUT
OUR LACK OF PROGRESS SO FAR?

WHY DO WE EXPERIENCE A
LET-DOWN AT THIS PHASE IN OUR WORK?

WHAT'S STOPPING US FROM TAKING
THE NEXT STEP TOGETHER AS A TEAM?

Figure 9.2 The Back Side of the Energy Map Lends Itself to Strategic and Important Questions for Processing Emotions and Thinking Related to Problems/Issues/Challenges

NEUTRAL FOCUS QUESTIONS

WHAT IS THE CURRENT ASSESSMENT OF OUR PROGRESS?

WHAT ESSENTIAL DATA WILL WE NEED TO GATHER FROM THIS OUTCOME?

WHAT ELSE DO WE NEED TO TRANSPARENTLY DISCUSS BEFORE WE MOVE FORWARD?

Figure 9.3 The Middle of the Energy Map Lends Itself to Strategic and Important Questions for Assessing Data and Aligning on Facts, and Framing a Shared Reality

Middle of the Energy Map Questions: These inquiries are neutral emotionally and stimulate the focus on data, info, and facts in the middle of the Energy Map. Figure 9.3 shows some examples.

Forward Focus Questions: These types of open-ended questions trigger a focus that leads team members to the front side of the Energy Map, as shown in Figure 9.4.

If you have ever spent time on or around a team like Dan's, where people are more consistently inspired, it doesn't take long to notice that they're having different types of discussions compared to most teams. Importantly, they're not waiting for an event to talk about the vision and motivation for the future; instead, they sprinkle their daily discussions with questions that activate their hearts and minds forward so the collective vision is consistently being crafted and reinforced.

They do this by using what we identified in our book, *ONE Team: 10-Minute Discussions That Activate Inspired Teamwork*, as a specific type of forward focus question that applies key words.[13] The highlighted portion of

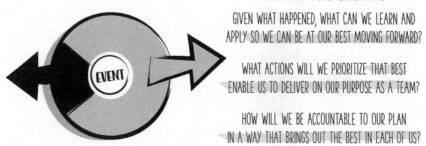

FORWARD FOCUS QUESTIONS

GIVEN WHAT HAPPENED, WHAT CAN WE LEARN AND
APPLY SO WE CAN BE AT OUR BEST MOVING FORWARD?

WHAT ACTIONS WILL WE PRIORITIZE THAT BEST
ENABLE US TO DELIVER ON OUR PURPOSE AS A TEAM?

HOW WILL WE BE ACCOUNTABLE TO OUR PLAN
IN A WAY THAT BRINGS OUT THE BEST IN EACH OF US?

Figure 9.4 The Front Side of the Energy Map Lends Itself to Strategic and Important Questions for Discovering and Focusing on the Path Forward in a Manner that Brings People Together

the three forward focus questions leverages and elevates the actions of your team by putting heart wisdom into motion.

Of the three directional questions, which are your team asking the most frequently? Your answer correlates to how frequently your team is shaping a shared and inspired future.

What Does Your Team Anticipate?

We can promise you this much: Dan's team is utilizing forward focus questions. That's because he knows that if a team is not focused together, it's not due to a lack of focus; it's because the members of the team are not focused together. They haven't collectively developed the discipline of focusing on what will best support the team's purpose. Such an inability is easy to observe, too. Perhaps you've seen it: Like members of a symphony all playing their instruments following different sheets of music, some teams attempt to have meetings with teammates scattered across the Energy Map.

If left adrift to focus anywhere they want without any strategic focus-guiding questions, things can quickly get scary for a team. According to Daniel Goleman, the periods of our day when our minds wander the most are when we're at work, using a computer at home, or driving to and from work. To add more emphasis to this step in the Do Big Things Framework, in this I'll-let-my-brain-determine-where-I'll-focus state, the average mind generally skews to the back side of the Energy Map. Even when provided with seemingly neutral content, Goleman said, the undisciplined mind shades that content with negative emotional tones.[14]

Dan Robinson and his team members did not let the future success of their new hospital be determined by minds that were adrift. For example, consider this all-too-common scenario that plays out in hospitals around the world: A highly educated and trained physician named Dr. Smith is entrusted with the lives of her patients. Routines among the doctor, nursing staff, and administrators are established. An event occurs, perhaps a nurse hands the doctor the wrong instruments during surgery, or over time the equipment becomes outdated. The doctor gets upset and demands to speak to the CEO of the hospital.

Dan has encountered similar discussions many times and succeeds in mobilizing the team forward by using all parts of the DBT Framework. "I stay focused on the best ways forward," Dan told us. "I've learned that when people get frustrated, it's because they have a very high bar of expectations—which is precisely what we want. My job is to facilitate and bring out their expertise and move us beyond egos to a future that's team driven."

While Dan would rather meet with the entire team, often calendars won't allow that. Using the common scenario just described, here's what Dan looks like in action in a one-on-one discussion with Dr. Smith.

Dan's first question is this: **"What's upsetting you, Dr. Smith?"** (This is a backward focus question, designed to safely allow Dr. Smith to tell her truth and process emotions.) Then he asks, **"Tell me what you're seeing?"** (A middle of the Energy Map question that Dan likes to ask. He told us, "I want us all to be able to see the real problem we're attempting to solve.")

Then Dan goes with two forward focus questions: **"What would make this better, Dr. Smith?"** and **"What's your vision to better care for the patient?"**

"Every time I ask these questions, in this order, they shift their focus to where they want us to go rather than staying stuck," Dan reported.

The value of "where they want us to go" is enormously important for any team that wants to do big things. Experts in Appreciative Inquiry—a method of asking questions to leverage what's working and other strengths—identify what they call the Anticipatory Principle.[15] Because humans always project and have expectations of the future, deliberately shaping the image of that future is a tremendous mobilizing agent. Because our mind goes toward its focus (Mind Factor #3), an entire team will move in the direction of what they collectively believe about the future. A more positive and optimistic image of the future correlates to more positive actions today.[16]

When Dan asks forward focus questions, he further develops an image of the future. His team doesn't paint abstractly like Kandinsky; they create an impression of what's to come like Monet.

What is your team talking about? Whatever they're talking about, this much is certain: Their words reveal where they're going and what you can anticipate in the future.[17] At any moment of your choosing, you can focus the team on what they need to talk about to do big things. All you have to do is ask them the question that will take them where the business needs them to go on the Energy Map.

As you think about the question you'll ask, consider this: The hearts and minds of your teammates are waiting.

To Execute Masterfully, Use these Classes of Mobilizing Questions

Six minutes into the meeting, we knew exactly why the team we were observing was nearly immobilized and struggling to improve productivity. These scientists and engineers led an R&D organization that took three times longer than their competition to get a new product to market. The pressure to execute their plan was intense: Losing market share always gets every stakeholder's attention.

We sat at a large table with 15 members of the team. Three other teammates were on the phone when a fourth caller "beeped" in.

"Who just joined the call?" Terrell, the team leader, asked.

"Oh hello, Terrell. This is Alex," the voice on the phone said. "Sorry I'm late. I got double-booked for this meeting. I've got my other meeting on a separate phone line, but I've got them on mute. Your meeting will be the only one I participate in."

We thought it was a joke, so smiles crossed our faces. In fact, however, the fourth caller wasn't attempting humor. Everyone else's face in the room stayed straight as they stared blankly at Terrell.

As the one-hour meeting carried on, we tracked the ratio of information exchange: Three people in the room, including Terrell, spoke a combined 75 percent of the time; one person on the phone spoke 15 percent of the time; and three others in the room combined for 10 percent of the verbal engagement. The remaining 12 people sat on the shore, reluctant to get in the boat.

In defense of this team, they didn't know they were close to flatlining. As one member of the team told us later, "This is how we've always run meetings here." Like a person who enters the hospital with a bit of fatigue, only to discover that three of the four valves of their heart are clogged, this team wasn't aware that the energy of their team could be significantly stronger than they were experiencing day-to-day.

Sandy Pentland, who directs the MIT Connection Science and Human Dynamics labs, made it clear what sort of information flow and patterns are necessary for teams that want to do big things. In his *Harvard Business Review* article, "The New Science of Building Great Teams," he cited these variables as paramount.[18] We're aligning these criteria with the 3 DBT Decisions your team is now more equipped to make.

- The team communicates frequently. (Contributor and Activator Decisions)
- Members of the team talk and listen in equal measure. (Contributor and Activator Decisions)
- The team engages in frequent informal communication. (Contributor and Activator Decisions)
- Members explore for ideas and information outside the group. (Connector Decision)

Few of these criteria were being accomplished by the team members we'd just observed. When we met with them later in the day, we told them, "You run expensive meetings!" The salaries invested in the 12 people who made little or no meaningful contributions to the team's efforts were significant. Plus, there was little wonder why so few people were not participating in delivering the future of the business: They couldn't see it.

The team for which Terrell is responsible is humble and hungry. Each team member has incredible passion and commitment to the team's purpose. All they needed was a mechanism to bring that energy forward as they executed their plan.

Researchers make it clear: The human brain only works with activated thoughts. Information that isn't retrieved from the recesses of our mind (and heart) might as well not exist.[19] The members of a team may be people with good intentions, but unless something occurs to bring forth and put those good intentions into action, potential productivity is never realized.

That *something* is this: the forward focus questions teams use during their meetings to mobilize hearts and minds. To be certain, Terrell's team was asking and discussing what we call the boilerplate or standard execution questions. See if you recognize this sample list:

- What's our plan?
- What needs to be done in this meeting to enable us to meet our objective?
- Who's heading this project, and what role clarity do the rest of us need?
- What resource commitments are we making?
- How will we communicate updates?
- Where and when will we reconvene to assess progress?

You likely recognize this list and have a few favorites of your own that you'd add. That's because these questions are standard; if you want to be a team that does *anything*, your team has to be well-versed in boilerplate execution questions. Yet, from our observations, there are three insights that are critical if you're going to do big things:

1. A minority of teams use questions, like those above, as the primary method to improve the team's ability to execute. Most teams rely on the old-fashioned telling method: the person in charge mandates what needs to be done. These teams are far more likely to struggle in their ability to execute.

2. Those teams that do ask the boilerplate execution questions improve their execution; yet, they still struggle to differentiate themselves as a team that's capable of doing big things. Clear and obvious potential remains unactivated.

3. As we've studied teams that do big things, this is clear: They go beyond boilerplate execution questions and mobilize hearts and

minds with questions that are in classes of their own: purpose, vision, motivation, accountability and objective. What's striking in organizations that *underperform* is that discussions that address these classes of thinking are relegated to upper management. Conversely, teams that do big things, regardless of where they are in the hierarchy, effectively integrate this higher-level thinking into their daily work. This is how you accelerate enterprise thinking, developing the team to think of their work in the context of the organizational whole. The improved results are undeniable. Let's explore.

Imagine that the big plan your team must execute is the running of a river, just like the Colorado that Powell's team took through the Grand Canyon. To succeed, it's going to take hearts to be all-in and sharp minds that are focused and able to adapt to changing conditions. In other words, you're going to need different and elevated types of thinking or consciousness. All too often teams get stuck in basic thought patterns typified by the boilerplate execution questions: "How will we do it?" Or, "What do we do now?" While these are essential questions to answer, that level of sustained thinking, however, doesn't create a Monet-like impression of the future. It doesn't get hearts pumping, nor activates the energy needed to do big things. Much more is needed to succeed.

Research supports the fact that for your team to do significant things it's going to require the focus and thinking triggered by the strength of five classes of mobilizing questions. Those who raft down actual wild rivers know that the rapids they encounter are categorized by classes. The higher the number or class, the greater the danger and risk to the boater. Class I rapids signify a ripple. Nearly any boater can safely and comfortably move through such rapids. Ultimately, Class V rapids have the most extreme torrents of crashing water, requiring master-level skills to navigate. When you enter a Class V rapid, every person in the boat better have a clear understanding of their purpose and a vision for how they'll succeed or risk being thrown from the boat.

The classes of questions that mobilize hearts and minds work the same way. The more severe the circumstances a team faces, the higher the class of questions will be necessary to persevere. Another way of looking at it: The higher the class of question, the greater the level of consciousness activated within team members—resulting in an increased effectiveness to execute even through the most challenging situations.

CLASSES OF QUESTIONS THAT TRIGGER HEARTS AND MINDS

CLASS V - PURPOSE

CLASS IV - VISION

CLASS III - MOTIVATION

CLASS II - ACCOUNTABILITY

CLASS I - OBJECTIVE

Figure 9.5   Classes of Questions That Trigger Hearts and Minds

When a team encounters an intense challenge (such as the loss of a customer, product recalls, or a vendor who can't provide materials on time), only those teams that are deeply motivated and clear on their vision and purpose will thrive. Those teams that aren't, flatline.

The focus points of the five classes of questions are outlined in Figure 9.5. These are all execution questions that go beyond the boilerplate questions. They are proven to demystify what's necessary to improve a team's performance, because they're categorized in a way your mind wants and needs to make sense of the world.

Class V Questions: Identify, clarify, or support *purpose*. Importance: To execute and deliver big things, the team must comprehend and internalize its reason for being.

Examples:

- What specifically is our purpose as a team in the broader context of our organization?
- How does the purpose of our team align with your purpose as a person?

Class IV Questions: Establish, illuminate, or simplify *vision*. Importance: While the directive of what the team must accomplish is likely mandated, what it looks like to arrive at that objective must be clear to all team members in order to execute effectively.

Examples:

- What exactly does success look like for us when we reach the next milestone?
- What do you see our customer doing differently or better because of our efforts?

Class III Questions: Determine, reinforce, and amplify *motivation*. Importance: Only when team members are intrinsically motivated by their personal *why* do they put their heart into the work they must do for the team to successfully execute.

Examples:

- Beyond external rewards, why are each of us so committed to succeeding in this effort?
- Why is it important to you that we consistently put our values into action?

Class II Questions: Enable and ensure *accountability*. Importance: Because being accountable is a personal choice, team members often exceed expectations in delivering on targets when they are involved in defining what success looks like and the consequences of failing to execute.

Examples:

- How will we measure success in a way that exceeds expectations others have of us?
- In moments when we think we may miss a target, how will we use the Energy Map to model high integrity and accountability?

Class I Questions: Articulate and align to the *objective*. Importance: Efficiencies, quality, and other aspects of strong performance better occur when all team members have a common understanding and fully comprehend what must be achieved.

Examples:

- What is our ultimate business imperative from your perspective?
- As a team, what is our shared and common objective?

Terrell's team readily admitted that they were not asking anything beyond basic "how do we do this" boilerplate execution questions. **In fact, from our observations, many teams know how to execute a task, while still not knowing how to succeed.** This precedent means certain doom for any team attempting to execute the raging river-of-a-plan in front of them.

Terrell's team didn't flatline. Far from it. His team accepted our challenge of applying Questions that Trigger Hearts and Minds, representing each of the classes. With practice, they realized some important lessons:

- **The needs of the team determine the class of question they should use.** As an example, it's best to ask Class V questions regarding purpose only when the team needs that focus. To ask too many Class III, IV, and V questions when the team only needs I, II, or III can feel manipulative and have a counter, de-energizing effect. (For example, if someone is repeatedly asked "What's our purpose?" or similar Class V questions while the team is experiencing smooth sailing, that person is likely to tune-out questions asked in the future.) The timing of which questions should be asked is important.

- To be certain, questions with a hidden agenda or desire to manipulate someone to behave a certain way are not mobilizing questions because they ruin trust. True forward focus questions work because they allow team members to cocreate the path forward together (Monet versus Kandinsky). Any of us can better see what we discover and create on our own—and doing so together builds trust.

- When a team member generates his or her own idea, it comes wrapped in the emotions of ownership. The heart and mind are more likely activated. And that's the energy needed to get through difficult rapids.

- Sincerity in hearing answers to questions asked is paramount. In fact, if you aren't interested in hearing an answer to a question, or the person already knows the answer, the question shouldn't be asked.

- Forward focus questions are not about masking what's not working or being positive. When perfectly timed after discussions on the back side or middle of the Energy Map, they're perfect for mobilizing the team toward positive outcomes.

The tools of the DBT Framework work because they're based upon how the brain is naturally wired. It wasn't a surprise to us when we shadowed Terrell's team in a meeting just a few months later and found remarkably different circumstances.

In contrast to the previous experience, this time seven people were in the meeting, five in person, with two remotely connecting. Terrell started with a Class III motivation question, "We're slammed. Given we've got more projects in our portfolio than we've ever had as a team, I want to ask you: What is it that drives each of you to make certain we succeed yet again?" Instantly, a short discussion ensued that activated motivations and gave them the confidence to adapt to the challenges they were about to discuss.

Of the seven people in the meeting, five combined to speak 65 percent of the time. Terrell spoke 20 percent, while one person spoke 15 percent. They expertly spent only a few minutes on the back side of the Energy Map; they were feeling a bit overwhelmed and stressed and needed to say so. Then, nearly half of their meeting was focused in the middle of the Energy Map, assessing the current state of all projects.

The remainder of the time was spent on the front side of the Energy Map, predominantly using Class I- through IV-type questions.

Teams that masterfully execute are those whose members find more meaning in their work. Their hearts and minds have been mobilized. This is accomplished by asking higher classes of questions that activate a greater consciousness.

The impact to the business Terrell's team has had by elevating the team's consciousness through asking forward focus questions has been significant. Once three times slower than their competitors in developing new products, in just one year they leapfrogged the industry and are now twice as fast. They've delivered seven new products in twelve months, while only delivering one in the previous year.

Equally important, they didn't have a heart attack while they did these things. The business unit's employee turnover dropped from 12 percent to just over 4 percent. Their culture and engagement scores registered the best across the division. As Terrell said, "We always had talented people here. We had the leadership. Once the culture piece was put in play the results came."

Achieve Something Bigger

Here's a fact that may or may not startle you: During the day, the discussions you have with a teammate influence the type of discussions they will have with their family when they go home in the evening. When you make the Activator Decision and ask Questions That Mobilize Hearts and Minds, you increase the odds your teammate will bring their best to their family, too.

Then, later in the day when a child pulls his or her chair up to the dinner table, and their eyes search Mom and Dad for clues about their mood, something important will happen. Because of the experience your coworker had with you, a ripple will have been created. And an inspired, more joyful discussion will occur. As a result, the child will receive a crucial gift: They will know that life is good.

Are you startled? What does it mean to you knowing that you influence the quality of others' lives in this way?

The members of Do Big Things teams don't just care about the results their teammates are producing. Because they intend to make an epic impact, they also care about the quality of lives their teammates are leading. That doesn't mean they take it easy on their teammates or lower their expectations of their effort and work to protect their feelings. Indeed, from our experience, we know the opposite is true. DBT team members set and expect a higher standard of living for each other, knowing that the work each person does is a key expression of that life. They insist that team members bring their best and bring out the best in others everywhere they go.

You can wait years—a career—to finally be on a team where people function this way. Or, you can get there faster by intentionally creating these relational dynamics.

There's no doubt that it sometimes requires emotional courage to ask powerful forward focus questions, especially those in Class III, IV, and V. Sadly, doing so is not common in the workplace, but for reasons we believe many people misinterpret. Such questions are not asked because people don't believe in mobilizing hearts and minds—they simply don't know how.

The truth of the matter is that this work of doing big things is eclipsed by something bigger: the opportunity to discover who each of us is as a person. The business imperative in front of us is a gift in disguise. It's in the pursuit of achievement that we get to discover and experience what each of us craves—the richness of a human experience only possible when collective hearts and minds are mobilized. It's this actualization, this fulfillment that's at stake. It's why your team needs you to step forward.

Go ahead. Ask the bigger question. Then another. As you stay the course, the reward is bigger than can be imagined.

Big Ideas in This Chapter and 3 Recommended Actions

- Teams that do big things have clarity about what the future looks like. This is a result of not relying solely on the leader to download a vision; it's a function of cocreating the image of the future collectively as a team. **Recommended Action:** Survey your team to determine their clarity of what the future looks like. (Simply ask!) Then determine—together—in what ways that image needs to be enhanced.

- **It's a fact: The human mind cannot resist a well-timed and well-phrased question.** You can shift a person's focus (indeed, the entire team) instantly by asking questions.

- There are three types of focus questions that create distinctly different directions in thinking on the Energy Map: (1) backward focus questions, (2) neutral questions, and (3) forward focus questions. **Recommended Action:** Determine what type of directional questions your team asks the most. What outcomes in thinking and actions is that creating for the team?

- A team's ability to execute masterfully is contingent on their level of focus, awareness, and consciousness. The classes of questions that mobilize hearts and minds provide users with the five points of focus and thinking essential to masterfully execute plans.

- Many teams know how to execute a task; few know how to succeed. To do big things a team must go beyond boilerplate execution questions.

- Every team will anticipate what it thinks about, discusses, and therefore *sees* the most. For a team to do big things, it's required that they anticipate a successful future. This way, hearts and minds are better mobilized. The most effective way to accomplish that is to ask Class III, IV, and V questions. **Recommended Action:** Ask your team the following questions. What class of questions do we ask the most? Where might we improve in this area? And, how do we develop our skill and confidence to ask higher class questions?

- Every interaction you have with a teammate influences the experience they have after their time with you. By activating the best in others through forward focus questions, you create a ripple of energy that can extend even to a teammate's home.

10 Is Your Team Ready to Do Big Things?

Like the Colorado and Green Rivers that John Wesley Powell and his crew were on during their exploration of the Grand Canyon—many rivers eventually find their way to bigger bodies of water. Those of us who have been to an ocean know there are very good reasons why in certain locations signs are posted warning, "Danger! No Swimming." On the surface the water often has waves that roll in and splash noisily on the beach. The invitation to jump in for a swim and play in the surf lights up the faces of those who walk by.

But danger lurks in those inviting waters.

From the beach the water appears to be coming into shore where every swimmer ultimately wants to go. In such places, however, if you jump in the water, your life is imperiled. Hidden underneath the surface is a riptide that overpowers even the strongest swimmers: a massive current of water pulling everything in its grip out to sea. The invisible, powerful force of energy puts you in a fight for your life.

To varying degrees, every team faces this same dynamic within the organization it operates. Unsuspecting and well-intentioned team members commit to do big things and enthusiastically jump into their work. But the system around them, the most powerful of which is the company culture ("this is how we do things around here"), grabs and overwhelms them like a riptide. Just as in the ocean, even the strongest are powerless in such currents.

The well-documented riptide of wrongdoing at organizations like Enron and others (a weekly read of business news highlights several) pulled employees to places many of them didn't want to go. All too often, in many organizations, the daily pressure to deliver business imperatives mounts a stunning force that, left unabated, engulfs people and teams.

While most of us won't break the law, far too many of us are susceptible to demonstrating behaviors that betray our better nature. Complacency, apathy, or even disdain for our fellow man become norms as the riptide pulls us away from our ability to practice our values. The promise of our potential is spoiled. This is epic in its most tragic form.

In these cases, the Do Big Things Framework becomes a lifesaver.

Stop Trying to Be a High-Performing Team

What does it mean if being on a high-performing team requires driving home at night questioning who you're becoming as a person? And wondering if your family will recognize you when you get home?

If this is the case, stop trying to be a high-performing team. We know doing so sounds like an act of heresy, yet consider the following scenario. Imagine you are swimming in that inviting ocean we just described and you find yourself caught in a vicious riptide. As you're being pulled out to sea, away from your objective (the shore), bystanders on the beach shout, "Swim harder! Swim harder!" So you do. But rather than making progress toward safety, you only feel yourself being pulled farther away from what's important to you.

As your muscles lose their strength, the fatigue feels like an anchor. You wonder if you will survive.

Within many organizations, well-intentioned trainings are launched for the purposes of developing high-performing teams. The basics of swimming are covered: Establish the team's purpose, set and align to objectives, determine strategies, ensure role clarity and methods of accountability. And always remember to communicate and trust your teammates. These basics are critical to the success of your team. They've been covered and reviewed in a plethora of resources, including the now classic work by Katzenbach and Smith in their 2005 *Harvard Business Review* article, "The Discipline of Teams."[1] Yet, what was needed for teams to succeed 10 years ago (heck, even five years ago), is not enough for teams to break free from stronger and different currents today.

In short, in many ways the term "high-performing teams" has become merely a cliché, a term meant to market or identify standard practices. Add to this the fact that participants in such trainings too infrequently return to do business as usual, and it's easy to understand why the term is beginning to fall out of favor.

Our study of the resources on the topic of high-performing teams that are being consumed by the majority of organizations shows a glaring omission. The ability for the team to deliver on its commitment to the human imperative is conspicuously absent. While the quality of the content is strong, it too often only appeals to the intellect. In other words, it activates only the brain. Changing behaviors, however, is not an intellectual exercise. It's the business of the heart.

When a team leaves a high-performing team training program that fails to include steps and tools to deliver the human imperative, it doesn't take long for them to discover they're not fully equipped to do big things. Thrown into the ocean of the real world, they're now exposed to an invisible undercurrent comprised of human emotions demonstrated in the countless interactions among team members and with those outside the team. Left unable to effect change in those areas, the members of the team swim harder, thinking that more effort is the answer.

To their horror, though, the team members look up and realize they're not making progress. In fact, it feels like they're getting pulled backward. So they call a team meeting and go over the team's purpose, objectives, plans, roles, measurements, and so forth, with the good intentions gaining the breakthrough they need.

But nothing is strong enough to counter the cultural riptide under the surface of all those spreadsheets and flipchart papers filled with numbers. The team needs more. They need to be equipped to deliver the human imperative.

The day most of us have been talking about for the past few years has arrived. By itself, business performance no longer defines success nor fulfillment. **We all want more. We want to deliver big results** *and* **enjoy the process of doing so. We want to be productive technically** *and* **contribute as human beings. We want to succeed as a team in business** *and* **be fulfilled in life. Doing both is how we define what it means to make an epic impact. It means we do more because we are more, certainly as individuals, and all the more so as a team.**

If you're caught in a riptide, to save yourself you must do what seems counterintuitive. The lifeguard will coach you not to swim toward the beach. Instead, they will tell you to swim parallel to the beach, so you can swim out of the harmful current.[2] Then, once you've cleared the opposing energy and created the conditions to be more effective as a swimmer, you begin to angle toward the beach.

To succeed as a team, you must go beyond the traditional definitions of high-performing teams by first swimming parallel to the shore—in other words, creating the human conditions needed to succeed. This is precisely why the DBT Framework equips teams to prevail. It makes sure the water is safe for everyone to be their best by maximizing the efforts of all.

As you effectively take the practical steps of the DBT Framework, here's what you can expect to see as your team goes beyond high performance.

Your Assessment: The Team Heart Quotient

You can effectively predict how well prepared your team is to do big things by measuring the level of technical and aligned capabilities the team possesses in proportion to how much the team's whole heart is in the matter at hand. The device to do this is the Team Heart Quotient (THQ), depicted in Figure 10.1, which measures essential elements that contribute to teams that Do Big Things as compared with teams that have only heart, or only high capability—or teams that lack either one.

At this moment, your team is one of four types of teams—(1) DBT, (2) High-Performing, (3) Heart Attack, and (4) Despondent—as depicted in Figures 10.2 through 10.5.

1. **Do Big Things (DBT) Teams:** Capable of sustained, robust, and regularly improving results. Team members are aligned with strong

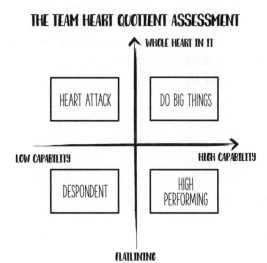

Figure 10.1 The Team Heart Quotient

technical skills, *and* they have the ability to put into practice essential whole-heart behaviors, including emotional courage, empathy, and a one-team approach. Simply, they care about one another while being very good at what they do in their jobs. The members of such teams may drive home physically tired, yet they're internally energized.

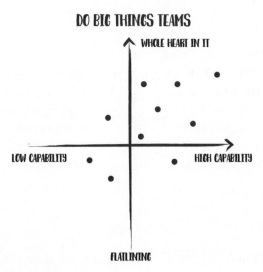

Figure 10.2 Do Big Things Teams

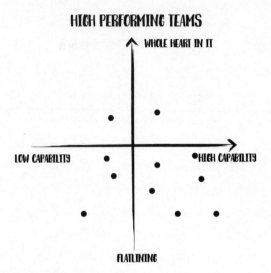

Figure 10.3   High-Performing Teams

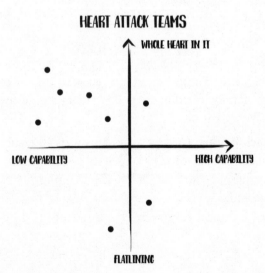

Figure 10.4   Heart Attack Teams

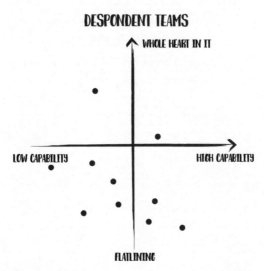

Figure 10.5 Despondent Teams

2. **High-Performing Teams:** Capable of short bursts of high performance. The team has top talent that is aligned, *yet* team members too infrequently have their hearts and minds mobilized. Consequently, the team is at a high risk of being overwhelmed by negative human behaviors in the working environment. Because team members are increasingly fatigued, pessimistic, and disillusioned, these teams have difficulty adapting to new requirements and suffer from dwindling capacity to get big jobs done. The members of these teams are at the highest risk of not being recognized by family members upon arriving home and asking the question, "What's it all for?"

3. **Heart Attack Teams:** Capable of small spurts in results. Such teams possess a lack of skill or aligned talent, *yet* they demonstrate huge amounts of heroic courage, passion, and commitment. These teams work extraordinarily hard because of their big hearts, but because they lack aligned technical capabilities the heavy lifting only leads to little progress, quick burnout, and turnover. The members of this team drive home with the chronic pain of disappointment.

4. **Despondent Teams:** Capable of only mediocre outcomes, at best. This team lacks skill or the talent they do have is not aligned, *and* they

are generally disheartened. Team members often conceal reality by focusing only on what they will do someday with little attention to how they will effectively improve. Their busy schedules give the illusion they are making progress. Yet, they lack a vision or a process for success. (Note: It's not uncommon for despondent teams to have team members with top talent or passion join them. Soon, however, these new people only want one thing from the team and that is to be off the team.)

The THQ assessment equips teams to measure the current state for your team and builds the awareness necessary for your team to take constructive steps forward. As a gift to our readers, you can take your free short THQ assessment at www.VerusGlobal.com/DoBigThings.

Once your team has assessed where it stands with regard to THQ, it's important to take the next step of improving. And to be sure, no matter where your team is on the THQ assessment, you can improve—and do so quickly. Use these five strength-based questions as a recipe to facilitate a transformative discussion so your team can evolve toward being a stronger DBT team:

1. Considering our current state as a team, what strengths do we possess that are necessary to become a DBT team?

2. How have we achieved the progress we've made in developing our team? (Study successes so they can be leveraged.)

3. Which specific step of the DBT Framework must we better apply to become more effective as a team and make an epic impact?

4. In what ways will developing our strength in the DBT Framework better equip us to do the big things in front of us? (Motivations must never be assumed.)

5. How will we achieve the objective outlined in question three and measure our progress? (Hint: Gaining mastery in the tools outlined in each step of the DBT Framework, such as the 3 Mind Factors and the Energy Map, are critical to include in your plan.)

The most effective way to change behaviors of any team is not by training the team about targeted values, but by equipping teams to use their values to deliver on the human imperative. The difference between these two approaches is subtle; teams that regularly do big things understand that difference.

The DBT Framework, Beginning to End: How a Team Went from Worst to First

As we near the close of *Do Big Things* and you advance your team's ability to make an epic impact, let's look at the DBT Framework in its entirety (Figure 10.6). To do so, we'll share another example of how one of our clients used the Framework. As you read their story, if your instincts tell you your team can do big things, too—trust your instincts. They're right.

Things were bad for this North American commercial team. When considering all the regions of the global medical device company, their performance was the poorest. Then, just before we began equipping them to do big things, worse news came, and the Grand Canyon they had to pass through got even deeper and more treacherous. The company's number-one product, positioned to compete with the top device of the leading competitor in their space, was recalled. The vision of closing the gap of 22 share points between them and the leader in the market now seemed insurmountable.

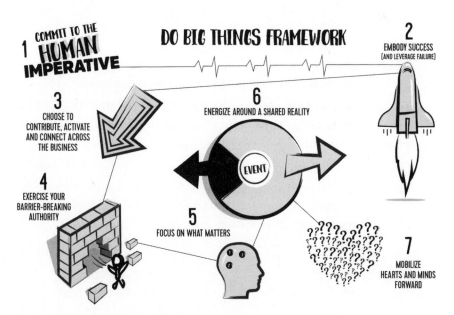

Figure 10.6 The DBT Framework

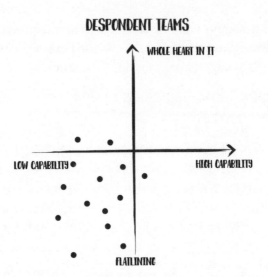

Figure 10.7 Despondent Teams in the THQ Assessment Matrix

Was flatlining imminent? Under such pressure, would a riptide of wrongdoing form and sweep this despondent team up in a current they couldn't overcome as a team?

"Morale was low. Results were poor. We felt like we were dragging the entire company down," said Jay, the vice president of sales. He's the sort of person who is built for authenticity. When Jay speaks, you can feel his words because he cares both about people and business success. As we heard him speak, that's when we knew that despite their severe challenges, this team would prevail, as long as they used a process for success.

Teams that do big things are neither distracted nor daunted by the size of the task in front of them. Rather, they stay focused on the plan to deliver their business imperative and the size of the heart within the team. High expectations by the business translate into high expectations as humans.

This commercial team, made up of Jay's salesforce, and his peers on the marketing team, and with supporting functions like HR and finance, had a sound business plan to get back to growing the business. Because plans are only as good as the team that will execute them, they only needed to answer this question: How do we operate in a way so we can quickly deliver the big thing that needs to get done? They used the DBT Framework as their solution.

There would be no flatlining for this team. We interviewed several members to learn their story. Here's a focused examination of key ways they applied the seven steps of the DBT Framework.

Step 1: Commit to the Human Imperative

"We knew we needed to take a stand as a team," a sales director named Ken told us. "Our plan was bold: Coming out of the product recall, we decided to no longer bring a device to market that consumers were asking for. Instead, we would go to market with a new device. On the surface our plan looked suicidal. But we'd done our research, and the data showed us that we could change the market by bringing the doctors a product that was better for their patients."

Being bold means breaking the limits of traditional thinking or actions. No one at corporate headquarters would have blamed the team for continuing to play in their space the same way their competitors were. But that isn't how big things are achieved.

"We got all-in," Ken said when describing the human imperative. "And not just for the plan, but for each other. No one straddled the fence. Everyone on the team committed their heart and soul because we felt that what we were doing mattered in our industry."

Jay added, "I've always believed that connecting people's emotional involvement and their intellectual drive is the key to unlocking success. People don't want to come to work and be average."

If a company is going to ask employees to be all-in, it works far better when employees know the company is all-in for them, too. "So we invested in developing the whole person within each team member," Jay said. "We made sure that the tools we equipped them with to be successful at work would also enable them to be more successful *people*, even at home. The Energy Map does that."

Committing to the human imperative by combining the emotional with the intellectual "is an additive," Jay told us. "It's a multiplier."

Step 2: Embody Success

Is your team losing? Or is the team a loser? Teams that do big things may compare themselves to the competition and realize they are losing. They never, however, define themselves as losers. Ken made sure of this. Early on, he and others on the team created experiences for the team that drove insights into what it looked and felt like to succeed.

"We showed a chart of the current state for our industry, in terms of what products customers were purchasing," Ken said. "Then we showed the next chart that had the product we were bringing to market listed as highest in volume sold across the industry. We said, 'When the market looks like this in the future, it will mean we'll have delivered on our plan, and we'll win.'"

As the plan began to work, the team seized the evidence. "When we took an account from our competitor in their own backyard, we celebrated in big ways. Then we all agreed: If we can do this there, we can do it anywhere," Ken said. "It was truly a symbolic moment because the team really began to believe."

Moving from thinking about how to be a success to knowing what it feels like to be successful is a team's transformative step to making an epic impact.

Step 3: Choose to Contribute, Activate, and Connect Across the Business

Imagine for a moment that you're a salesperson. You work out of your home a thousand miles away from headquarters. Suddenly, through rumors and leaked information, you're informed: The company is no longer going to give you a product to sell that most customers want.

This is a salesperson's nightmare, one that causes a lot of teams to flatline. Sales team members have made plans. Lives have been established that are contingent on bonuses earned for achieving those plans. How can someone be "all-in" when the rules keep changing?

But this isn't how it's done on teams that do big things. "We knew we had to successfully connect with the people in the field if we were going to succeed," Jay's colleague, Rhea, told us. As the lead HR person on the team, she focused on making sure every step the team took activated the best in others and people felt connected across the business.

Far too many organizations default into thinking that sharing information across the business means people are connecting across the enterprise. Not so. Information only satisfies the intellect; to connect is to deliver the experience of caring, which includes ensuring everyone understands the "why" and "how" of decisions made.

"We were all-in," said Rhea. "We've got a tremendous passion to improve the lives of those we serve." Face-to-face meetings, personal phone calls, and other interactions were no longer simply exchanges of information to get a job done. Now, such moments were used to develop cross-functional relationships and establish a common language and shared vision. Each interaction among team members was targeted as an opportunity to bring the best out of others. The impact was immediate.

"Once people realize they have the capacity to activate others, every interaction changes," Rhea told us. "And that awareness doesn't go away. You can choose to ignore it, but that's tough to do when everyone around you is modeling it."

Step 4: Exercise Your Barrier-Breaking Authority

"Our mantra on the team became, 'Control what you can control,'" Marcus, an executive sales director on the team, told us. Rather than spending time discussing the merit of the decisions executive leadership were making, he said, "We had to focus on those things that we could truly influence." The 3 Mind Factors, always turned on, now were being put to greater use.

A team can only do big things when the individuals on the team own their response to their circumstances. When enough people on the team exercise their natural authority to respond in a healthy and productive way to issues and events that occur, greater change can occur.

A key moment for this medical device commercial team occurred early at a company conference. Standing on the stage, Ken asked everyone to write 70 on a piece of paper. Then he told them, "That's the percentage of our customers who say that out of all the companies in our industry, they trust us the most."

Next, they were asked to turn the paper over and write 30 on the other side. Ken then told the team, "That's the percentage of market share we possess."

The room was silent. "You could have heard a pin drop," Ken reported to us. "You could *feel* the fact that everyone knew this gap wasn't right. Very honestly, we told them, 'We're number one in our customers' eyes, but number two in the market,'" Ken said. "We didn't have to tell them that wasn't right. They already knew that. All we had to say was, 'You are empowered to change this.'"

Step 5: Focus on What Matters

It's impossible for a team to effectively focus its energy on executing a plan when team members are distracted by poor or ineffective relationships with one another. "If we're not working together, we're not working," Rhea said, laughing at the common sense.

Several team members had been in the organization for more than a decade. Unfortunately, some of them had reputations that weren't in service to the team's goals; instead, these people were the flag bearers for cliques that had formed over time. The Doofus Principle (when people choose to focus on and collect evidence that is destructive to people, partnership, and performance) was pervasive. Groups of people under separate banners were focused on what they didn't like about each other, which meant discussions were rarely focused on the business imperative. Instead, priceless time was spent discussing why "those people" were wrong.

All of this changed for the better when those who were carrying the flags were equipped with the 3 Mind Factors. Together, they looked at each other and said: This isn't working. This isn't who we want to be.

Within days the flag bearers of cliques proved what brain researchers say is true. As they began to focus on and talk about what they *did* appreciate and respect about one another, a transformation occurred: They saw each other differently. Trust expanded, and they delivered on their commitment to the human imperative.

"No longer were discussions about 'gotcha,' where people were trying to catch others doing things wrong," Rhea told us. "People began to actively see people fight for the right things, instead of fighting each other. The speed with which we could tackle tough issues immediately improved because of the relationships we were building with each other. Now we could talk honestly about how we were getting the results we were getting."

It's impossible for a team to adapt to changing circumstances or a new plan when team members are locked in old or destructive relationships with one another. **If you want your team to have an epic focus, you increase your odds by equipping team members to have epic relationships.**

Step 6: Energize Around a Shared Reality

Bold plans are often not executed because they involve extraordinary risk. Had this commercial team correctly interpreted the data? Would the doctors and patients truly respond to the new device as they expected? And what if the competition beat them to market with a more innovative product?

While those questions reveal the risks the team was taking, the greatest danger for any plan (bold or not) is having a team that halfheartedly executes the plan. As this team wrote their success story, the Energy Map proved vital in enabling the team to function in a shared reality that elevated the whole heart within the team.

"Our general manager could see it clearly," Marcus said. "The reality of the situation was that our culture was going to have to get stronger if we were going to get through this." To ensure they could better make the Connector Decision and see the needs of the entire enterprise, "We put a time line up on the wall of everything that had happened to the company up until that point," Marcus said.

The Energy Map was then used naturally to process their focus and emotions so the team could prepare itself to move forward. "After telling a bunch of stories about what used to be, we finally stepped back, looked at the entire time line. And then we said, 'Good or bad, the past is the past. We have to focus forward from now on,'" Marcus told us.

"I truly believe that was the turning point for the team," he said. "By that I don't mean things suddenly became easy, either. We just had the same frame of mind and more energy to do the job we knew we needed to do."

Step 7: Mobilize Hearts and Minds Forward

"I had a dream team," Roberto said. As a regional sales manager, he and his team were on the front lines, engaging directly with the customer. "We'd worked incredibly hard to get to where we were. Everyone was talented and dedicated. And then," he paused as he told us the story, "when they introduced the new business plan, they realigned the regions. Overnight, we had a 65 percent disruption to the sales force. Now, most of the people on our regional team were people I didn't hire, nor even knew well."

Disruptions often mean that the path the team used to see as the direction forward no longer exists. Things get messy, and results can suffer as a consequence. "It wasn't a surprise to me that in the early stages of delivering the plan, our regional team ranked twentieth out of 24 teams in sales," Roberto told us.

Don't feel sorry for Roberto or his team, though. Regardless of the challenge, they always prove they can adapt—because they have a proven process to ensure the team operates in way to succeed at whatever challenge they're thrown. Observing Roberto and the team meant seeing each step of the DBT Framework modeled impeccably.

"The key was keeping the new team focused on executing a simple plan," Roberto said. "We concentrated on training ourselves on the new device, executing a plan to educate our customers, and then regularly tapping into the natural energy we all have to get the job done."

Roberto is wise. He knew the team would need to address more than the typical boilerplate questions. As well, it wouldn't be enough if he was the only one asking Questions that Trigger the Hearts and Minds of the team. To do this big thing in front of them, he needed the entire team equipped with the ability to use effective questions. "So we made the conscious and strategic decision to slow down so we could speed up by developing everyone's skill to use questions," he said. Here's a sample of those they used:

- What mindsets, capabilities, and skills do we absolutely have to have right now to overcome our challenges and deliver our objective?
- How must we shape the narrative on this challenge?
- How can we immediately strengthen our focus and execution to ensure we achieve our goal?
- Given the challenge we just got hit with, how high do you believe we can bounce as a result? And why?
- How will this challenge and our success make us stronger and better as a team?
- How do we strengthen the inner core of our team to get this job done?

You're right if you think that these questions aren't typical in most workplaces. This is why so few teams do big things: Hearts and minds are mobilized forward too infrequently. The questions Roberto's team used were strategic Class III through V questions. Like those listed, they elevate consciousness by tapping into motivation, vision, and purpose.

"Anyone who joins our team quickly learns we're not trying to be just another high-performing team," Roberto said. "We're going to push the performance boundaries and establish new benchmarks of success.

"The right questions asked at the right time light up the soul and spirit of people at a deep and primal level. And that's the only part of each of us that brings forth a superhuman strength," Roberto told us. "No team can do anything significant without a laser focus and a compelling reason to achieve. And forward focus questions achieve that."

By executing their plan with mobilized hearts and minds, in 18 months Roberto's region had an epic impact on the company's success story. "We became the second fastest growing region in the country," he reported. "To see members of the team recognized for their contributions was exciting. Winning as a team, though, and knowing how close we all became as a team creates powerful memories that will last a lifetime."

The Epic Impact

Teams that do big things deliver high performance *and as they do so* **the members of the team become better people and stronger together.** Over the next five years, this medical device commercial team closed a 22–point gap in market share between them and their top

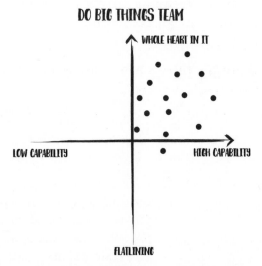

Figure 10.8 Teams that Do Big Things in the THQ Assessment Matrix

competitor. They did their big thing: They went through their Grand Canyon and became the market leader.

Visiting with Ken afterward, as he reflected on the success of the team, he said, "We stayed focused on the big things that would have the greatest impact. As a result, we changed the way the game was played in our industry. Who gets a chance to say that? It's an incredible feeling."

When Ken, Jay, Rhea, Marcus, and other members of this team interact with one another, there's a striking camaraderie that continues to this day. Trust, laughter, and lots of listening are apparent. As well, immediately noticeable are two things they don't do. They don't talk about themselves. And no single person acts as if they are bigger than the team. As a result, you find yourself wishing you could spend more time with them. Forward-focused energy is always infectious.

The rewards for the team were many, including Country of the Year honors bestowed in consecutive years by the parent company. But for this team, there is more to their epic results than the plaques they can put on their wall.

"More importantly," Jay said, "our doctors, the people we serve, are enjoying seeing their businesses grow because of the greater focus we're putting on them."

Then, Jay paused, thought for a moment, and finished: **"I'm proud of the business results. But I'm most proud of people coming up and saying thank you for investing in me professionally and personally. I'm a better person, even at home."**

The Only Reason Big Things Are Achieved

At noon, on August 29, 1869, 99 days after their epic journey began, Powell's band of explorers emerged from the Grand Canyon. The emotions were intense as the men brought their boats to their final landing. "The relief from danger and the joy of success are great," Powell wrote in his journal. "Our joy is almost ecstasy."[3]

As a crew that had accomplished what seemed impossible, no one should be surprised by what the men discussed around the campfire their first night removed from the canyon. While they talked about what they had just done, about home, and their scant supplies, what was discussed most centered around relationships among team members, including those who were no longer with them. "We sit till long after midnight . . . talking chiefly of the three men who left us,"[4] Powell noted.

One of the crew members, George Bradley, added in his journal, "All we regret now is that the three boys who took to the mountains are not here to share our joy and triumph."[5]

They cared. They knew they were better together. And it showed.

Should Major Powell, as the leader of the expedition, be given the credit for creating this dynamic? In fact, was the entire success of the expedition a result of Powell's leadership? In an age that glorifies individuals, especially those in the position of leadership, it's tempting to heap praise on the expedition's commander. Doing so, however, would be to deny certain facts.

The journals of those people who accompanied Powell, as well as the history books written by those who have made it their purpose to study Powell and the expedition, make it clear that the man had his foibles and deficiencies.[6] For all his visionary work, optimism, and bravery, he was also noncommunicative, demanding, distant, and, many say, self-centered.

This, then, reinforces the power of the DBT Framework: Powell would have been forgotten (perhaps even killed) if it hadn't been for a team, a group of individuals coming together to do something more significant than any one of them alone. Indeed, the team is the only reason the big thing was achieved.

This means that **for a team to succeed, leaders do not need to be superhuman. Nor do the members of a team need to qualify as exclusive specimens of humanity.**

Historian Donald Worster, in his book, *A River Running West: The Life of John Wesley Powell,* summarized this point perfectly. What Major Powell's crew represented was:

> . . . a triumph of ordinary people confronting an extraordinary landscape.
> The Major and his men, with few exceptions, successfully answered the old challenge . . . could people of no particular status or breeding or elite education, through diligence and ambition, achieve something special? They could and they did.[7]

People being at their best, bringing out the best in others, and partnering across the business to deliver shared objectives—this is how teams do big things. This is how you make an epic impact.

Your team is ready for its Grand Canyon.

POWELL'S MAP

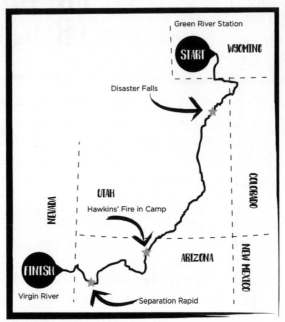

YOUR MAP

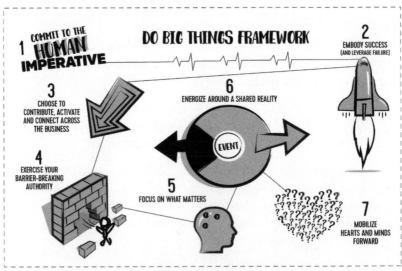

WHERE WILL YOU BEGIN?

WHAT BIG THINGS WILL YOUR TEAM DO?

FOR ADDITIONAL IDEAS, STORIES AND RESOURCES FOR LEVERAGING THE DO BIG THINGS FRAMEWORK WITH YOUR TEAM, VISIT **VERUSGLOBAL.COM/DOBIGTHINGS**

We want to hear your stories too!

- What challenges is your team facing and how have you applied the concepts in this book?
- What impact has the Do Big Things Framework had on your team and how you approach the big things right in front of you?
- How can we support you and your team as you set out to do big things?

Email Craig, Angie and Victoria at
DoBigThings@VerusGlobal.com

VerusGlobal.com
🐦 Follow us on Twitter @verusglobal
f Like us on Facebook.com/letsdobigthings

NOTES

Throughout the book, we use full names and company names where possible. In some examples, we cite a single name, different names, or anonymous companies to avoid revealing confidential or private information on behalf of our clients.

Introduction

1. A quote by John Wesley Powell, 1834–1902, www.qotd.org/search/single.html?
   qid=71838.
2. Diane Coutu, "Why Teams Don't Work," *Harvard Business Review*, May 2009, https://hbr.org/2009/05/why-teams-dont-work.
3. University of Phoenix, "University of Phoenix Survey Reveals Nearly Seven-in-Ten Workers Have Been Part of Dysfunctional Teams," UOPX News, January 16, 2013, www.phoenix.edu/news/releases/2013/01/university-of-phoenix-survey-reveals-nearly-seven-in-ten-workers-have-been-part-of-dysfunctional-teams.html.
4. Anita Bruzzese, "How to Create Trust Among Cross-Functional Teams," QuickBase (Blog), September 6, 2016, www.quickbase.com/blog/how-to-create-trust-among-cross-functional-teams.

Chapter 1: Teams That Do Big Things

1. Edward Dolnick, *Down the Great Unknown: John Wesley Powell's 1869 Journey of Discovery and Tragedy Through the Grand Canyon* (New York: Harper Collins, 2001).
2. Chris McChesney, Sean Covey, and Jim Huling, "How to Set Wildly Important Goals, and What They'll Do for You," *Fast Company*, April 24, 2012, https://www.fastcompany.com/1835210/how-set-wildly-important-goals-and-what-theyll-do-you.
3. Scott Berinato, "A Framework for Understanding VUCA," *Harvard Business Review*, September 5, 2014, https://hbr.org/2014/09/a-framework-for-understanding-vuca.

4. "Report: State of the American Workplace," Gallup, February 28, 2017, www.gallup .com/services/176708/state-american-workplace.aspx.

5. Deloitte, "Global Human Capital Trends," Deloitte University Press, 2016, https:// dupress.deloitte.com/dup-us-en/focus/human-capital-trends/2016/human-capital-trends-introduction.html.

6. Deloitte, "Global Human Capital Trends," Deloitte University Press, 2017, https:// www2.deloitte.com/us/en/pages/human-capital/articles/introduction-human-capital-trends.html.

7. John P. Kotter, "Leading Change: Why Transformation Efforts Fail," *Harvard Business Review*, January 2007, https://hbr.org/2007/01/leading-change-why-transformation-efforts-fail.

8. Diane Coutu, "Why Teams Don't Work," *Harvard Business Review*, May 2009, https://hbr.org/2009/05/why-teams-dont-work.

9. "Apollo 13," NASA, last modified September 19, 2013, https://www.nasa.gov/ mission_pages/apollo/missions/apollo13.html.

10. Paul Sullivan, "Chicago Cubs Win World Series Championship with 8–7 Victory over Cleveland Indians," *The Chicago Tribune*, November 3, 2016, www.chicagotribune .com/sports/baseball/cubs/ct-cubs-win-world-series-sullivan-spt-1103-20161102-story.html.

11. Linda Hill, Greg Brandeau, Emily Truelove, and Kent Lineback, "The Capabilities Your Organization Needs to Sustain Innovation," *Harvard Business Review*, January 14, 2015.

12. Author interview with Jim Kouzes.

13. Angela Maiers, "The YOU MATTER Manifesto," Angelamaiers.com, January 10, 2012, www.angelamaiers.com/2012/01/the-you-matter-manifesto/.

Chapter 2: Teams That Flatline

1. John Wesley Powell, Don D. Fowler, and Catherine S. Fowler, "John Wesley Powell's Journal: Colorado River Expedition 1871–1872," *Canyon Legacy* 5, no. 1 (1990): 2–12.

2. Laurie Miller, *ASTD's 2013 State of the Industry Report: Workplace Learning.* T+d 67 11 (November 8, 2013): 40.

3. Jack Zenger, "Does Leadership Development Really Work?" *Forbes*, May 2, 2012, www.forbes.com/sites/jackzenger/2012/05/02/does-leadership-development-really-work-2/#2f0431bc6135.

4. Michael Irwin Meltzer, David Sirota, and Louis A. Mischkind, "Why Your Employees Are Losing Motivation," *Harvard Business School*, April 10, 2006, http://hbswk.hbs.edu/archive/5289.html.

5. Theresa Minton-Eversole, "Virtual Teams Used Most by Global Organizations, Survey Says," Society for Human Resources Management, July 19, 2012, https://www .shrm.org/resourcesandtools/hr-topics/organizational-and-employee-development/ pages/virtualteamsusedmostbyglobalorganizations,surveysays.aspx.

6. Ibid.

7. Gianluigi Cuccureddu, "Lack of Collaboration or Ineffective Communication Cause of Workplace Failures," *Damarque*, May 19, 2013, www.damarque.com/blog/gianluigi-cuccureddu/lack-collaboration-or-ineffective-communication-cause-workplace-failures.

Chapter 3: Commit to the Human Imperative

1. Alex "Sandy" Pentland, "The New Science of Building Great Teams," *Harvard Business Review*, April 2012, hbr.org/2012/04/the-new-science-of-building-great-teams.

2. Bruce W. Tuckman, "Developmental Sequence in Small Groups," *Psychological Bulletin* 63, no 6 (1965): 384–399, doi:10.1037/h0022100.

3. Wayne Dyer, "When You Change the Way You Look at Things," YouTube Video, 3:36, April 19, 2008, www.youtube.com/watch?v=urQPraeeY0w.

4. Michael Beer, Magnus Finnström, and Derek Schrader, "Why Leadership Training Fails and What to Do about It," *Harvard Business Review*, October 2016, hbr.org/2016/10/why-leadership-training-fails-and-what-to-do-about-it.

5. Ibid.

6. Willis Towers Watson, "How the Fundamentals Have Evolved and the Best Adapt," 2014, www.towerswatson.com/en-US/Insights/IC-Types/Survey-Research-Results/2013/12/2013-2014-change-and-communication-roi-study.

7. Ibid.

8. Deloitte, "Global Human Capital Trends," Deloitte University Press, 2017, www2.deloitte.com/us/en/pages/human-capital/articles/introduction-human-capital-trends.html.

9. Stephen R. Covey, *The 7 Habits of Highly Effective People: Powerful Lessons in Personal Change* (New York: Free Press, 1989).

10. A. H. Maslow, "A Theory of Human Motivation," *Psychological Review* 50. no. 4 (1943): 370–396, doi:10.1037/h0054346.

11. John Wesley Powell, Don D. Fowler, and Catherine S. Fowler, "John Wesley Powell's Journal: Colorado River Expedition 1871–1872," *Canyon Legacy* 5, no. 1 (1990): 2–12.

12. Edward Dolnick, *Down the Great Unknown: John Wesley Powell's 1869 Journey of Discovery and Tragedy Through the Grand Canyon* (New York: Harper Collins, 2001).

13. Gary Topping, "Colorado River Controversies," *Utah Historical Quarterly* 51, no. 3 (6) (1983): 300–301.

Chapter 4: Embody Success (and Leverage Failure)

1. Heidi Chatfield and Allison Wooten, "Who Is in Control of Your Employee's Behavior?" All Star Incentive Marketing, June 2012, c.ymcdn.com/sites/www .incentivemarketing.org/resource/resmgr/imported/Locus%20%20of%20Control% 20%20final.pdf.

2. Daniel H. Pink, *Drive: The Surprising Truth About What Motivates Us* (New York: RiverHead Books, 2011).

3. Simon Sinek, "How Great Leaders Inspire Action," September 2009, TED Talks, 17:57, www.ted.com/talks/simon_sinek_how_great_leaders_inspire_action#t-784406.

4. "Engaged Employees Infographic," Dale Carnegie Training, www.dalecarnegie.com/ employee-engagement/engaged-employees-infographic/.

5. Jakob Rogstadiusa, Vassilis Kostakosa, Aniket Kitturb, Boris Smusa, Jim Laredoc, Maja Vukovicc, "An Assessment of Intrinsic and Extrinsic Motivation on Task Performance in Crowdsourcing Markets," AAAI (Report compiled by Association for the Advancement of Artificial Intelligence, Palo Alto, CA).

6. Ibid.

7. "Locus of Control," Changing Minds, changingminds.org/explanations/preferences/ locus_control.htm.

8. "Executives Don't Think Employees Understand Strategy," *Holmes Report*, June 28, 2015, www.holmesreport.com/research/article/executives-don't-think-employees-understand-strategy.

9. Zeno Group, "Zeno Group Study Explores Reasons Why Employees Are So Disengaged," *PR Newswire*, June 10, 2015, www.prnewswire.com/news-releases/zeno-group-study-explores-reasons-why-employees-are-so-disengaged-300096754.html.

10. Sting, *Lyrics* (New York: The Dial Press, 2007), 4–5.

Chapter 5: Choose to Contribute, Activate, and Connect Across the Business

1. Nancy Armour, "Jason Heyward's Speech Spurs Cubs during World Series Game 7 Rain Delay," *USA Today*, November 3, 2016, www.usatoday.com/story/sports/mlb/ cubs/2016/11/03/world-series-championship-game-7-rain-delay-jason-heyward/ 93226544/.

2. Ibid.

3. Joel Hoomans, "35,000 Decisions: The Great Choices of Strategic Leaders," Roberts Wesleyan College, March 20, 2015, go.roberts.edu/leadingedge/the-great-choices-of-strategic-leaders.

4. Jennifer Briggs, *Strive to Excel: The Wisdom of Vince Lombardi* (Nashville: Rutledge Hill Press, 1997), 76.

5. Dominique Jones, "The Dollars and Sense of Employee Engagement," Talent Space (Blog), March 6, 2012, www.halogensoftware.com/blog/the-dollars-and-sense-of-employee-engagement.

6. Steve Crabtree, "Worldwide, 13% of Employees Are Engaged at Work," Gallup, October 8, 2013, www.gallup.com/poll/165269/worldwide-employees-engaged-work.aspx?version=print.

7. "Report: State of the American Workplace," Gallup, September 22, 2014, www.gallup.com/services/176708/state-american-workplace.aspx.

8. "The Impact of Employee Engagement on Performance," *Harvard Business Review*, www.yorkworks.ca/default/assets/File/analyst-insights-HBR_Achievers% 20Report_TheImpactofEmployeeEngagementonPerformance(1).pdf.

9. Willis Towers Watson, "The 2014 Global Workforce Study," August 2014, www.towerswatson.com/en/Insights/IC-Types/Survey-Research-Results/2014/08/the-2014-global-workforce-study.

10. Jones, "The Dollars and Sense of Employee Engagement."

11. Oriana Negulescua and Elena Doval, "The Quality of Decision Making Process Related to Organizations' Effectiveness,"*ScienceDirect*, 2014, ac.els-cdn.com/S2212567114005486/1-s2.0-S2212567114005486-main.pdf?_tid=fcf9513c-fd36-11e6-8244-00000aacb361&acdnat=1488232509_0f009bc0319887ad42165ff9b591dcbf.

12. Ibid.

13. Briggs, *Strive to Excel.*

14. MacMillion Dictionary, s.v., "Moral Imperative," accessed March 21, 2017, www.macmillandictionary.com/us/dictionary/american/moral-imperative.

15. William Nevins, "We Are Too Prone to Judge Ourselves by Our Ideals and Other People by Their Acts," Quote Investigator, March 19, 2015, quoteinvestigator.com/2015/03/19/judge-others/.

16. German Lopez, "George W. Bush in Dallas: 'Too often we judge other groups by their worst examples,'" *Vox*, July 12, 2016, www.vox.com/2016/7/12/12164176/george-bush-dallas-shooting-speech-video.

17. Michael Fullan, *Leadership and Sustainability: System Thinkers in Action* (Thousand Oaks, CA: Corwin, 2004), 27.

18. John Wesley Powell, Don D. Fowler, and Catherine S. Fowler, "John Wesley Powell's Journal: Colorado River Expedition 1871–1872," *Canyon Legacy* 5, no. 1 (1990): 2–12.

Chapter 6: Exercise Your Barrier-Breaking Authority

1. John Wesley Powell, Don D. Fowler, and Catherine S. Fowler, "John Wesley Powell's Journal: Colorado River Expedition 1871–1872," *Canyon Legacy* 5, no. 1 (1990): 2–12.

2. Denis Waitley, *The Psychology of Winning: Ten Qualities of a Total Winner* (New York: Berkley Books, 1979), 3. Also, "Why Are so Many People Quitting Their Jobs?" Pacific Crest Group, www.pcg-services.com/people-quitting-jobs/.

3. Alan Hall, "'I'm Outta Here! Why 2 Million Americans Quit Every Month (And 5 Steps to Turn the Epidemic Around)." Forbes.com, March 11, 2013. www.forbes.com/sites/alanhall/2013/03/11/im-outta-here-why-2-million-americans-quit-every-month-and-5-steps-to-turn-the-epidemic-around/#6e14c71c6484.

4. Michael Beer, Magnus Finnström, and Derek Schrader, "Why Leadership Training Fails and What to Do about It," *Harvard Business Review*, October 2016, hbr.org/2016/10/why-leadership-training-fails-and-what-to-do-about-it.

5. "Overwhelming Majority of Companies Say Soft Skills Are Just as Important as Hard Skills, According to a New CareerBuilder Survey," Career Builder, April 10, 2014, www.careerbuilder.com/share/aboutus/pressreleasesdetail.aspx?ed=12/31/2014&id=pr817&sd=4/10/2014.

6. Hans J. Thamhain, "Influences of Environment and Leadership on Team Performance in Complex Project Environments," Project Management Institute, 2010, www.pmi.org/learning/library/influences-environment-leadership-team-performance-6482.

7. Shep Hyken, "Drucker Said 'Culture Eats Strategy for Breakfast' and Enterprise Rent-a-Car Proves It," *Forbes*, December 5, 2015, www.forbes.com/sites/shephyken/2015/12/05/drucker-said-culture-eats-strategy-for-breakfast-and-enterprise-rent-a-car-proves-it/#6f6cd4272749.

Chapter 7: Focus on What Matters

1. Stu Woo, "Against the Wind," *Wall Street Journal*, February 28, 2014, www.wsj.com/articles/SB10001424052702303393804579312803907849782.

2. "2013 America's Cup," Wikipedia, en.wikipedia.org/wiki/2013_America's_Cup.

3. Oracle Team USA, "The Comeback," YouTube Video, 9:06, November 18, 2013, hwww.youtube.com/watch?v=t3vRMRnSbys&feature=youtu.be&t=1m.

4. Ibid.

5. Ibid.

6. Ibid.

7. Susanna Huth, "Employees Waste 759 Hours Each Year Due to Workplace Distractions," Telegraph.co.uk, June 22, 2015, www.telegraph.co.uk/finance/jobs/11691728/Employees-waste-759-hours-each-year-due-to-workplace-distractions.html.

8. Kristin Wong, "How Long It Takes to Get Back on Track After a Distraction," Life Hacker, July 29, 2015, lifehacker.com/how-long-it-takes-to-get-back-on-track-after-a-distract-1720708353.

9. Alison Green, "Team Productivity—Stories of the Week," Quickbase (blog), January 26, 2017, www.quickbase.com/blog/team-productivity-stories-of-the-week-12.

10. Hara Marano, "Our Brain's Negative Bias," *Psychology Today*, June 9, 2016, www .psychologytoday.com/articles/200306/our-brains-negative-bias.

11. Ed Oakley and Doug Krug, *Getting to the Heart of Change: Enlightened Leadership* (New York: Touchstone, 1994).

12. Daniel J. Simons and Christopher F. Chabris, "Gorillas in Our Midst: Sustained Inattentional Blindness for Dynamic Events," *Sage Journals* 28, no. 9 (1999), 1059–1074, doi: 10.1068/p281059.

13. Ibid.

14. Daniel Kahneman, *Thinking, Fast and Slow* (New York: Farrar, Straus and Giroux, 2011).

15. Daniel Goleman, *Focus: The Hidden Driver of Excellence* (New York: HarperCollins, 2013).

16. Ibid.

17. Ibid., 203.

18. Daniel Wegner, "How to Think, Say, or Do Precisely the Wrong Thing for Any Occasion," *Science* 325, no. 5936 (2009): 48–50, doi: 10.1126/science.1167346.

19. George Lucas, *Star Wars, Episode I, The Phantom Menace: Illustrated Screenplay* (New York: Ballantine, 1999.

20. Goleman, *Focus,* 4.

21. Ibid., 69.

22. Ibid., 124.

23. Ibid., 125.

24. Ann Japenga, "Against the Current," *Los Angeles Times*, February 4, 2002, articles. latimes.com/2002/feb/04/news/lv-river4.

25. John Wesley Powell, Don D. Fowler, and Catherine S. Fowler, "John Wesley Powell's Journal: Colorado River Expedition 1871–1872," *Canyon Legacy* 5, no. 1(1990): 2–12.

Chapter 8: Energize Around a Shared Reality

1. Interview with Pam Lindwirth.

2. The Energy Map is inspired by a concept described as the Net Forward Energy Ratio in Doug Krug and Ed Oakley's book, *Enlightened Leadership* (New York: Touchstone, 1994).

3. Steven W. Vannoy and Craig W. Ross, *Stomp the Elephant in the Office* (Ashland, OH: Wister & Willows, 2011).

4. Bethany Brookshire, "Dopamine Is," *Slate*, July 3, 2013, www.slate.com/articles/ health_and_science/science/2013/07/what_is_dopamine_love_lust_sex_addiction_ gambling_motivation_reward.html.

5. Dalai Lama, "Dalai Lama Quotes," www.dalailamaquotes.org/an-open-heart-is-an-open-mind/.

6. From Shakespeare's play, *Hamlet* (HM.2.2.234-235).

7. Jeff Boss, "6 Truths on Why Introverts Make Great Leaders," *Fortune*, October 7, 2015, fortune.com/2015/10/07/introverts-make-great-leaders/.

8. Thomas Wedell-Wedellsborg, interview by Sarah Carmichael, *Harvard Business Review*, December 22, 2016.

9. Greg Satell, "The Little Known Secret to Pixar's Creative Success," *Forbes*, May 29, 2015, www.forbes.com/sites/gregsatell/2015/05/29/the-little-known-secret-to-pixars-creative-success/#2f49813938b2.

10. Barbara L. Fredrickson, "The Broaden-and-Build Theory of Positive Emotions" (London: The Royal Society, 2004), 170.

11. Barbara L. Fredrickson, *Positivity* (New York: Harmony Books, 2009), 170.

12. Sonja Lyubomirsky, Laura King, and Ed Diener, "The Benefits of Frequent Positive Affect: Does Happiness Lead to Success?" *Psychological Bulletin* 131, no. 6 (2005): 803–855, www.apa.org/pubs/journals/releases/bul-1316803.pdf.

13. Elizabeth Cabrera, "The Six Essentials of Workplace Positivity," Innovation Eco-system, n.d., innovationecosystem.pbworks.com/w/file/fetch/63566498/Cabrera-6essentials.pdf.

14. Daniel Kahneman, *Thinking, Fast and Slow* (New York: Farrar, Straus and Giroux, 2011), 105.

15. Jennifer Lawler, "The Real Cost of Workplace Conflict,"*Entrepreneur*, June 21, 2010, www.entrepreneur.com/article/207196.

16. Ibid.

17. Kathy Caprino, "How Happiness Directly Impacts Your Success," *Forbes*, June 6, 2013, www.forbes.com/sites/kathycaprino/2013/06/06/how-happiness-directly-impacts-your-success/#2d327098618b.

18. Nicole Torres, "Looking for Problems Makes Us Tired," *Harvard Business Review*, March 30, 2015, hbr.org/2015/03/looking-for-problems-makes-us-tired.

19. Robert Leahy, "Is Dwelling on the Negative Hurting You? The Cognitive Costs of Rumination," *The Huffington Post*, December 30, 2010, www.huffingtonpost.com/robert-leahy-phd/dwelling-on-the-negative-_b_799103.html.

20. Daniel Goleman, *Focus: The Hidden Driver of Excellence* (New York: HarperCollins, 2013), 150–151.

21. In Scottsdale, Arizona, on March 28, 2017, during his talk at the Annual Business Retreat for membership organization, ISA, the authors heard Joe Brown from IDEO share this statement.

22. Bradley P. Owens, Wayne E. Baker, Dana McDaniel Sumpter, and Kim S. Cameron, "Relational Energy at Work: Implications for Job Engagement and Job Performance," *Journal of Applied Psychology* 101, no. 1 (2016): 35–49.

23. Richard E. Boyatzis, "Managing a Negative, Out-of-Touch Boss," *Harvard Business Review*, March 28, 2014, hbr.org/2014/05/managing-a-negative-out-of-touch-boss.

24. Kahneman, *Thinking, Fast and Slow*, 55.

25. Ibid., 60.

26. Author interviews with Jim Kouzes.

27. Author interview with Mike Taigman.

Chapter 9: Mobilize Hearts and Minds Forward

1. John Wesley Powell, *The Exploration of the Colorado River and Its Canyons* (New York: Dover Publishing, 1961).

2. Mark Davis, "Lost in the Grand Canyon," PBS, www.pbs.org/wgbh/amex/canyon/filmmore/transcript/transcript1.html.

3. Powell, *The Exploration of the Colorado River and Its Canyons*

4. Ibid.

5. Craig W. Ross and Angela V. Paccione, *ONE Team: 10-Minute Discussions That Activate Inspired Teamwork* (Littleton, CO: Verus Global Leadership Press, 2015), 22.

6. "Percentage of Children Asking Questions," Right Question Institute, 2017, rightquestion.org/percentage-children-asking-questions/.

7. I. Senay, D. Albarracín, and K. Noguchi, "Motivating Goal-Directed Behavior Through Introspective Self-Talk: The Role of the Interrogative Form of Simple Future Tense," *Psychological Science* 21, no. 4 (April): 499–504.

8. Sterling A. Bone, "Mere Measurement 'Plus': How Solicitation of Open-Ended Positive Feedback Influences Customer Purchase Behavior," *Journal of Marketing Research*, 2016, www.researchgate.net/publication/299403296_Mere_Measurement_Plus_How_Solicitation_of_Open-Ended_Positive_Feedback_Influences_Customer_Purchase_Behavior.

9. B. Dervin and P. Dewdney, "Neutral Questioning: A New Approach to the Reference Interview," *Research Quarterly*, 25, no. 4 (1986): 506–513.

10. Dan N. Stone, Edward L. Deci, and Richard M. Ryan. "Beyond Talk: Creating Autonomous Motivation through Self-Determination Theory," University of Kentucky, November 24, 2008, sdtheory.s3.amazonaws.com/SDT/documents/2009_StoneDeciRyan_JGM.pdf.

11. Interview with Dan Robinson.

12. "Principles of Appreciative Inquiry," Center for Appreciative Inquiry, www.centerforappreciativeinquiry.net/more-on-ai/principles-of-appreciative-inquiry/.

13. Ross and Paccione, *ONE Team*.

14. Daniel Goleman, *Focus: The Hidden Driver of Excellence* (New York: HarperCollins, 2013), 30.

15. "Principles of Appreciative Inquiry."

16. Ibid.

17. Ross and Paccione, *ONE Team*, 44.

18. Alex "Sandy" Pentland, "The New Science of Building Great Teams," *Harvard Business Review*, April 2012, hbr.org/2012/04/the-new-science-of-building-great-teams.

19. Daniel Kahneman, *Thinking, Fast and Slow* (New York: Farrar, Straus and Giroux, 2011).

Chapter 10: Is Your Team Ready to Do Big Things?

1. Jon R. Katzenbach and Douglas K. Smith, "The Discipline of Teams," *Harvard Business Review*, July–August 2005, hbr.org/2005/07/the-discipline-of-teams.

2. "How to Survive a Riptide,"WikiHow, www.wikihow.com/Survive-a-Rip-Tide.

3. John Wesley Powell, *The Exploration of the Colorado River and Its Canyons* (New York: Dover Publishing, 1961), 284–285.

4. Ibid.

5. "John Wesley Powell's First Expedition Down the Colorado River," PBS, www.pbs.org/wgbh/amex/canyon/maps/maptext.html.

6. John Wesley Powell, Don D. Fowler, and Catherine S. Fowler, "John Wesley Powell's Journal: Colorado River Expedition 1871–1872," *Canyon Legacy* 5, no. 1 (1990): 2–12.

7. Ibid.

KEY TERMS AND LIST OF TOOLS

ACKNOWLEDGMENTS

It's a fascinating and humbling experience to write about how to do big things. Consistently, as we observed teams, interviewed leaders and team members, and sharpened the focus on how these people were able to achieve epic outcomes, we learned. While bringing this book to you, the gift given to us has been significant. Every team's and leader's story inspired us.

As we translated their experiences and wisdom into these pages, repeatedly we found ourselves identifying what we can do ourselves to become even more effective team, community, and family members. The two decades it's taken to put this work together have been filled with remarkable and transformative awe.

We are indebted to many. In particular, we want to give special recognition to our teammate, Theresa Letman, who shepherded this project from start to finish while completing a myriad of other responsibilities. As well, we're grateful to Lacey McMahan, who led the efforts for our graphics, some key endorsements, and marketing. While it's impossible to acknowledge the hundreds of others who have played a role in doing this big thing, we're particularly grateful to the following for supporting our efforts:

Our client partners are the reason we get to do big things. Their inspiration activates the best in us. Without their willingness to share these stories and their wisdom with the world, this book wouldn't be in your hands. We remain as committed to their success as we are to our own.

Our home team is the best there is. This book may have the authors' names on it, but it has this team's heart in it. In particular: Bob Burgess, Denise Pushnik, Molly Kemmer, Celes Phillips, Sundi Ford, Bea Raemdonck, Sherilyn Jayne, Mollie Chacon, Anissa Gil, and Cindy Main.

The great partners, who assisted in refining a big idea into a book that can do big things, deserve special recognition. Many of you navigated early drafts that required patience and a belief in us. We are forever grateful for your contributions. Specifically, we want to thank: our editor, Liz Gildea, and our agent, Esmond Harmsworth, for thinking big; Sandy Wendel for both challenging and cheering us; our graphic designer, Amy Shenton; our photographer and videographer, David Cummings of Outer Woods Media; and our pre-readers: Jessica Amortegui, Jim Calhoun, Andrew Collier, Rich Crawford, Nuri Dimler, Joe Hannigan, Blane Harding, Mark Helton, Julie Hunt, James Kaw, Franck Leveiller, Burak Malkoc, Kevin McEvoy, Matt McNair, Roy Nickerson, Kristina Nattoch Dag, Ed Oakley, David Olshansky, Doug Reeves, Patti Trautwein, and Anne Watson.

Our delivery team, both past and present, make the 3 Do Big Things Decisions in ways that better our world. Thank you: Steve Vannoy, Noreen Broering, Broc Edwards, Brett Kleffner, Burke Miller, Lisa Teets, Steve Drury, Natalie Sayer, Lisa Marie Main, Peter Stoltz, Tom Miller, Pilar Pardo, Sue Taigman, Sheryl Alstrin, Brenda Trejos, Kevin Gray, J. Victor McGuire, and Paul Zaffiro.

And finally, thank you to the research interns from BYU: Aaron Allred, Melissa Andelin, Tommy Anderson, Tiffany Burke, Ashley Correa, Luis Hernandez, Jacob Howarth, Michael Jarman, William Kongaika, Marinda McKenzie, Caden Morgan, Jeff Orgill, Christian Serafin, Tyler Welch, and Seth Wetsel.

ABOUT THE AUTHORS

Photo Credit: David Cummings, Outer Woods Media

Craig W. Ross

As CEO of Verus Global, for 20 years Craig has partnered with c-suite executives and leadership teams in global organizations across numerous industries. Combining a passion for uniting people and a conviction that organizations achieve extraordinary things through teams, Craig delivers practical and real-world expertise to those he serves. He and his family call Colorado home.

Other books authored by Craig: *Stomp the Elephant in the Office*, *Degrees of Strength*, and *One Team*

Angela V. Paccione, PhD

As an executive facilitator and powerful keynote speaker for Verus Global, Angie is "all-in" and 100 percent committed to the success of the partners she serves. A former professional athlete, college professor, two-term state representative and Congressional candidate, Angie is a performance expert who activates the greatness within people and teams. Angie enjoys being single in Colorado.

Other books authored by Angie: *One Team*

Victoria L. Roberts

As president of Verus Global and former head of organizational effectiveness for a large medical device company, Victoria is passionate about bringing humanity to the workplace and beyond. Her experience transferring cognitive behavioral psychology practices across organizational systems enables her to build lasting solutions for partners with immediate and sustainable results. Victoria and her family live in Colorado.

INDEX

For additional resources, tools, and to download a
free version of the Do Big Things Framework, visit:
www.VerusGlobal.com/DoBigThings

We equip teams to do BIG things.™